WHAT IS GOOD AND WHY

WHAT IS GOOD
AND WHY

The Ethics of Well-Being

Richard Kraut

HARVARD UNIVERSITY PRESS

Cambridge, Massachusetts

London, England

2007

Library of Congress Cataloging-in-Publication Data

Kraut, Richard, 1944–
    What is good and why : the ethics of well-being / Richard Kraut.
        p. cm.
    Includes bibliographical references (p.   ) and index.
    ISBN-13: 978-0-674-02441-0 (alk. paper)
    ISBN-10: 0-674-02441-9 (alk. paper)
    1. Good and evil.   2. Well-being.   I. Title.
    BJ1401.K73 2007
    171′.3—dc22   2006049655

For my students

Contents

Acknowledgments

Having devoted much of my academic life to the understanding of a few texts of Plato and Aristotle, I entered the rough terrain of contemporary moral philosophy with trepidation. Were it not for the encouragement of a few people—David Copp, Raymond Geuss, Douglas MacLean, Judith Jarvis Thomson, and Susan Wolf—I might not have made the decision to pursue, more fully than I had before, the ideas that led to this book. It is a pleasure to acknowledge my debt to these colleagues and friends. To Northwestern University I am obliged for the leave of absence that allowed me to write a first draft. And to the Rockefeller Foundation I am grateful for the ideal working and living conditions of the Bellagio Study and Conference Center. I received help from many people who were kind enough to read portions of the manuscript and to give me guidance or criticism. In particular, I would like to thank Robert Audi, Reid Blackman, Chris Bobonich, Bruce Brower, Brad Cokelet, David Copp, Pierre Destrée, Ed Feige, Sam Fleischacker, Jon Garthoff, Raymond Geuss, Dan Hausman, Douglas MacLean, Curtis Matthews, Jason Raibley, David Reeve, Steven Skultety, Michael Slote, Christine Swanton, Judith Jarvis Thomson, Julie Ward, and Susan Wolf. Two anonymous referees for Harvard University Press took great pains in their critiques of the manuscript, which led to many improvements. Finally, thanks to Ann Twombly for valuable editorial assistance.

Hoc est ergo primum praeceptum legis, quod bonum est faciendum et prosequendum, et malum vitandum. Et super hoc fundatur onmia alia praecepta legis naturae.

This therefore is the first precept of law, that good is to be done and pursued, and bad is to be avoided. And on this all other precepts of the natural law are founded.

—Aquinas, *Summa Theologica,* Pt. 1.2, q. 94, art. 2

ONE

In Search of Good

1. A Socratic Question

"Good," its linguistic relatives ("better," "best," "well"), their opposites, and corresponding terms in other languages pervade the vocabulary of everyday life. With their help, we arrive at conclusions about what to choose and what to do. We want not just to eat, but to eat good food; not just to make plans, but to make good plans; not just to have friends, but to have good friends. If we lacked a vocabulary for making such evaluations and still finer distinctions ("good, but not as good as"), decision making would be an impoverished enterprise.

"Good" goes even deeper than that. When followed by the preposition "for" or "of," it purports to tell us where our interests lie. To deliberate about what is good *for* someone, or the good *of* someone, is to ask about what is beneficial or advantageous—not what is beneficial or advantageous in general, but *for* or *to* him in particular. It is to inquire about how to place that person in a more favorable position than he would otherwise occupy. If we lacked words like "good for," "in his interest," "to his advantage," "beneficial to," we would have no linguistic resources for thinking about how to improve our circumstances or how to prevent them from deteriorating.

Without such terms, we would lose the grounding for the evaluations we make. For when we use "good" as a grader of members of a kind (good food, plans, friends), we are guided by our ideas about what is good *for* this person or that. Food is good by being good *for* the person who eats it.[1] Plans are good when their results are likely to be good *for*

---

1. I set aside complications for now and return to good things of a kind in sections 69 and 70.

those affected by them. A good friend is good *for* the person to whom he is a friend. Behind our evaluative practices and our practical reasoning lie countless assumptions, normally unexamined, about which things are good *for* us.

In this study I reflect on those assumptions in order to find their underlying rationale. Common sense, we will see, tends to make systematic errors about what is good for us, and philosophers have sometimes incorporated those errors into their theories. If we learn how to guard against these tendencies, we should arrive at a better understanding of how to live our lives. In doing so, we will not be entirely abandoning common sense—far from it. Much that will be said here about what is good for us will be obvious. The trouble with common sense, in this area, is that it accepts too many ideas; they cannot all stand up to scrutiny. We have to lay bare our underlying assumptions about what is good for us in order to see that our house is not in order and to set about rebuilding it.

We will be moving to a level of abstraction that seems far removed from the exigencies of daily life. We want to know not only which things are in fact good for someone, but what is being said about a thing when it is judged to be good for someone. What, in fact, is the nature of the relationship that holds between G and S when G is good for S? ("G" will be our placeholder for goods, "S" for individual subjects.) Since we want to scrutinize the assumptions we make about what is good, we should ask what we commit ourselves to when we call something good for someone. We should, in other words, try to understand the nature of goodness.

That abstract question is the sort we can imagine Socrates asking an interlocutor in a Platonic dialogue. In *Meno* he tries to discover which property all the virtues have in common—a property that justifies calling each of them a virtue—and he might have asked the same sort of question about what is good. "When you say that eating certain kinds of food is good for you, and that making certain plans is good for you, and that having these friends is good for you, what is it that you are asserting about each of these things? What justifies your claim that each of these things is good for you?"

There is no guarantee that this is a fruitful question to ask—that it is well formulated, that it has an answer, or that we need an answer. Perhaps there is nothing that all good things (things that are good for someone) have in common. Perhaps nothing is amiss if they do not. Perhaps we would do better to think in terms of what is good absolutely—just plain good—than to inquire about what is good *for* us. Or, even if what is good for us is a matter of great importance, perhaps the assumptions we make about this matter in our everyday lives are entirely in order as they stand. There is no way to tell, at the start, whether philosophical reflection that presses, as this study does, toward greater abstraction and systematicity will bear fruit by detecting pervasive errors in our thinking. There is no guarantee that we are asking a good question when we ask about the nature of goodness. We simply must be on guard to avoid unwarranted assumptions as we seek a theory that withstands all the critical tests we can bring to bear upon it.

2. Flourishing and Well-Being

The question we are pursuing in this study is extremely broad—perhaps, it will be said, too broad. What is good for S? What do we commit ourselves to when we say that G is good for some individual, S? These questions leave entirely unspecified who or what S is. S need not be a human being; it might be a plant or a nonhuman animal. For an immense variety of living things—trees and shrubs, no less than every member of the animal kingdom—certain things are good and others bad. They can be healthy or diseased. It is good for them to be healthy, bad to be diseased, to be stunted, to die before they mature.

S does not have to be a living creature for it to be the case that G is good for S. Dry air is bad for pianos. Sugar is bad for gas tanks. Sand is bad for watches. Whatever enhances the performance of an artifact or its ability to play its role is good for it; whatever damages it or detracts from its suitability to achieve its purpose is bad for it (sections 34, 68).[2]

But the word "good" does not vary in its meaning as it is applied to these many diverse subjects. We say, "That kind of barley is good for horses but not for human beings." But we do not mean that it is good-in-a-horsey-sense for horses and bad-in-a-human-sense for humans. A certain kind of food may be good for human beings whose stomachs have certain enzymes and bad for other human beings who lack those enzymes. But that does not require us to suppose that "good" or "good for" takes on different meanings when applied to different human groups.

---

2. We also speak of what is good for activities: fair weather is good for flying, knives for cutting, wet snow for making snowballs. These will not call for separate treatment.

We sometimes distinguish senses of a word as a way of saving ourselves from contradiction, but there is no need to do so in this case, for the relativization we bring about by tacking "for" onto "good" already allows us to avoid contradicting ourselves. We can say that this barley is both good and bad, and then add that there is no contradiction here, because our statement is elliptical: it is good for horses, bad for humans. There is no need to relativize a second time, by saying that it is horsey-good for horses and human-bad for humans.

Should we confine our inquiry to an examination of what is good *for human beings?* Similarly, should we limit ourselves to an examination of what we are committed to when we say of something that it is good *for a human being?* If we did so, no one could accuse us of being narrow-minded. A theory of what is good for human beings is precisely what we humans should be eager to find, and this study will therefore pay special attention to that kind of self-knowledge. Nonetheless, there is no reason to overlook the larger framework to which such an inquiry belongs. To understand the human good, we are asking about a certain property—goodness or, more precisely, a certain relation—the one that holds between G and S when G is good for S. We want to improve our understanding of what that relation is. It is one and the same relation, whether it is entered into by humans, animals, plants, or artifacts. Having understood it, we will be better equipped to apply what we have learned to the human case.

A theory about what is good for human beings will of course have to say something about human beings, and not just about what it is for G to be good for S. Similarly, there is no saying what is good for some particular individual living being, unless we know a great deal about him or her or it. Some of what we must know pertains to the peculiar circumstances and idiosyncrasies of that particular individual, though other facts we must know pertain to the species to which S belongs. Because we want to say what is good for any human being, we must in some way reckon with human nature (sections 22, 35–53).[3] Even so, we should not overlook what is obvious: to know whether G is good for S, we must have

3. A theory of human nature also lies at the heart of Thomas Hurka's *Perfectionism*. But his theory makes claims about which properties of human beings are essential to them, whereas I do not. For doubts about Hurka's approach, see Philip Kitcher, "Ethics and Perfection." The position adopted here also differs from Hurka's in its rejection of maximizing approaches to ethics (sections 4, 12), and the importance it attaches to the role of "for" in "good for" (sections 16–24). Hurka defends maximizing consequentialism (*Perfectionism*, pp. 55–68) and accepts what I will call (section 21) a "locative" reading of "good for" (ibid., pp. 17–18, 58).

some understanding of *each* of three items: not only the purported good, not only the being for whom it is good, but also what is involved in one thing being good for another.

It is striking that we have a single term—"flourishing"—that we use to evaluate how well any living thing is doing. For most living things, to flourish is simply to be healthy: to be an organism that is unimpeded in its growth and normal functioning. Organic development, health, and proper physical functioning are also important components of human flourishing; but for us, faring well includes healthy *psychological* development and functioning as well. Could it be that the notion of flourishing is involved in the very idea of what is good for a living organism? That the things that are good for us human beings are the ones that play a role in our living flourishing lives—lives that go well for us in a way that is comparable to the way the lives of other sorts of creatures go well for them? That, at any rate, is the hypothesis that will be explored in this study.[4]

That is one reason for keeping the term "good for" at the center of our attention: doing so serves to remind us that the relationship we are investigating is not one into which only human beings enter. The range of a relationship—the variety of relata held together by it—should shape our understanding of what that relationship is. Other authors who investigate the same subject that we are exploring here—what is advantageous, beneficial, in someone's interests—hardly use such terms as "good" or "good for" at all; they prefer instead "well-being" or "welfare" or "utility."[5] Those terms can be useful tools, and they even have some advantages that "good for" lacks. When one announces that one is in-

4. The notion of flourishing first receives attention in contemporary ethical theory in G. E. M. Anscombe, "Modern Moral Philosophy," pp. 43–44. It has recently been exploited for the purposes of political theory by Martha Nussbaum in *Frontiers of Justice.* The good of animals plays an important role in the thinking of Rosalind Hursthouse, *On Virtue Ethics,* pp. 197–231, 247–265; and Philippa Foot, *Natural Goodness,* pp. 5, 16, 40–46, 92, 109. Note especially Foot's statement: "It is . . . possible that the concept of a good human life plays the same part in determining goodness of human characteristics and operations that the concept of flourishing plays in the determination of goodness in plants and animals" (ibid., p. 44). The approach I propose has similarities to those of Robert Adams, *Finite and Infinite Goods,* pp. 83–101; David Brink, *Moral Realism and the Foundations of Ethics,* pp. 217–236; John Finnis, *Natural Law and Natural Rights,* pp. 59–99; and Amartya Sen, *Development as Freedom,* pp. 70–77. Like Adams, I reject the maximization of value and the construction of well-being out of a person's real or hypothetical desires. But we differ in that I treat flourishing as the central concept of practical thought, whereas he gives pride of place to excellence (in terms of which he defines well-being) and defends the thesis that all finite excellences are images of a divine exemplar.

5. I have in mind James Griffin, *Well-Being;* and L. W. Sumner, *Welfare, Happiness, and Ethics.*

quiring into the nature of well-being, for example, one will be understood to be discussing something that is in itself desirable (for someone, of course—the one who attains such well-being). When one claims that well-being consists in X (for example: pleasure, or virtue, or knowledge), one cannot justify that claim by holding that X is an effective means to something else. For something to constitute well-being, entirely or partly, it must be noninstrumentally valuable (though it can be both such a constituent and *also* instrumentally valuable).

Not so for all that is good. The class of things that are good for S includes items that are admitted to that class by two very different routes: some of them are included only because they are effective means to the acquisition of others that are already in the class. And the rest are there on their own merits, as it were. The former are merely good instrumentally. The latter we can call "intrinsically" good—meaning simply that it is not merely by virtue of being instrumentally valuable that they are good.[6]

In this study, when it is asked whether something is good for someone, or claimed that it is, it is noninstrumental goodness that is being talked about. "Is it good for someone to know how to swim?" If we construe that as a question about whether swimming is a useful skill for anyone to have, it becomes the sort of practical question that philosophy is not well equipped to answer. But it becomes a more difficult and interesting question if it asks whether swimming should be included among the noninstrumental goods—that is, whether it is a component of a person's well-being or welfare.[7] Before we can satisfactorily reply to that question so interpreted, we are forced to wonder: how should we go about answering questions of this sort?

Such terms as "welfare," "well-being," and "utility" are seldom, if

---

6. Although this is what I shall mean by "intrinsically good" in this study, I will for the most part use the more cumbersome phrase, "noninstrumentally good," because it is less likely to cause confusion. It is not clear what the contrast between intrinsic goodness and extrinsic goodness amounts to when "intrinsic" is not used, as I use it here, interchangeably with "noninstrumental." Is something intrinsically good, for example, when its being good is somehow grounded in its intrinsic rather than its extrinsic properties? (See Jonathan Dancy, *Ethics without Principles*, p. 168.) In that case, one must clarify what an intrinsic property is. If, for example, it is claimed that a marriage is intrinsically good for its two partners, and this is taken to mean that its goodness is grounded in the intrinsic rather than the extrinsic properties of marriage, we must determine which properties of this institution should be counted as intrinsic to it.

7. Throughout this study, I will use "component of well-being" merely as a variant for "noninstrumentally good for someone."

ever, applied to plants. But it is just as obvious a point about plants as it is about animals that some things are good for them and others are not. If something can flourish or fall short of flourishing, that by itself shows that we can speak of what is good or bad for it; for S's flourishing is good for S, and what stands in the way of such flourishing is bad for it. Perhaps some living things (single-celled organisms, for example) are too simple to be properly spoken of as flourishing. If so, nothing counts as good for them or bad for them.[8]

The linguistic awkwardness that might be felt in talking about the welfare of a plant has no practical or philosophical significance.[9] To see this, consider a child who plans on lighting a fire and destroying a forest, simply for the sake of such destruction. Should we stop him? Certainly. But why so?—is it only because he may endanger human lives, kill the animals that live in the forest, and prevent it from serving human purposes? Why should not the fact that his act is bad for trees and a great many other living things—in fact, *all* the things in the forest that are flourishing—also be counted as a reason for interfering with him? Would we not be concerned, and rightly so, about his destructiveness, even if we knew that the forest is uninhabited by animals? After all, the child is not innocently rearranging the world; he is deliberately inflicting harm on all those forms of life for its own sake. That state of mind should disturb us, and so there must be something objectionable in what he is trying to do. That we do not normally speak of the welfare of trees should not diminish our concern about what the child does. We should say that since his act is bad for a great many be-

8. I am thus committed to saying that if merely being alive is not by itself a constituent of flourishing, but only a prerequisite for having one or more such constituents, then it is not intrinsically good for the creature whose life is in question. Destroying a single-celled organism would in that case no more be bad for it than would pulverizing a pebble be bad for it. After all, if a pebble's going out of existence is not counted as bad for it, and so ceasing to exist is not in all cases a bad thing, why consider an amoeba's demise bad for it? In any case, our temptation to speak of what is good or bad for an organism is far stronger when we can describe it as something that can be not only alive or dead but also flourishing—that is, capable of developing properly and being in a healthy condition. Readers who are convinced that it is always bad for a living thing to be destroyed can nonetheless accept my theory, if they agree that bare living is, at least for certain organisms, at least one component of their flourishing. I cannot, however, accommodate those who insist both that living is good and that it is not a component of flourishing.

9. Contrast this with Sumner, who, by emphasizing the term "welfare" rather than "good for," places plants at the periphery of his study (*Welfare, Happiness, and Ethics*, pp. 14–15, 74–75). He notes (ibid., p. 75) that "there are animal welfare groups, but no plant welfare groups."

ings (including those that are not classified as members of the animal kingdom), and good for none, that settles the matter: he should not light the fire.[10]

3. Mind and Value

Some philosophers hold that all value is, in some way, a creation of the mind.[11] Accordingly, if G is good for S, that must be because S pursues it, or desires it, or likes it—or would, under certain conditions, pursue, desire, or like it. Pain is bad for the animal that feels it because the animal is averse to it. The food it eats is good for it because it seeks and enjoys it. Similarly, according to this way of thinking, what is good for human beings is made good by their attitudes, emotions, desires, plans, goals, and the like (section 25).

There is a grain of truth in this doctrine, but it will take some work to extract it (section 30.) What we can say for now is that when a creature has a mind (that is, sensations, feelings, thoughts, desires), what is good for it depends on the kind of mind it has and its peculiar constitution.[12] That should not be the least bit surprising: what is good for S depends a great deal upon facts about S; and if S is the sort of being that has desires

10. We return to the good of plants in sections 12 and 56. My claim that living things should not be wantonly destroyed, because we should not do what is bad for something without adequate reason, does not imply that we should take steps to benefit every living thing (section 56). Admitting that there is such a thing as what is good for S does not commit one to enhancing, even to some small degree, S's good.

11. For a survey and critical assessment of this "constructivist" conception of value, see Russ Shafer-Landau, *Moral Realism*, pp. 13–14, 41–52. The thesis that value is a mental construct not only is accepted by a few academic philosophers but pervades many parts of our culture and sometimes provides the framework for research in the social sciences. For example, Jonathan Haidt, a social psychologist, writes: "Good and evil do not exist outside of our beliefs about them" (*The Happiness Hypothesis*, p. 71). The outlook I defend here is what Christine Korsgaard calls "substantive moral realism . . . the view that there are answers to moral questions *because* there are moral facts" (*The Sources of Normativity*, p. 35, her emphasis). She holds, against this, that "value is grounded in rational nature . . . and it is projected on to the world" (ibid., p. 116); "the value of humanity [is] the foundation of all value" (ibid., p. 145).

12. There are difficulties lurking here, but they will not be addressed in this study. Is it possible for the mind of an individual to change so much that what was once good for it (because it had one kind of mind) is no longer so (because its mental life is now so different)? Presumably if a cat, for example, could be transformed into a dog, then what is good or bad for it would, to some extent, be different. But what of some inchoate genetic material that could be developed

and thoughts, then what is good for it will depend, at least to some degree, on the fact that it is a desiring and thinking being.

But we can already see that the doctrine that all value is mind-dependent is a gross oversimplification. Plants do not have minds. And yet some things are good for them: to grow, to thrive, to flourish, to live out the full term of their lives in good health. Whatever impedes this—diseases, drought, excessive heat and cold—is bad for them. What is good for a plant is not made good for it by the fact that some human being takes up a certain mental attitude toward it. Most plants—the ones that exist now and all those that predate human existence—are beyond the ken of human beings; but that does not entail that nothing that happens or happened to them is good or bad (for them). Before human beings came into existence, the sun gave off light and heat, many species of plants arose, some members of those species flourished, and others did not. Good and bad—that is, the relationship that exists between any two things when one of them is good or bad for the other—are not brought into being by, or dependent on, human attitudes or minds in general. One kind of value is already "out there" in the world, existing independently of any mind.

It is worth bearing in mind that it is not only human beings who should do certain things and avoid others. We can also sensibly talk about what an animal should do. The vocabulary of "should" and "should not" is not grounded on human norms. To see this, consider a wolf that is searching for food and sniffs out two alternative paths at a fork in the road. If it selects A, it will find food; if B, it will be killed in a mud slide. What should it do? Obviously, it should proceed along A. And there is an argument to support this conclusion: "It is good for it

---

into either an ape or a human being, depending on the way it is manipulated? Is there reason to say that one course of development would be better for it than the other? Many would be tempted to say that it will be better for it to become human (at any rate, if it will live in circumstances favorable to human life). That position rests on assumptions about what kind of mind it is best for a minded being to have. It thus goes far beyond the more modest idea I endorse here—that if a living thing already has a mind, its well-being depends on the kind of mind it has. (We are, with good reason, far more confident about certain judgments that weigh the lives of human beings against those of other living things. A pilot guiding a disabled plane to the site of its crash will keep it away from human habitations, even if doing so results in the death of animals and plants. And medical research can justifiably sacrifice the lives of certain animals, if doing so saves a large number of human lives.)

to move along A, bad for it to move along B. Therefore it should choose A." The terms of the argument are the same as the ones we use all the time in thinking about our own lives. They apply with no less force to the wolf.[13]

Should it choose A over B because it wants food and wants to avoid death? We rightly hesitate to say that animals want to avoid death. (The objects they fear are other animals, not the possibility of annihilation.) But in any case, it should be clear that nourishment is good and untimely death bad for any healthy being. The wolf's appetite is what makes it seek food, but the food it seeks is good for it whether or not it seeks it. (If the wolf loses its appetite for food, that is bad for it.) We should remind ourselves that nourishment is good for plants as well, though they have no desires. An animal's mind has no bearing on the fact that food is good for it and death bad. Some truths about what is good or bad for a creature that has a mind are grounded in facts about that creature that are not facts about its mind. And since this is true of animals, we should not be surprised to find that it holds true of human beings as well.

The roots of many (not all) plants will rot if they sit in water for too long. That is bad for those plants. And so they should be located in a place where they will not be exposed to excessive water (assuming that this harms no other living thing). The little argument just rehearsed is the same in form as those that apply to animals and humans. Facts about what is good need not be grounded in a human mind or any other kind of mind. When there are facts about what is good (and the good of one being brings no harm to another), there are also at the same time facts about what should be the case, and these too are not grounded in any mind. Value is not the sort of thing that is, by its very nature, a human or a mental construct.

---

13. Animals that are impeded in their power to detect sources of nourishment are thereby defective. But it would be difficult to understand why this counts as a defect if there were no such thing as what an animal should do. Of course, when there is a conflict between the good of several creatures, it often becomes difficult to reach conclusions about what any one of them should do or what should happen. If a wolf were to kill a rabbit, that would be good for the wolf, but bad for the rabbit. What should happen? What should the wolf do? These questions do not always have answers (section 10). But that does not mean that it is never the case that there is something that an animal should do.

4. Utilitarianism

It is evident that claims about what is good (better, best, and so on) for someone have *some* bearing on the conclusions we reach about practical matters. "It will be good for your children if you read to them. That's why you should do it." That is a homely but exemplary piece of practical reasoning. Appealing to what is good for someone is one of the routes by means of which we legitimately arrive at practical conclusions. But what of other routes—those that steer clear of what is good for someone and advert to other sorts of considerations that speak against or in favor of doing this or that? Are there any such routes? Or, when we reason soundly toward a practical conclusion, must we always travel by way of goodness, badness, and their congeners?

We use many other kinds of words than "good," "bad," and their ilk when we reason our way to a conclusion about what to do. "Killing is morally wrong, so you must not take his life." "Lying to him would be dishonest, so you ought not do so." "He deserves more money, so you should increase his wages." "You promised to help him, and so you should." Important as "good" and "bad" are, they seem to be only two among a large and motley assortment of terms that figure in the premises we use to arrive at practical conclusions. Nonetheless, one of the leading ethical theories of the modern age—utilitarianism—has sought to give "good" and "bad" a kind of primacy over all the other terms of our practical vocabulary. It holds that we should take into account only two types of consideration when we ask what someone should do: what is good for someone, and what is bad for someone.[14] The fact that an act is dishonest, for example, does not in itself count against it, according to the utilitarian. Nor does the fact that an act would break a promise. But if an act of dishonesty or the breaking of a promise is bad for someone (the agent or someone else), or if such an act has results that are (or are

---

14. Sometimes utilitarianism is formulated as a doctrine that advocates producing the best *states of affairs;* what is good *for someone* is then counted as only one factor that contributes to the goodness of a state of affairs. I leave aside this alternative, which I regard as less appealing than the version of utilitarianism that I discuss. For the idea that utilitarianism rests on a mis-understanding of the proper role to be played in our practical thinking by judgments about the best states of affairs, see Philippa Foot, "Utilitarianism and the Virtues"; and *Natural Goodness,* pp. 48–50.

likely to be) bad for someone, then *that*—the harm done to someone—is what counts against it.

Utilitarianism embraces a second striking principle: the *quantity* (or expected quantity) of good that we produce is the only thing that should matter to us, and we should strive to make this quantity (or expected quantity) as large as possible.[15] We have not yet given an adequate justification for what we do if the only point we have made in its favor is that it does some amount of good for someone. We must consider our alternatives, and if an alternative is available to us that brings about a larger quantity of good, that is the option we should choose. To determine which alternative does the most good, we are to subtract the bad each does from the good it does, and choose the one that has the highest sum. Evil must be done that good may come—if the total amount of good done (less the harm) is a greater sum than would be brought about by any alternative. Killing, for example, is not only permissible but a necessity when whatever harm it does is so greatly outweighed by the good it causes that the total amount of good in the universe is greater than it would have been had any alternative been chosen. Goodness and badness have magnitude; and the proper way to arrive at a practical conclusion is to pay attention solely to those magnitudes.[16]

Nonetheless, the philosopher who did more than any other to bring utilitarianism to the forefront of philosophical discussion—John Stuart Mill—incorporated into his defense of that doctrine a distinction that puts him at odds with other members of this "school." In Chapter 2 of *Utilitarianism* he argues that all that is good is pleasure and all that is bad

---

15. For the sake of simplicity, I leave aside the question raised by the phrase placed in parentheses, "expected quantity." One form of utilitarianism finds, for each person, the outcome that has the highest expected desirability and then, aggregating this information, directs us to produce the largest quantity of expected "utility." The tactic of combining a desirability matrix and a probability matrix to arrive at a ranking of estimated desirability is one of the hallmarks of Bayesian decision theory. See Richard Jeffrey, *The Logic of Decision,* for an accessible exposition. For a lucid introduction to utilitarianism, see Shelly Kagan, *Normative Ethics,* pp. 25–69, and esp. p. 44, on the utilitarian's need to find a quantitative measure of well-being.

16. Throughout this study, I construe utilitarianism as a theory about what practical reasons there are and hence about factors that should be taken into account when one deliberates about what to do. Whether one is engaged in abstract ethical inquiry or is coping with a difficult and concrete decision, one wants to know not only what to do, but why one should do it. Utilitarianism, I assume, purports to tell us what shape those reasons should take. Nonetheless, it can instead be formulated as a theory that assesses only what people do and not as a prescription for practical reasoning. For people might, on the whole, be poor deliberators about how to

is painful.[17] But some types of pleasures, he claims, are of higher quality than others, and that difference should play an important role in our practical thinking. Suppose one alternative brings a smaller quantity of pleasure than another, but the quality of the pleasures of the first alternative is higher than the quality of the pleasures of the second. (For example, one might be choosing between an hour of writing poetry and a week of passively sitting on the beach.) The first alternative's qualitative superiority might more than compensate for its quantitative inferiority; and if it does, that is the alternative Mill thinks one should choose. His idea, then, is that although no consideration speaks in favor of an action except its goodness and its productiveness of goodness, we should not think of goodness as something that has no important feature other than magnitude. The goodness and badness (goodness and badness *for* someone) of an act and of its consequences are the only features of it that are of practical importance, but goodness is not to be maximized.[18]

Hedonism—the claim that all and only pleasures are good, and that all and only pains are bad—can be set aside for now. (We return to it in section 32.) Nor does it matter whether we use the word "utilitarianism" narrowly, as a name for the doctrine that good is a quantity to be maximized, or broadly, so that it includes Mill's nonmaximizing version of

---

maximize the good; they might produce the greatest amount of good by aiming not at this in their deliberations, but at something else. The utilitarian can say, in that case, that people should not aim at maximizing the good, even though the criterion by which their "actions" should be judged is whether they maximize the good. (I put "actions" in scare quotes because actions are undertaken for a reason and are therefore normally assessed not as mere happenings but also as an expression of one's purposes. But utilitarianism, so construed, does not recommend itself to deliberators as a basis for deliberation.) This point is emphasized by Derek Parfit, *Reasons and Persons*, pp. 3–51; see too R. Eugene Bales, "Act-Utilitarianism: Account of Right-Making Characteristics or Decision-Making Procedure?" Some of the difficulties I will raise for utilitarianism in section 12 do not tell against it when it is construed as a thesis about how our doings should be assessed, but not about how we should reason toward concrete practical conclusions. But it pays a price when it is formulated in this way.

17. John Stuart Mill, *Utilitarianism*, pp. 210–213.

18. Kagan's discussion of what he calls "qualitative hedonism" raises the possibility that quality might be measured and factored into an equation that caters both to the quantity and quality of pleasure. "Perhaps a new formula could achieve this [accounting both for quality and quantity] by multiplying intensity times duration times a 'quality rating'" (*Normative Ethics*, p. 32). According to this version of Mill's idea, goodness *is* to be maximized. I know of no sensible "quality rating," however. To treat quality as one more factor (along with intensity and duration) to be numerated is to perpetuate rather than abandon a quantitative approach to well-being.

it.[19] What is most significant about Mill's moral philosophy, for our purposes, is that it affirms a kind of primacy for goodness as a practical consideration, but without advocating the maximization of goodness. Mill does not believe that there are multiple routes by which we can validly arrive at practical conclusions, some proceeding by way of goodness and badness, and others by way of entirely different sorts of considerations—such considerations as rights, duties, desert, justice, or equality. Rather, his idea is that what counts in favor of or against an action is *only* the good or harm it does for someone. (Some harms, he thinks, should be punished; that, according to Chapter 5 of *Utilitarianism*, is what is meant when we say that we have a *duty* to refrain from them.[20] But there is no duty to refrain from what does no harm.) That is why one must always proceed toward practical conclusions by way of good and bad: no considerations that are independent of them can have any importance.

There is another possibility, though it is not one that utilitarianism countenances. Perhaps in arguing well toward a practical conclusion one must always advert to some good that is done or harm that is avoided, but something else must be added as well: namely, a reason one should do what is good, or avoid what is bad, for *this* person rather than that. "Because he is my son." "Because he deserves it." "Because I promised." "Because justice requires it." These are all factors that weigh heavily in our practical reasoning because they are the normal ways in which we allocate our attention and resources. Each of them can figure as fragments of a larger justificatory argument that adverts to what is good and the avoidance of harm; they need not be conceived of as self-standing reasons that come into competition with considerations having to do with good and bad. We might think of sound practical reasoning as always having to do with someone's good—but *who* that someone is, and

19. Throughout this study I shall always use "the maximization of good" to name the policy of thinking of all goods as possessing some magnitude (a measure of how good they are), comparing one's options by measuring those magnitudes, and selecting whichever option yields the greatest quantity of good. The term can be and sometimes is used more loosely to designate any policy of making decisions by ranking one's options (the best alternative, the second-best, and so on), and choosing whichever ranks highest. The latter policy requires no quantitative measure of alternatives: by whichever standards one evaluates one's options, some of them will be no worse than the others, and one is to select from among those. No one could reasonably object to *that* policy. (Why choose the second-best alternative, when one can as easily attain the best?) It might be called a policy of maximization insofar as it seeks not merely a good alternative, but the best among them (or, at any rate, one that is unsurpassed).

20. Mill, *Utilitarianism*, p. 246.

not just what kind of good that good is (or how much good is done), makes a great difference. Such factors as justice, merit, associative ties, obligations, and duties determine whom it is that we should be helping.

Such a conception of good practical reasoning would not urge us to think *exclusively* in terms of good and bad, eliminating all the other factors (justice, obligation, affiliation) that play so large a role in everyday social transactions. Rather, it would insist on the necessity—indeed, the centrality—of good and bad. According to this way of thinking, the *point* of social institutions, social interactions, and individual projects should be to enhance someone's well-being or to eliminate impediments to well-being. What is good for someone is a *central,* and not only a *necessary,* reference point of practical reasoning because it is what we should be aiming at. That, I believe, is the place that good should occupy in our thinking.

With this conception of the centrality of goodness any utilitarian would agree, and that is the element of utilitarianism that accords most fully with common sense. But the utilitarian takes a radical step by attaching no intrinsic importance to the allocative considerations recognized by common morality, that is, to the weight that is ordinarily attached to giving priority, when we do what is good, to one person rather than another, on grounds of affiliation, merit, prior commitment, and so on. A still more radical step is taken by most utilitarians (though not Mill) when they hold that the quantity of good that one does is the only consideration that should matter.

That there is just one legitimate route—the route of goodness—for arriving at practical conclusions is a thesis that was widely accepted by the moral philosophers of the ancient world. All actions, they supposed, are undertaken on the assumption that they are or lead to what is good for someone.[21] The project of ethical theory, as they conceived it, is to determine whether the things thought to be good by ordinary people or so-

---

21. The clearest expression of this idea is the Stoic identification of goodness and advantage or benefit. See, for example, Diogenes Laertius *Lives of Eminent Philosophers* 7.94. Plato, in raising the question whether justice is good for the just person, implies that the question "What is good for us?" is the fundamental practical question. Similarly, Aristotle can be reasonably interpreted to be placing that question at the center of practical reasoning in the opening sentences of both the *Nicomachean Ethics* and the *Eudemian Ethics.* I will not pursue interpretive difficulties here, but I concede that there are ways of taking both Plato and Aristotle to be giving primacy to absolute rather than relative goodness—that is, to what is good, but not good for anyone.

phisticated thinkers really are such—and if they are not, to seek a re-
placement for these misunderstandings. What we deliberately undertake
must have a goal, and that goal must be something that is good for
someone. Since good rightly occupies a central place in our deliberations, the most urgent practical task of philosophy is to discover what
the content of goodness is—to discover, in other words, what concrete
goal (whether it be knowledge, or virtue, or pleasure) should be placed
at the center.

By contrast, the idea that practical questions are always to be resolved
by dismissing all qualitative distinctions among alternatives, and choosing among them solely on the basis of a purely quantitative superiority, is by no means a commonplace of ancient ethical theory. It is, on
the contrary, an idea that one rarely, if ever, encounters in that period.
Socrates seems to be proposing something like this hypothesis in Plato's
Protagoras[22]—and that feature of the dialogue is not lost on Mill, who refers to it on the opening page of *Utilitarianism*. But in other dialogues,
Socrates and Plato's other leading interlocutors cannot be found looking for something to maximize. On the contrary, Socrates suggests in the
Philebus[23] that what is good is produced when limit, structure, and form are
imposed on something, thereby preventing it from becoming excessive.

In any case, it is difficult to believe that finding something to count,
and choosing among alternatives by finding the alternative that brings
about the greatest amount of some magnitude, is the key to all good decision making. When we grade things of a kind—deciding whether this
will be a good marriage, whether she will be a good attorney, or if this es-
say best deserves the prize—we do not suppose that all qualitative distinctions must be set aside, and that we must look for some magnitude
to be maximized by that marriage, attorney, or award. No one can plausibly suppose that the best novel is the one that has the greatest number of
words, or the greatest amount of some other factor. Whether a novel is a
good novel is not a question that is determined by quantitative considerations. Similarly, no one supposes that whether a life is a good one is a
question that can be settled entirely by asking how long it is, or by some
other purely arithmetic test. A good G is not necessarily made good by
having more of something than a bad G. That should put us on guard

22. Plato *Protagoras* Stephanus pp. 353–357.
23. Plato *Philebus* Stephanus p. 64d–e.

against assuming that questions about what is best for someone are to be settled by finding something with magnitude and increasing that magnitude as much as possible. Counting something and increasing it as much as one can might be as poor a way of making decisions regarding what is good for someone as it is a way of making decisions about what a good thing of its kind is.[24] (We will return to grading things that belong to a kind in sections 17, 20, 69 and 70.)

It is nonetheless possible to slip into utilitarianism by sheer inattention. That can happen in the following way. To make decisions, we must make comparisons. Not only must we know what is good for someone; we must also know how to compare the many different types of things that are good for someone. Are some of them better than others? Is there one, or a group, that is best? To say that one good is better than another is simply to say that it is more good. To say that one good is best is to say that it is the most good. And it seems that the very logic of goodness—the fact that it admits of comparison (good, better, best)—forces us into using a quantitative method for making decisions about what is advantageous for someone. That is, we seem forced to suppose that if X is better for someone than Y, then there must be some third thing, Z, that X has a larger amount of than Y.

That, however, is a non sequitur. To say that X is better for someone

24. John Rawls is more sympathetic to maximization: "It is natural to think that rationality is maximizing something and that in morals it must be maximizing the good. Indeed, it is tempting to suppose that it is self-evident that things should be arranged to lead to the most good" (*A Theory of Justice*, p. 22). He of course rejects the principle that good is to be maximized, but the context of this passage suggests that the only reason for rejecting it is that its acceptance would require us to violate principles of moral rightness. Doubts about treating good practical thinking as the search for the maximum of something are expressed by Elizabeth Anderson (*Value in Ethics and Economics*, passim), T. M. Scanlon (*What We Owe to Each Other*, pp. 78–107), and Adams (*Finite and Infinite Goods*, pp. 97, 119). I do not believe that the fundamental difficulties encountered by utilitarianism are alleviated if it is formulated as a theory about which *rules* we should follow. According to this approach, often called "rule utilitarianism," we are not to choose the act that will maximize the good, but are instead to discover the ideal set of moral rules—namely, those rules the general acceptance of which would maximize the good—and abide by them. But there is no more reason to assess moral rules by means of a simple quantitative formula than there is to assess actions in this way. And if one is attached to the idea that good is to be maximized, then it would be odd to abstain from an act that *will* maximize the good merely for the reason that it violates a rule the general acceptance of which *would* maximize the good. Rule utilitarianism is an unstable compromise: it retains an important place for maximizing good, but recoils from those optimific acts that could not be permitted by an ideal code. Some of its difficulties are discussed by Bernard Williams in *Morality: An Introduction to Ethics*, pp. 99–107. For a recent defense, see Brad Hooker, *Ideal Code, Real World*.

than Y—that it is more good for someone than Y—is simply to assign to X a higher grade than Y with respect to their goodness for that person. But that higher grade need not be more fully deserved by X than Y because X has a higher quantity of something, Z, than Y does. The phrase "more good" means "better than"; and one thing can be better than another in that it is of higher quality. There need not be some third good, lying in the background—the good that X has more of than Y.

To illustrate: a philosopher might hold that two things are good for us, virtue and pleasure. He might argue that virtue is the greater good, and that no amount of pleasure would compensate for the loss of virtue. He thinks that a good person who feels no pleasure is better off than a bad person, however much pleasure the bad person feels. A philosopher who adopts this high-minded position might find it difficult to defend his theory, but he is not forced by the very logic of goodness to admit that there is something that both virtue and pleasure produce or involve, something that virtue has much more of than pleasure.

To illustrate again: it is worse for someone to suffer through the death of a close friend than to be deprived of the pleasure of eating a strawberry. It is better for a lonely person to make a new close friend than to have the pleasure of eating that strawberry. It would be a mistake to suppose that, for such statements as these to be true, there must be some single thing that one gets from friendship and from strawberries, and that friendship is better for someone because it has a larger quantity of that thing.

The point can be made more general, so that it covers all uses of "better": there is no reason to think that they can be supported only by quantitative considerations. When we judge that one poem is better than another, we can fully support our evaluation by pointing to the good features of the first and the bad features of the second. There need not be some single feature that both share, the greater quantity of which is what accounts for the superiority of the one to the other. Any attempt to reduce the evaluation of the quality of a poem to the mere counting of something would show a failure to understand how poems are to be appreciated.

The utilitarian holds that we should increase the total amount of good in the universe, making whatever sacrifices are needed to do so. Some people might have to suffer, but their suffering is justified if it is a necessary means for achieving the highest possible balance of good over bad. That is precisely what makes some philosophers hostile to utilitarianism: they think that its interpersonal implications—its views about how people are to treat each other—are morally offensive. But the utilitarian has already made a mistake if he starts from the assumption that when we consider what is good for a single individual, we should look for some quantitative measure by means of which we can assess that person's options. That sort of utilitarian thinks: "Without addressing the question of which things are in fact good, we can see that goodness has magnitude, and that more of it is always better for someone than less. Quantity of good, in fact, is the only factor that needs to be weighed, whether a decision affects only one person or several. Now, we ought not to care only about what is good for some one person, or some restricted group of people; rather, it is the good of all (that is, the largest possible number) that should be our concern. Therefore, whatever we happen to think is good, it must be something that we try to produce the greatest amount of, throughout the universe."

The interpersonal component of utilitarianism—its claim that the gains of some need only be large enough to compensate for the losses of others—is deeply problematic (section 12). But even aside from that, even in its application to decisions that affect only a single individual, utilitarianism is unacceptable. It claims that what is best for any single individual is the maximization of something or other—namely, whatever is good for that individual; and it claims that we do not have to decide which things are in fact good to recognize that this is so. In effect, that is to claim that "X is better for someone than Y" can be true only if X is quantitatively superior to Y. There is no reason to accept this as a formal principle—a principle that we affirm, regardless of what we think is in fact good.

What a utilitarian will have to do to salvage his principle of maximization is to proceed in a less abstract fashion. That is, he will have to propose a substantive theory about what is in fact good for someone. Then he will have to argue that since *this* is what is good, the most sensible way to make decisions about what is good for any individual is to look for ways of producing the greatest possible amount of *this* thing that has been shown to be good. For example, the utilitarian might proceed as follows: "What is good for anyone is pleasure and pleasure alone. Furthermore, what makes one pleasure better for someone than another is simply its quantity—its intensity and duration. Therefore, to decide what is best for one individual, look for the alternative that brings the greatest quantity of pleasure." That, of course, is the way in which

Jeremy Bentham presents utilitarianism.[25] He does not ask us to accept the abstract proposition that whatever is good—whether it be pleasure or something else—must be something that it is best to have the greatest amount of. He argues that pleasure, and pleasure alone, is good; and this, he hopes, will lead us to see that there can be no reason not to have as much of it as possible. When we are deciding among competing pleasures, he assumes, the only reasonable basis for choice is to find the alternative that offers the most.

Hedonism, we will see, is unacceptable (section 32). Nor is there any other plausible conception of what is good that can sustain the idea that what is best for someone is to attain the greatest quantity of something. When we decide what is best for someone, we necessarily look for the alternative that is more good for him than any other; that is a tautology. But once we clarify our ideas about what is in fact good, we will see that it is nothing that one should seek the largest possible quantity of. Simple quantitative goals—the largest number of friends or the greatest amount of power, or wealth, or prizes, or satisfaction, or virtue—are too simple. They deform rather than enhance our lives.[26] The things that are good for us are not items toward which the proper attitude is: as much of that as possible (section 44).[27]

---

25. Jeremy Bentham, *An Introduction to the Principles of Morals and Legislation,* chap. 1.

26. The Bayesian framework for decision making assumes that what is better for S is what is preferred by S and then provides a method for moving from preference orderings to a cardinal ranking of all of an individual's options, ranging from 1 (one's first-ranked preference) to 0 (one's least preferred option). One can then numerate and not merely rank one's options and thus give exquisite precision to the consideration of alternatives. See Jeffrey, *The Logic of Decision,* pp. 41–53. But this serves as a theory of what is better for someone (and not merely what is preferred by him) only if what is good for someone is a construction out of what he wants. That approach to well-being will be discussed in sections 25–31.

27. Even the more limited project of maximization to which W. D. Ross subscribes strikes me as misguided. He holds that one of our prima facie duties is to bring into existence as much knowledge, virtue, and ("with certain limitations") pleasure as possible (*The Right and the Good,* p. 24). That is, we are to maximize these goods whenever doing so would not break a promise or violate any other principle of moral rightness. Ross writes as though we are to be devoted to knowledge, virtue, and pleasure *themselves* and to their maximal increase; the prima facie duty to increase these values without end treats the people in whom they reside as mere vessels through whom the project of maximization operates. My opposition to even this limited form of maximization should be compared with Scanlon's rejection of a "teleological" conception of value, according to which "what we have reason to do . . . is to act so as to realize those states of affairs that . . . have the greatest value" (*What We Owe to Each Other,* p. 80). Nonetheless, the position I am defending here could be called "teleological" simply because it is, in a sense to be explained, good-centered.

And yet in a way the project pursued in this study is akin to the one pursued by the utilitarian. Utilitarianism is the ethical theory of the modern world that upholds the centrality of goodness in practical thinking. It claims that all reasoning to practical conclusions should proceed by finding a way to do what is good for someone or to avoid what is bad for someone, and that attempts at practical justification fail if they advert to no good or to no avoidance of harm. It is *the* modern advocate of that ancient and appealing idea. It is unfortunate that utilitarianism also weds itself to more questionable philosophical programs: the elimination of common methods of allocating goods (justice, desert, affiliation, promising, and so on) and the relentless quantification of value. For good-centered ethical theories—theories that require all practical justification to proceed by way of what is good because this is the point of all that we do—deserve careful examination.[28]

But perhaps even this good-centeredness is misguided. We should be wary of all monisms: all philosophical doctrines that deny the multiplicity of the world and of values and seek to fit seemingly disparate items into one mold. There seem to be many different ways of arriving at the conclusion that something should be done or not done. ("It is wrong." "He deserves it." "You promised.") That some good will be done for someone is certainly one of them, but why believe that there are no others?

It would be absurd to say, at this point, that we already know what role goodness properly plays in our practical thinking. To achieve a greater understanding of this matter, we must consider what is being said about something when it is claimed that it is good for someone, and we must decide which things are in fact good. Those will be the topics of Chapters 2 and 3. Then, in Chapter 4, we will be better able to decide whether our practical thinking should be good-centered.

5. Rawls and the Priority of the Right

John Rawls holds that "the two main concepts of ethics are those of the right and the good,"[29] but that rightness has priority over goodness. He explains what he has in mind as follows: "An individual who finds that

28. A theory of this sort might aptly be described as an "ethics of well-being," and that is what the subtitle of this study is meant to convey.
29. Rawls, *A Theory of Justice*, p. 21.

he enjoys seeing others in positions of lesser liberty understands that he has no claim whatever to this enjoyment. . . . The principles of right, and so of justice, put limits on which satisfactions have value; they impose restrictions on what are reasonable conceptions of one's good. . . . We can express this by saying that in justice as fairness the concept of right is prior to that of the good. . . . The interests requiring the violation of justice . . . [have] no merit in the first place [and therefore] cannot override its claims."[30]

When Rawls says that acts that violate "the principles of right" have no "value" or "merit," and that a person who enjoys harming others does not have a "reasonable" conception of the good, he does not mean to deny that those wrongful satisfactions are good for the person who feels them. On the contrary, to say that rightness is prior to goodness is to grant that those wrongful satisfactions *are* good.[31] Rawls believes that "the good is . . . the satisfaction of rational desire."[32] Or, as he puts it: "A person's good is determined by what is for him the most rational long-term plan of life given reasonably favorable circumstances. A man is happy when he is more or less successfully in the way of carrying out his plan."[33]

Let us elaborate on Rawls's example of someone who "enjoys seeing others in positions of lesser liberty." Imagine that he has disdain for certain people, and his goal is to deny them the freedoms of citizenship by arranging for their capture and enslavement. Rawls thinks that if such a person is successful, more or less, in the pursuit of his plan, then—provided that it is a rational plan—his success is good for him. A plan is rational if it conforms to certain principles of rational choice and would be chosen "in the light of a full knowledge of [one's] situation."[34] Neither of these conditions is necessarily violated by someone who aims at the en-

30. Ibid., pp. 27–28.

31. My reading sets aside Rawls's later statement that "something is good only if it fits into ways of life consistent with the principles of right already on hand" (ibid., p. 348). By this I do not believe that Rawls means that if it would be wrong for S to do V, it cannot be good for S to do V.

32. Ibid., p. 27.

33. Ibid., p. 79.

34. Ibid., p. 359. For the principles of rational choice that Rawls has in mind, see ibid., pp. 361–365. They are to take effective means to one's ends, to achieve more of one's ends than fewer, and to develop a larger number of ends. The last, which Rawls calls "the principle of inclusiveness," will be discussed and rejected in section 46. At this point it is enough to see that those who aim to hold slaves need not be in violation of Rawls's principles of rational choice.

slavement of others. And so, according to Rawls, we have to concede that the successful execution of such a plan would be good for the person who carries it out, provided the plan is one he would have chosen had he "assess[ed] his prospects with care in the light of a full knowledge of his situation."[35]

No doubt, if the enslaver succeeds, he not only does good (for himself) but brings about great harm (for the person he enslaves). Rawls assumes that the person who is forced to accept a reduction in his liberties is made worse-off because his rational desires or plans will be impeded (section 63.) But his thesis that the right is prior to the good rests on the idea that some other sort of consideration, besides what is good or bad, must be brought into play if we are to come to the correct conclusion about what should be permitted by a society's constitution and laws. It is a mistake, he thinks, to adopt the utilitarian principle that the proper way to resolve the conflict between the good of one person (the person who aims at enslaving others) and another (the person who would be enslaved) is simply to assess how much good and harm would be done by permitting slavery. There is another factor at play: the moral *wrongness* of such an institution. That, he thinks, is not merely one consideration among others; rather, it has a special kind of weight. It makes irrelevant the good that comes to the person who "enjoys seeing others in positions of lesser liberty." Seeking to enslave others is good for people who like that sort of thing (provided their plan is one they would arrive at were they to think with care and knowledge). But it is wrong, and that settles the question. Good draws us forward. Wrongness pulls us back: it imposes a "constraint," a "boundary," a "restriction."[36] To which should we pay greater heed when they conflict? Rawls replies: wrongness. The practical significance of goodness sinks to nothingness when it comes up against the boundaries set by right and wrong.

Rawls is no doubt correct in his claim that simply counting up the quantity of good and bad, as the utilitarian does, is objectionable. But his thesis that right is prior to good—like his claim that goodness sinks to insignificance when it is wrong—rests on a mistaken conception of what is good, as we will see in Chapters 2 and 3. What is good for a person is not the satisfaction of that person's rational desires, or the achievement

35. Ibid., p. 359.

36. These are the terms Rawls uses when he explains what is meant by the priority of the right (ibid., p. 27).

of his rational aims. Before we can know whether something trumps goodness, as Rawls believes, we need a better understanding of the nature of goodness. (We will return to the alleged priority of rightness to goodness in sections 60, 62, and 65.)[37]

6. Right, Wrong, Should

Not every case in which someone does something right or goes wrong falls within the domain that is studied by moral philosophy. If, for example, someone is baking bread, and it comes out of the oven burned, then he probably did something wrong. But no one is likely to accuse him of wrongdoing. He made a mistake, of course; but he did no wrong. He did something wrong, but he did no wrong: that sounds like a contradiction, but of course it is not. We can easily sort things out by distinguishing different kinds of rightness and wrongness, or perhaps even different senses of these terms.[38] We apply "right" and "wrong" whenever we are assessing the correctness or incorrectness of an action in some dimension. But on occasion to speak of right or wrong is to speak of what is morally right or morally wrong. When Rawls says, "The two main concepts of ethics are those of the right and the good; the concept of a morally worthy person is . . . derived from them,"[39] he is claiming that *moral* rightness is one of the central concepts of ethics. A good cook must know about how to go right and avoid going wrong in the preparation of food. But a good person—that is, a person who is "morally worthy," as Rawls puts it—must know something about which actions are morally

37. The thesis that rightness is prior to goodness might be construed as a principle that does not rest on any particular conception of what goodness or rightness is. It might be said, in other words, that whether goodness is the achievement of rational aims or not, it can be seen that it is nullified by considerations of moral rightness and wrongness. That is not in fact how Rawls introduces the priority of rightness: the utilitarian conception of goodness as the satisfaction of rational desire is accepted first (ibid., p. 27), and then the priority thesis is explained as the nullification of goodness so conceived (pp. 27–28). But perhaps Rawls is nonetheless best interpreted to be proposing the more abstract claim—that right is prior to good, however good is understood. I believe that the arguments to be given in sections 60–65 cast doubt on even that more general formulation of the priority thesis. For when goodness is understood as flourishing, it is doubtful that some other type of reason can nullify its force; and so it is doubtful that goodness, whatever it is, has this inferior status.

38. I move back and forth between saying that "right" has different senses and saying that there are different kinds of rightness. These are not equivalent claims, but for my purposes, it is not important to distinguish between them.

39. Rawls, *A Theory of Justice*, p. 21.

right and which are morally wrong. By making this distinction between two different meanings of "right," or two different kinds or rightness, we can make it clear that there is no contradiction in saying that when someone burned the bread he did something wrong, even though he did nothing that was wrong: in its second occurrence, but not its first, the wrongness in question is moral wrongness.

"Right" and "wrong" have both broad and narrow uses: rightness, broadly speaking, embraces every sort of correctness (the correct time, the correct train, the correct gift), including the special species of correctness that we call "moral." You will not incur the charge of being an immoral person, or acting immorally, if the only thing that can be said against you is that your act displayed some form of incorrectness; it is only one particular kind of incorrectness—doing something that is not merely incorrect but morally wrong—that will support the charge that you are a wrongdoer and not without moral blemish.

The use to which we put "should" in our normative thinking differs in an important way from the use to which we put "morally right" and "morally wrong." They play different roles in the inferences we make. To see this, consider the following sociological platitudes. Many people attach great weight to doing what is morally right and avoiding what is morally wrong. They think that rightness and wrongness should figure in our deliberations in a special way: there are few, if any, circumstances, in which they allow considerations other than right and wrong to be given greater weight in their practical thinking. They say: "It would be morally *wrong,* and for that reason alone I *should* not do it." Or: "I *should* do it, if only because it is the morally *right* thing to do."

Notice how differently "should" and "right" operate in these sentences. The moral rightness of an act is what is referred to in the premise of their argument; by contrast, the sentence "I should do it" does not state their argument in favor of doing it, but instead reports the conclusion at which they arrive, on the basis of the consideration that doing so would be morally right.

It is intelligible, though chilling, to say, "You should do it precisely because it is wrong." When we decide what we should do, all things considered, we must determine how much weight to attach to the fact that some of our options are morally right and others are morally wrong. But once we have come to the conclusion that we should V, there is no further question to be raised about how much weight we should attach to the fact that we should V. It is self-stultifying to admit, "I should V," and then to ask, "But should I V?" There is no similar problem about asking, "It is morally wrong to V, but nonetheless, should I?" If the wrongness of an action always, or nearly always, gives the strongest possible reason against doing it, then the answer will be "No, you should not do it, because it is wrong."

7. The Elimination of Moral Rightness

The moral use or sense of "right" and "wrong" have so fully entered the vocabulary of ordinary discourse and moral philosophy that it may seem that any ethical theory worth taking seriously must put forward a view about what moral rightness and wrongness are, or about which actions are morally right and which are morally wrong. The frequency with which these terms are used in philosophy is partly the result of the fact that it is not only philosophers in the Kantian tradition who typically assign a central role to such phrases as "morally right," "morally permitted," and "morally required." Classical utilitarians and their contemporary followers often do the same. A typical formulation is that every "agent is *morally required* to perform the act with the best consequences." And "the optimal act is the only act that is *morally permissible; no other act is morally right.*"[40]

But, in fact, utilitarians can tell us how we should act without using such terms as "morally right," "morally wrong," "morally required," and "morally permissible." They hold that each person *should,* or *ought to,* or *must* maximize what is good. It does not matter which of those modal terms they use; for practical purposes, the important thing is to determine which alternative will produce the most good, for in every case that is what we should (ought to, must) do. So, if moral rightness and moral wrongness are thought of as additional features of actions that we must attend to, beyond the amount of their goodness and badness, the utilitarian will say that there are no such things. Of course, utilitarians may, if they so choose, continue to use such terms as "morally right" and "morally wrong." Whatever maximizes the good, they may say, is morally right, and whatever falls short of that is morally wrong. But for them, what makes it the case that we should choose one alternative over

40. Kagan, *Normative Ethics,* p. 61, my emphasis.

another is always the greater quantity of good that it involves. Moral rightness and wrongness do no work, for utilitarians, in the premises that support conclusions about how one should act.[41]

Much that we do, and should do, would not happily be described as "morally required" or "the morally right thing to do." There is a time and a place for going to a party, or for playing golf, for example—at any rate, it would be a radical departure from common sense to hold that such innocent and healthy pleasures are never to be enjoyed. If utilitarians do not want to deny that there is a time and a place for these sorts of activities, then they must say that, upon occasion, one can do no more good than by playing golf or going to a party. But it is implausible to suppose that whenever one should go to a party or play golf, one is morally required to do so, and that it would be morally wrong not to do so. That is because it rarely, if ever, happens that the reasons for playing golf or going to a party are considerations that would normally be classified as moral reasons. When none of the reasons that favor choosing such activities can be thought of as a moral reason, there is no basis for arriving at the conclusion that these activities are morally required or morally right. The utilitarian should feel no discomfort in accepting the idea that some of the things that should be done are not *morally* demanded of us.[42]

Rawls should therefore have said that, as he and many other anti-

41. When a utilitarian is asked, "Which am I to do: follow my inclinations, whatever they happen to be, or maximize good?" he will of course advocate the second of these alternatives. But his advocacy need not consist in saying that one has a moral duty or obligation to pursue the second policy rather than the first; he can merely say that this is what one should or ought always do. (Why should he take on the burden of showing that this is not only what one should do, but what one has a moral duty to do?) Beginning with the appealing idea that doing something good speaks in favor of an action, he need "only" persuade us that nothing could speak more in favor of an action than the fact that it does the most good. Utilitarians may nonetheless take common ideas about which sorts of actions are morally right or wrong to be reliable guides to utility and disutility—an approach that goes back to Mill's treatment of justice, duty, and morality in Chapter 5 of *Utilitarianism*.

42. Henry Sidgwick holds that all practical thinking characterizable as "ethical" or "moral" must recognize a "quality of conduct discerned by our moral faculty as 'rightness'" and holds that "this term, and its equivalents in ordinary use . . . [implies] the existence of a dictate or imperative of reason, which prescribes certain actions either unconditionally, or with reference to some ulterior end" (*The Methods of Ethics*, p. 105). Utilitarians, Sidgwick insists, no less than other sorts of moral philosophers, must express their ethical theory by making a claim about what end we *ought* to adopt and pursue, and he takes "ought," "right," "duty," and "moral obligation" as more or less equivalent ways in which ordinary speakers show their recognition of a "dictate or imperative of reason" (ibid., pp. 32, 34–35). I do not share his assumption, drawn no doubt from Kant, that all these terms, insofar as they express the idea of a "dictate" or "im-

utilitarians think about moral philosophy, the right and the good are its two main concepts.[43] Instead, he writes as though this point is common ground among *all* moral philosophers, including utilitarians. For the utilitarian, there is only one source of justification—only one route by which to arrive at a conclusion about what one should do. In that sense, the utilitarian holds that the good is the main concept of ethics. Rightness, for the utilitarian, can be eliminated; or, if he does not mind stretching "morally right" beyond its normal limits, he can continue talking about moral rightness by identifying moral rightness with the maximization of the good.

As we have seen, the good-centeredness of utilitarianism must be distinguished from its commitment to maximizing something. One can reject maximization and still investigate the possibility that all practical justification proceeds by way of goodness. It is not a datum—a fact that must be accepted by all ethical inquiry—that moral rightness and wrongness are no less important, or more important, for acting well than are goodness and badness. When we develop a theory of what is good that replaces the one Rawls proposes—goodness as the satisfaction of rational desire—we will see how little need we have to talk about moral rightness and wrongness (section 65). We can reason satisfactorily to

---

perative," connote a "possible conflict of motives" between reason and nonrational inclinations (ibid., p. 34). For there is nothing *linguistically* amiss in the statement that one ought to act on passing impulses, or that this is the right thing to do, whatever deliberative reason may think. (Nor would it be *linguistically* amiss to make the rather different claim—one that is even more dubious—that one has a duty or a moral obligation to act on impulse.) Sidgwick sees that modal terms like "ought" play an indispensable role in practical thinking, and that the characterization of a course of action as "good" does not yet constitute an "authoritative prescription to do it" (ibid., p. 106). But he does not make fine enough discriminations among these terms ("ought," "duty," "moral obligation"), and his discussion is marred by the idea that "ought" has different senses: the "narrowest ethical sense" (in which "ought" implies "can"), the "political" sense (in which it does not have this implication), and the "absolute" sense (which carries no implication that reason may conflict with impulse). These different senses are introduced on pp. 33–35.

43. This aspect of Rawls's thinking owes a great deal to Sidgwick and Kant; and it is no doubt also influenced by the work of Ross (*The Right and the Good*) and H. A. Prichard, particularly "Does Moral Philosophy Rest on a Mistake?" and "Duty and Interest," (both in his *Moral Writings*). The partisan nature of the thesis that goodness and moral rightness are the two main concepts of ethics can be appreciated if one reflects on the absence of the concept of moral rightness from Aristotle's ethical writings. But that claim about Aristotle is by no means universally accepted; it is proposed by Anscombe ("Modern Moral Philosophy," pp. 26–27) and defended by me in "Doing without Morality: Reflections on the Meaning of *Dein* in Aristotle's *Nicomachean Ethics*."

conclusions about what we should do without them. Of course, there
will always be a place for the right thing to do, where this simply means
what one should do or (more emphatically) what one must do (section
9). But *moral* rightness—the special kind of reason that is alleged to support conclusions about what one should do, the kind of reason so potent
that it can nullify goodness—does not exist.

8. Rules and Good

The rules and codes of conduct by which some of our institutions are
governed have a transparent purpose: when those governed by these
rules abide by them, some result comes about that is good for them.
Consider a simple example: every respectable university has a code of
academic honesty that prohibits plagiarism by specifying what it is,
which procedures will be used to adjudicate allegations of plagiarism,
what the penalties will be for violations, and so on. The promulgation
and enforcement of these rules play an important role in promoting the
goods around which higher education is organized. Students must be
taught to think on their own, to develop the skills of good writing, careful inquiry, and reflection. They must learn how to make their own judgments and assessments, to carry out independent research, to develop
their imaginations. When they copy the work of others, they fail to
achieve the many goods that the university offers them. Because they
promote the good of every member of the academic community (and
those outside it as well), the rules that prohibit plagiarism have a transparent rationale. That is what makes them good rules. We can say, correctly, that plagiarism is morally wrong. But the reason one should abide
by a university's code of academic honesty does not lie in the wrongness
of plagiarism but in the harm it does.[44]

If a student protests that plagiarism is good for *him*—he has adopted
that as his goal, because he finds it much easier and more enjoyable than

---

44. I assume that the reasons that any specific set of good rules should be obeyed include
the reasons that there should be those rules. Often the goods promoted by means of a system of
rules—for example, by a code of honesty—cannot easily be achieved by institutions that have
no such rules. Plagiarism must be defined; an academic institution cannot simply tell students
to be honest in their work. It would be a mistake for students to treat the code of academic honesty as a mere assemblage of rules of thumb that can be set aside whenever they believe creativity and judgment require doing so. These same points apply to many other rules: a legal system
and fair procedures are needed if the goods served by social rules are to be achieved.

doing his own work—we should not immediately concede his point. The code of academic honesty exists to serve the good of *all* students, his good no less than any other's; it is good for him, as it is for any student, to develop the skills that can be acquired only by honest academic work. At any rate, we should look for a theory of well-being that accords with the common belief that a student who plagiarizes is cheating himself no less than others. He may be satisfying his desires, enjoying himself, achieving his goals; but he fails to develop his mind, and that is bad for him to some degree, whether he realizes it or not.

What we have just said about the rationale for the rules of academic honesty might hold true of all good rules whatsoever—that is, of all those that deserve our respect. Social rules, when they are not mere taboos or instruments of oppression, are promoters of the good of all members of the community. Examples are not hard to find. We regulate the conditions under which a person may take a human life for an obvious reason: death is generally bad for the person whose life is lost, and it is a great good to exercise control over the conditions under which one's life continues (section 53). Similarly, if it is reasonable for societies to have a notion of individual property and to enforce property rights, that is because it is good for everyone to have that kind of control over material resources and to be protected against their loss. There are more examples. The norm that prohibits adultery can serve a useful purpose when it stops couples from acting in ways that would make it difficult or impossible for them to sustain the loving, cooperative relationships that are the principal good of a good marriage. Slavery, once widely accepted, is now prohibited because we recognize the great harm done to those who are treated as pieces of property (section 63). There are no human beings so limited in their capacities that their well-being is not damaged by the institution of slavery. In case after case, when we think of widely accepted and reasonable prohibitions, we are able to point to something that stands behind them and gives them their point, just as a university's prohibition of plagiarism has a point. What makes them good rules is the good they do for all the members of the community who abide by them.[45]

45. In saying this, I am drawing on a widely accepted idea about justice rather than on a conception of the human good: namely, that the rules that govern a community should equally serve the good of all. Justice in the family, for example, requires arrangements that do not favor some members over others. Justice in larger social organizations consists in serving the com-

Suppose that in a particular case it would be better for a person to die than to go on living. He has a painful disease and no prospects for recovery. He wants to die; no one would be made worse off as a result of his death. Not everyone agrees, but it is tempting to say that in such a case the general prohibition against taking life should be relaxed—because this is a situation in which killing would do good and no harm. That temptation must compete with the worry that a general acceptance of killing in these situations would lead to abuses: people might be killed even when it is not obvious that it is good for them to die. It is the good and harm that would be done by euthanasia that we attend to when we wonder whether allowing this practice can be justified.

In certain conditions, norms, rules, and laws do not serve the good of all. They may be components of an oppressive social system in which some people do extremely well, while others are forced to pay great costs. The property system may make it impossible for some to have the material resources they need to maintain their health, or to have a family, or to have control over their lives. The laws that prohibit theft in that case do much good for some and much harm for others. Our confidence that it is wrong for any member of such a society to steal should therefore diminish. What objection can be made to taking what is not yours if you need it to sustain the health of your children, and the person from whom you take it has so much that it would do him no good? The rule against taking what is not yours must be evaluated as a component of the social system in which it is embedded. It is when such a social system operates in a way that is good for all members that we feel most confident that anyone who steals is doing what should not be done.

Similarly, when the law that defines and prohibits adultery fails to promote the good of men, women, and children—for example, when it is part of a patriarchal system that gives husbands total control over their families, and women are severely constricted in their choices and opportunities—then it is no longer a good law. We should not insist that such

---

mon good of all those who are defined as members. In particular, a just political community must abide by rules and develop institutions that equally serve the good of all citizens. Justice across national borders serves all human beings. This identification of justice and the common good can be found in Aristotle (*Politics* 3.6–7) Cicero (*On Duties* 1.31), Aquinas (*Summa Theologica* 1–2 q.90 art. 2), and their followers. Something closely related can also be located in Rawls's *Theory of Justice:* the principles that emerge from the original position are principles of *justice* because the original position is so structured that each party is assured that his good will be served by them.

a law creates winners (husbands) and losers (wives); were that the case, our attitude toward such a law ought to be mixed (since it does both great good and great harm). We should rather say that when spouses treat each other as equals and loving companions, then the norm of sexual fidelity serves a useful purpose, and adultery inflicts psychological harm on both partners, particularly when it is detected (as it almost always is, though even when it is not detected it is corrosive; section 66.) On the other hand, when a marriage is dead, and both spouses recognize that this is so, one may reasonably ask whether any objection can be made to adultery (assuming no children or others under their care are harmed). By hypothesis, all the harm to the marriage has already been done, and so it is no longer evident that the restriction on extramarital sexual relations serves a useful purpose. Arguably, at that point, adultery is no longer wrong—that is, it is no longer the case that individuals in the circumstances described should not engage in extramarital sexual relations. At any rate, a defense of an absolute prohibition on adultery would have to appeal to some harm that might be done even in such cases as these, or perhaps to the difficulty of knowing that a loving or even a minimally amicable relationship between spouses cannot be reestablished.

I claimed earlier, in my discussion of plagiarism, that a student who engages in this practice may be acting against his own interests, whether or not he is willing to concede the point. There is a great good that he fails to acquire, and it may be of no value for him to satisfy his desire (however rational) to copy someone else's work and enjoy the ease with which he can do so. There is something amiss in a theory of well-being that denies this, or cannot explain why it is so, and we will be seeking a theory that does not have this defect. In connection with our discussion of adultery, we can add another example that creates difficulties for a theory of well-being that equates goodness with the satisfaction of rational desires. When a man engages in an extramarital affair, he may be doing exactly what he chooses and wants more than anything in the world. There may be nothing irrational in his desire, or in the plan of action he puts into effect. But by carrying out his plan, by satisfying his desire, by enjoying this forbidden pleasure (made all the more appealing because it is forbidden), he may permanently lose the love of someone whom even he recognizes as a wonderful human being, and so his act of infidelity may inflict great short- and long-term damage on himself (and not only on others). That may be a consequence he fully recognizes as he carries out his affair, and yet his desires, his emotions, his values, and his deliberations may nonetheless lead him to undertake this self-destructive act of betrayal. On balance (let us assume) his sexual adventure will be extremely bad for him—in fact, his bout of infidelity need not be supposed to be good for him *at all*. It accomplishes what he deliberatively and reflectively set out to do, but that will make no difference to his well-being if, from the start, his goal was one that, for his own sake, he should not have had. He himself may, either at the present or at a later time (or both), view his adultery in exactly these terms. (People do sometimes reflectively choose to do what they acknowledge to be self-destructive.) It is an odd theory of well-being that is forced to take issue with him on the grounds that since he deliberately planned to engage in this affair, and did so with his eyes wide open, it must have been good for him.[46]

We have seen that when we consider some of the most familiar social prohibitions—do not kill, do not steal, do not commit adultery—exceptions can be found. It is striking both that the exceptions occur in cases where following the rule does no good, and that the rule receives our respect and is acknowledged to be a good rule when we recognize the good it fosters or the harm it prevents. But it is also possible to concoct exceptionless rules. For example: One should never take the life of another human being merely for the pleasure of doing so. Nor should one blind another human being merely for the fun of it. Nor should one destroy another human being's capacity to remember merely for the sake of pleasure. And so on.

---

46. Here I reject the approach to well-being proposed by Sidgwick, who holds that "a man's future good on the whole is what he would now desire and seek on the whole if all the consequences of all the different lines of conduct open to him were accurately foreseen and adequately realised in imagination at the present point in time" (*The Methods of Ethics*, pp. 111–112). That idea is developed more fully in Rawls (*A Theory of Justice*, pp. 365–372). For I am assuming that one may reflectively judge that, all things considered, one should do something whose consequences one nonetheless foresees in this clear-headed, fully imagined way and correctly characterizes as entirely harmful to oneself. To defend the assumption that such a characterization can be correct, I must present a conception of how statements about well-being are to be justified if they are not treated, as Sidgwick and Rawls do, as propositions about what someone would "desire and seek on the whole" under certain conditions. I turn to this task in Chapter 3. My claim that when adultery is bad for the adulterer, that is to be explained not by any appeal to what he would ideally choose, but by the actual harm it does to him—the loss of goods he might have had—depends on assumptions I make about the value of love, friendship, intimacy, and honesty. See especially sections 41 and 66.

Why do these prohibitions immediately strike us as exceptionless? Because the damage done to the other person, depriving him of his basic faculties, is so great a harm that it could be justified, if at all, only by a good of immense magnitude. We would be justified in killing or blinding a Hitler, or ruining his basic cognitive capacities, if in doing so we could end his regime and save millions from suffering. But to kill someone or impair him in these basic ways, and to do so only for the pleasure of doing so, is beyond the pale because the good achieved—if that is what it is—does not come close to what would be needed to compensate for the harm inflicted. There are thousands of things that it would be better for someone to do—more in his interest—than taking pleasure in the blinding of another person. So it is reasonable to say that the pleasure a person takes in this act of destruction is not good even for him. But whether we say it is not at all good or good only to a small degree hardly matters (section 33). In either case, the harm that is done is enormous, and the pleasure felt by the person who inflicts it falls utterly short of compensating for it.

If every pleasure is good, no matter what kind, and no matter what its cause or object, and if it becomes better for someone to experience as it becomes more intense and enduring, then taking pleasure in blinding another person is extremely good for the perpetrator of this horrible act. Suppose a large number of people share in that project, each experiencing intense pleasure as they formulate their plan and execute it. Then, at some point of intensity, and as the group grows in size, the amount of good that comes into being will outweigh the harm done (particularly if the blinding is done painlessly). A philosopher who is worried that this conception of good (which counts all pleasure as good, and more intense pleasures as better) is correct, or at least no less defensible than any other, will be tempted to say: there must be some other kind of consideration having nothing to do with what is good or bad that stands behind our conviction that no one should blind another person simply as a way of having fun.

But why believe there is any such consideration? We saw no need for it, in our discussion of the familiar prohibitions against killing, theft, and adultery. It is more reasonable to question the assumption that every pleasure is good and that more intense pleasures are better. Recall our earlier example of the child who gets a thrill from lighting a fire and destroying all the animal life and vegetation in a forest (section 2). It is very bad, not good, for him to feel that pleasure; it would be far better for him if he had an entirely different attitude toward nature. Anyone who loves such a child and takes his well-being to heart would want to change him by eradicating his destructive urges. Similarly, an adult who enjoys inflicting great physical damage on other human beings would be far better off if he could root out his destructive desires and put in their place desires that are good for him to satisfy.

There is no reason to suppose that intensity of feeling, no matter what the feeling or its object, is by itself good. Consider laughter, for example. We rightly assume that a life that contains no laughter at all is for that reason deficient; but that does not entail that the more intensely we laugh (or the more time we spend laughing), the better off we are. Someone's sense of humor is unhealthy if he finds everything funny and laughs uncontrollably at what is not funny and not regarded by others as funny (section 39). That kind of sense of humor—if that is what it can be called—cuts one off from one's social world and displaces healthier responses. Cruel, obsessive, intense pleasure would be no less an impediment to a flourishing life than constant, maniacal laughter.

The survey we have conducted of rules that have a purpose—that safeguard or promote some good for all those governed by the rule—is the barest sketch. In Chapter 4 we will turn to other moral rules and principles that might be thought to have no connection to what is good. Before we can be confident in our judgments about whether a rule serves a good, we must find an adequate conception of what is good.

9. Categorical Imperatives

It sounds lame to say, "One should not kill people just for the pleasure of doing so." That is because "should not" does not do justice to the awfulness of doing such great damage for so little reason. It is not enough to say that one *should* not. One *must* not. It is *imperative* that one never do such a thing, or even think about it. Such terms as "must" and "imperative" indicate that the case to be made for or against some action is extremely strong, whereas "should" can be used even when the premise just barely makes the case for the conclusion. When a compelling case can be made for one of the alternatives under consideration, then one must choose it. A good that shines forth as superior to all competing goods is one that we should—indeed, must—choose. A harm so terrible that one should not even contemplate it is one that must be rejected.

We might follow Kant's lead by saying that "one must not kill for pleasure" is not only an imperative but a *categorical* imperative. It is not an imperative in the strict grammatical sense; it is a declarative statement. But it tells one what one must not do, as negative imperatives do. And it is different in character from rules of strategy and skill, rules that tell one how to achieve an end that one might or might not pursue, as one pleases. "One should not exchange a rook for a pawn" is good advice; if one ignores it, one will not do well as a chess player. But "Do not kill for pleasure" does not advise us about how to achieve what we are aiming at. It governs our behavior, regardless of what we are aiming at. If someone wants to kill, simply for the pleasure of doing so, it remains the case that he must not do so.

Kant would say that the maxim "Let me kill human beings for the pleasure of doing so" does not stand up to scrutiny—and with this we should wholeheartedly agree. But the idea we are exploring is that we can best explain what is defective about this maxim not by employing such concepts as rational willing, or self-legislation, or freedom, but by more carefully examining what is good and what it is to be good. We will find room for such notions as rational willing, self-legislation, and freedom in our theory: these things are indeed good for us (section 53). But they are not the only things that are good, nor are they in any way ultimate goods. They are not the "master values" of ethical life; that position is occupied instead by the good.[47]

But suppose we find someone who cares not one whit for doing what is good for anyone (himself included) or avoiding what is bad for anyone (himself included). Can we construct an argument that ought to be accepted by such a person, an argument that will lead him, if he reasons well, to the conclusion that he should care about these things? And even if we cannot, should he refrain from acting on the impulses he has—for example, his impulse to kill?

If it can be shown that all the routes by which we can legitimately ar-

---

47. The phrase "master value" is borrowed from Scanlon (*What We Owe to Each Other*, pp. 108, 142–143). He holds that there is "an element of truth" in the thesis that "well-being is a 'master value': that other things are valuable only insofar as they contribute to individual well-being." But he warns that the thesis "invites misunderstanding" if it is taken to mean that well-being is "a good separate from other values, which are made valuable in turn by the degree to which they promote it" (ibid., p. 142; see also p. 103). I too reject that thesis, but for reasons other than Scanlon's, since we propose different conceptions of well-being. The upshot is that for him "well-being is a 'master value'" is a truth of far less significance, practically and theoretically, than it is for me.

rive at practical conclusions advert to what is good or what is bad, then someone who is completely indifferent to good and bad is not someone who can be influenced by good practical reasoning. We might try all sorts of methods of changing him, but good reasoning is not one of them. Our inability to get through to him would not show that there is any defect in our conception of what is good, or in our conception of the proper role of goodness in practical reasoning.

Should he refrain from acting on his impulses—for example, on his urge to kill? Of course he should. Recall that a plant's roots should not sit in water for too long, because that is bad for the plant (section 3). What is good or bad for someone or something always supports a conclusion about what should be (provided no other organism is adversely affected). If someone's impulses do no good and do only harm, they should be suppressed. A person does not have to care about what is good or bad for it to be the case that he should do what is good and not what is bad.[48]

10. Conflicting Interests

The good of one person can come into conflict with the good of another. At any rate, there is nothing about the concept of goodness—of G being good for S—that prevents that from being so. Precisely *which* situations are conflictual depends on the assumptions one makes about what is good and what it is to be good. If one thinks that the satisfaction of desires is always good for the person whose desires are satisfied, then one will say that whenever S and T want to have the same thing, and only one can have it, their interests conflict. If S gets the object of his desire, that is good for him but bad for T.

Needless to say, *people* can come into conflict with each other, even when there is no conflict between what is good for one and what is good for the other. If two people disagree, their beliefs are in conflict with each other—but not necessarily their well-being. When S can get what he wants only if T fails to get what he wants, there certainly is a conflict

---

48. According to Bernard Williams ("Internal and External Reasons"), the individual in question has no reason to refrain from acting on his impulses. That thesis is compatible with the proposition that he should refrain for his own good. There is a reason that he should (namely, it would be best for him), but that is not a reason he possesses because it is beyond him to be moved by it. And surely it is a defect of his that this is beyond him.

between them—but not necessarily a conflict between what is good for one and what is good for the other. Conflicts in beliefs and desires can lead to bickering and hostility, but such animosity does not necessarily indicate that there is a conflict in goods.

The theory of well-being to be presented here does not agree that a conflict of desires is always a conflict of interests, but it nonetheless acknowledges that the good of individuals can easily conflict, when the world is not an entirely hospitable environment. It never has been entirely hospitable, and it is unlikely that it ever will be. Consider a simple example: a boat has capsized, only one life preserver is floating in the ice-cold sea, and only one of two survivors can make use of it. One will grasp it and live; the other will die. If one takes hold of it, that is good for him but bad for the other fellow.

Ideally, ships should have abundant life-saving equipment, so that such conflicts never occur. More generally, we should structure our social institutions in a way that minimizes conflict—not conflict in beliefs or desires, but in goods. But perfection in the provision of resources is a faint hope, and social institutions will never be able to make human relations so smooth that genuine interests never compete with each other. And so it might seem that it is one of the proper tasks of philosophy to propose a theory about how to solve the genuine conflicts that inevitably arise.

But philosophy cannot be asked to solve unsolvable problems. Consider the two men who are in danger of drowning. Suppose a third party (a stranger to both victims), hovering above the sea in a helicopter, can rescue only one. He has no information about either. The question "Which is it better for him to save?" is not one that he can answer. And even if a great deal of information is provided about each (one is a cook, the other a musician), that information may not be of the sort that makes a reasonable decision possible.

But suppose one of them does a great deal of good for the whole community and will continue to do so for many years if he lives, whereas the other does no good and will do no good for anyone—not even himself; suppose too that his life is not worth living, and that he makes no other life worth living. That information certainly helps. It makes it difficult to resist the conclusion that it is the first party who should be saved.

More often the information we have when we must make a choice about whom to rescue comes in the form of numbers, and in these cases it is tempting to say that the greater number of lives should be saved. That is not because the utilitarian principle is always the principle that should guide us. When the *only* distinctions we can make are quantitative, then it is not absurd to suggest that the right thing to do is to save the larger number.

11. Whose Good? The Egoist's Answer

Even if we knew everything there is to know about what is good, and how great a good each good is, we would not yet know how to act. When we do good, we do good *for* someone. And so, in addition to our deciding which things are good, we also must answer the question "Whose good should one promote?" There are many simple formulas that propose an answer to that question. The two that are most prominent are egoism and utilitarianism.

Egoism holds that there is only one person whose good should be the direct object of one's actions: oneself. It allows one to take an indirect interest in others, and to promote their well-being, but only to the extent that doing so is a means toward the maximization of what is good for oneself. And it does not adopt this position because it has any doubts about our ability to know and promote what is good for others. If one helps oneself only because one denies that one can know what is good for others, or doubts one's ability to help them, then one is accepting the view that ideally one should help others no less than oneself, if only one could.[49] Genuine egoism tells us that, as a matter of principle, we are to have no *direct* concern for the good of others. That is precisely why it is so implausible. For it advances no good reason in support of this principle, and there is nothing plausible or obvious about

49. Against this, it could be said that since "'ought' implies 'can'" (a common slogan of moral philosophers), someone who denies that he can help others should infer that he ought not to. But that slogan is too blunt. Everyone in the path of an oncoming fire should flee, including someone who is pinned to the ground and unable to do so. Similarly, someone who claims that he is unable to help others may regret this limitation; in fact, to see this as a limitation is already to acknowledge the attractiveness of helping others. More generally, the thought that human beings can never do any good for each other (by itself deeply implausible) can be combined with the belief that this is an imperfection in our nature (as it surely would be). Egoism, as I construe it here, finds nothing amiss when a human being has no direct concern for others: it says that such a person is acting in accordance with the correct principles of motivation and behavior and is not settling for some second-best mode of operation.

it.[50] We can grant, at least for the sake of argument, that it is reasonable to make one's own good a matter of some concern. But why must this be one's *only* direct concern?

The rejection of egoism leaves open that there may be, from time to time, people who are so situated that there is no one they should care for but themselves. During that period no one else needs them or has a claim to their assistance. They would not be happier, for that period of time, were they to minister to the well-being of others. In this situation they should look only to their own well-being. But it is implausible to suppose that all people are at all times in this situation.

One other reflection shows how weak a theory egoism is. No human being acting in complete social isolation will go far with the project of promoting his own good. As infants and children, we need to be protected, cared for, and educated by others. For one's own good, one must master the skills of social interaction so that one can determine, reasonably well, what others want, what they think, and what they are likely to do. A child who never develops any direct interest in the good of any other member of his community will be impeded in his efforts to master the social skills he needs. Having no love for anyone else, or even lukewarm affection, he will be handicapped in his interactions with those who expect that sort of emotional connection from him. When everything goes well for a child and he has all the emotional resources he needs to interact with his community in ways that are best for himself, he will have some direct interest in some other members of that commu-

50. No leading contemporary academic philosopher defends egoism (as it is construed here), but there are illustrious figures from the past who did—for example, Thomas Hobbes, Henry Sidgwick, and (going further back) Plato and Aristotle (as they are sometimes read—the interpretive issues are complex). Hobbes is generally taken to accept egoism on the grounds that one cannot help seeking one's good (and will help others only if this is in one's interests), and that if one cannot help acting in a certain way, one should. Both premises are doubtful; see Simon Blackburn, *Being Good,* pp. 29–37, on the first; and the preceding note on the second. Sidgwick holds in *The Methods of Ethics,* pp. 496–509, that egoism is as credible as utilitarianism, and that these are the two systematizations of our commonsense practical beliefs between which we must choose—though reason is unable to find a basis for favoring one over the other. He grounds the credibility of egoism not only on its ability to systematize commonsense moral beliefs, but also on the fundamental importance of the distinction between persons and the consonance between egoism and ethical thought in the England of the seventeenth and eighteenth centuries. I agree with the consensus of contemporary philosophy that none of these is a plausible basis for egoism. See Robert Shaver, *Rational Egoism,* for a historical study and critique of the egoism of Hobbes and Sidgwick. Even if Plato and Aristotle accept egoism (I do not believe they do), one can find no arguments in them to support it.

nity—namely, those who have manifestly expressed their love for him in ways that benefit him. So no one whose early education is as good for him as it can be will emerge from childhood as a person who is inclined to act as egoism says he should act. So fortunate a young adult will gladly help others for their sake, whether or not doing so is good for him. Egoism tells him to extirpate this desire. That will take considerable effort. And it will also require him to conceal from others that he is changing his personality in this way—for others are likely to be offended that they are no longer loved and that their well-being is no longer of any direct concern to him. Why should someone transform himself in this way? The egoist replies, "Because it will be good for him to do so." But the person it addresses cares about others besides himself, and egoism gives him no good reason to suppose that his desire to promote the good of others for their sake is misguided.

12. Whose Good? The Utilitarian's Answer

Utilitarianism is as simple a theory as egoism: instead of saying that there is one and only one being whose good should be the direct object of one's concern, it holds that there is no limit to the group of beings with whom one must have a direct concern. That includes all human beings, but there is no reason why the utilitarian should stop there. After all, there is such a thing as what is good for an animal. And as a matter of fact, utilitarians have indeed urged us to extend our concern to animals. *Classical* utilitarianism (as it is sometimes called) takes pleasure and pain to be the sole good and the sole harm; but *any* utilitarian who counts pleasure as merely one good among many, and pain as one bad thing among many, will urge us to extend our concern to any creature that can have these experiences. For any utilitarian, whatever his theory of well-being, the answer to the question "Whose good should one take into account when one acts?" is "Every being for whom something good can be done." Which beings are those? To answer that question, the utilitarian relies on a conception of what is good. If knowledge were the only good, the utilitarian would say that we should pay no attention to animals (assuming that, even when they are intelligent, they do not have knowledge).[51]

---

51. For an epistemology that counts the cognitive achievements of nonhuman animals as genuine cases of knowledge, see Hilary Kornblith, *Knowledge and Its Place in Nature*, pp. 28–69.

But if pleasure is not the only good and certain things are good for plants, the utilitarian must make plants, no less than sentient animals and human beings, the object of his concern. If the reason we should show consideration for other animals besides human beings is that they too are beings for whom there is such a thing as what is good and what is bad, then all living things must receive consideration. And indeed, as we noted (section 2), what is bad for plants does figure in ordinary practical reasoning, in that their wanton destruction is generally condemned.[52]

A utilitarian who wishes to exclude plants from his inventory of beings for whom we should all extend our concern might hold that it is all and only human beings—members of our species—whose good is to be promoted. But that would be an arbitrary limitation. A utilitarian can bring about a greater amount of good if he promotes the good not only of human beings but of other animals as well. Why should a utilitarian, of all people, not do so? His central idea is that one must increase the quantity of good in the universe. Furthermore, suppose we discover on some distant planet a race of beings who have cognitive and emotional lives as rich and complex as our own. We can increase the amount of good in the universe by helping them, and so the utilitarian is committed to saying that we should try to do so. It would be arbitrary to say that we should do nothing for them merely because they are not human beings. The maximizing thrust of utilitarianism drives it ever outward, to exclude nothing from its concern that can contribute to the total amount of good. That is the result of its fundamental commitment to quantitative thinking: the larger the sum total of good that exists, the better the state of the universe.

If one has a choice between doing good for individual S and doing that same kind and amount of good for S and in addition doing some good for someone else, then obviously one should choose the second alternative, which has every good feature of the first, and another as well. As strong as the reasons for choosing the first alternative are, the reasons for choosing the second are stronger because there is an additional reason that favors it. But, of course, the utilitarian does not confine himself to making this recommendation; if he did so, his theory would be trivial. He goes far beyond this piece of common sense by saying that we should lower the welfare of some in order to increase the welfare of others—

52. We also noted (section 2) that there is such a thing as what is good for an artifact. But no sensible ethical theory will give independent weight to what is good for them (sections 34 and 68). For further discussion of the good of plants, see section 56.

provided that doing so creates a greater sum of good in the universe. Utilitarianism is committed to a regime of constant sacrifice—sacrificing some for the sake of others—in order to increase the quantity of good. And the wider our circle of concern becomes—the more beings there are for whom some things are good and others bad—the greater must be our readiness to diminish the well-being of some. For that diminution of well-being will be outweighed by the greater amount of well-being we create as our beneficence is spread out over ever greater numbers.

We should recall a point made above (section 4): it is a mistake to suppose that commonsense ways of thinking lead inevitably to the utilitarian formula. It is a matter of common sense that if it is better for S that he V than that he W, that provides him with a weightier reason to V than to W. And it is a linguistic tautology that whenever it is better for someone that he choose one alternative over another, then it is more good for him that he choose it. But a mistake occurs if we infer from this that we should make decisions by looking for something that can be measured quantitatively and bringing about the greatest possible amount of it. As I observed above (section 4), we do not decide what a good poem is by counting something. Similarly, counting something and increasing it as much as possible is often a poor way of making decisions about how best to improve someone's situation.

Just as there is no reason to suppose that one can or must adopt a purely quantitative approach to deliberating about how best to promote one's own well-being, so there is no reason to think that we should adopt a purely quantitative approach to one's interactions with other beings. When one looks out at the world of beings for whom there is such a thing as what is good and what is bad and asks what, if anything, one should do about their good, there is no commonly accepted premise that supports the conclusion that one should maximize the total amount of good in the universe.

The complaint that utilitarianism goes astray by turning a blind eye to everything but the quantity of good has often been made before. W. D. Ross, for example, by making excellent use of commonly accepted ideas about promise keeping, points out that we are not at liberty at all times to choose the people who shall be the beneficiaries of our actions.[53] If one has made a commitment to deliver a certain good to a certain person, then one has voluntarily accepted a restriction on one's future

---

53. Ross, *The Right and the Good*, pp. 37–39.

beneficence: one is not free to bring about the greatest amount of good for the universe, because there is a small portion of the universe—the person to whom one has made a promise—to which one has agreed to pay special attention. There is a local good one should deliver—the good offered to the promisee—and global beneficence, however worthy a project, must not be one's only concern or a concern that always takes precedence over all others.

The point can be generalized. Often there are several small portions of the universe to which we should pay special attention. A small child needs to be protected, cared for, and nurtured. By whom? Generally, biological parents are assigned this responsibility, and for good reason: in many cases, they are the ones who will give a child the best care.[54] Now, if we ask about some person S, who happens to be a parent, "Whose good should this person be promoting?" part of our answer will have to be "His children's." Of course, there may be several or many other people to whom S should also give aid. But, since S is a parent and is for that reason assigned responsibility for the care of a certain child, S should not think of himself as free to, or obliged to, produce as much good as he can throughout the universe. Just as the promise-maker should give heightened attention to one small part of the world and should provide the good he said he would provide, so a parent who has a responsibility to care for his child should also give heightened attention to one small part of the world. If parents adopted the principle that they should produce the greatest amount of good for the universe, giving their children only as much attention as will contribute to this final sum and treating the needs of their children as having no more importance than anyone else's, then not only would the children of the world suffer greatly, but their parents would themselves lose the good that consists in having a special relationship with their children.[55]

54. I set aside the question whether alternative arrangements—for example, the system proposed in Plato's *Republic* 5—might be as good or better. If there is something better than the traditional family, there will be certain people, not biologically related to the children under their care, who are assigned the primary responsibility for their well-being. In that case, the point made here will apply to them rather than to biological parents.

55. Suppose the utilitarian concedes, at this point, that people should not think as utilitarians, but he nonetheless insists that utilitarianism best explains *why* they should not do so: because the amount of good in the universe would not be as high as possible were they to do so. If *no one* should put the utilitarian formula into practice, even though that formula is true, we are faced with a paradox: a truth about what to do that no one should believe or put into action. In any case, if the utilitarian formula is something that at least some of us should believe, we must

A similar point applies to all the other sorts of people with whom we have special ties, however close or distant: parents, brothers and sisters, lovers, close friends, companions, colleagues, coworkers, people with whom we share a village, or city, or nation. In each of these cases, we put the good of certain people ahead of the good of others, at least to some small degree and on some occasions. We give far more help to intimate friends with whom we share a long history than to strangers. We would lose the good that consists in special relationships with other people if we treated all human beings in precisely the same way, that is, as material for the maximization of the good. If we were to pay attention only to what can be measured—the quantity of good we produce for the universe—that would make it impossible for us to possess the several kinds of good that are constituted by the various intimate or cordial relationships we have with others. (This argument rejects conceptions of the good according to which one's relations to others are merely of instrumental value. More will be said about the good of personal relationships in sections 35 and 41.)

It is not only special relationships with other people that are good for us. As we will see (section 36), many sorts of tasks, jobs, and careers are good for those who undertake them because of the way they allow individuals to exercise the cognitive, emotional, and social skills they have spent so much time developing. It is, for example, good for someone to excel and take pleasure in such activities as writing poetry, cooking, running an organization, and playing a sport. But engagement in these demanding tasks requires a commitment to them that is incompatible with a readiness to maximize the amount of good there is in the universe.

Consider a talented and successful poet who is entertaining doubts about his profession, despite the enjoyment it gives him and the small circle of his readers. He thinks: "I could be doing so much more good for so many other human beings if I stopped writing poetry and spent that time giving humanitarian aid instead. And so that is what I shall do." We should be able to see an error in the way he arrives at his conclusion: al-

---

be led to it through a process of reasoning; we cannot be expected merely to accept it unquestioningly. If it denies the rational force of common patterns of deliberative inference (I should deliver this good because I promised to do so; I should help her because she is my child), it is left with too little material to support its thesis about why we should do what it claims we should do. Lacking a basis in ordinary practical reasoning, it can only hope that we see the great attraction of producing as much good as possible. When doubt is cast on the quantification of good that underlies utilitarianism, its credibility diminishes significantly.

though he may be correct in believing that the number of people he can help by means of humanitarian aid is far greater than the number of people he benefits by giving them the pleasure of reading his poetry, he oversimplifies his situation with his thought that by giving up writing he does more good for the world. Admittedly, he is entitled to say that he will affect a larger number of people as a humanitarian than as a poet. And he is entitled to say that there is one kind of good—the physical relief that comes through humanitarian aid—that he will create a greater amount of if he changes professions. But he makes the mistake of supposing that he can compare these two different kinds of good—writing and reading poetry on the one hand, humanitarian aid on the other— along a single dimension, and thereby arrive at the conclusion that the total quantity of good in the universe is increased by the change he is making. No sense can be attached to that idea. There is nothing that humanitarian aid is a certain amount of, and that the enjoyment of poetry is also a certain amount of. What the poet would be doing by changing careers is withdrawing from the production of one type of good, one that is enjoyed by a small number, and devoting himself to a different type of good, one that will be received by a much larger number. (More will be said in sections 47 and 69 about the kind of good poetry is.)[56]

Should he do so? Thus far, we have not discussed the conclusion of his argument that he should change professions, but only the faulty premise he uses to arrive at it. When we look at his conclusion and ask whether it is defensible in some other way, the only proper response is that this is not yet an answerable question because we have included so little information in our example. How good a poet is he? How few will ever read him? How many will actually be benefited by his humanitarian aid? Would they not be aided without his help? If we fill in the answers to these questions in a certain way, we can emerge with an example of someone whose decision to make this kind of career change is justified.

---

56. My claim is not that *no* two goods can be compared, but only that *some* cannot. When they are incomparable, that is because they are described so schematically that no basis for choice is available. Which is a better good: honesty or friendship? No comparison is possible, because the choice is too abstractly described. But that leaves open the possibility that a particular honest act does no good and should be rejected in favor of the particular act of friendship with which it is competing. See sections 35 and 53 for some examples of goods that are worth giving up in order to acquire or retain others. The comparability of goods is also accepted in section 45. For good guides to these issues, see Griffin, *Well-Being*, pp. 75–92, and "Incommensurability: What's the Problem?"

As we have just seen, its justification would not be one that appeals solely to the quantity of good that he does. Rather, the argument would be that the difference in the number of people affected by the two careers is extremely large; without his help, those to whom he gives aid would continue to suffer miserably; and the poetry he writes is mere doggerel.

But there would be a great loss to the world if all creative writers, musicians, dancers, and painters did the same. That would be bad for everyone whose circumstances allow them to enjoy the creations of these artists; and we should be putting more people, not fewer, into these circumstances (section 47). The world would contain a vastly diminished array of goods of various kinds. A way must be found of meeting the basic physical needs of those who live in misery without at the same time impoverishing the emotional lives of others. It is implausible to suppose that we must choose: either the needs of the starving and malnourished must go unmet, or the worlds of imaginative enrichment must be destroyed.

It is difficult to be entirely unsympathetic to utilitarianism because it is, for all its problems, one way of addressing a problem that cannot be dismissed. There are billions of people who need more help than they are receiving, and much more can be done for their good than is currently being done. If everyone were to embrace the utilitarian formula and adopt effective means to their goal of maximizing good, the condition of these needy people would improve. But that consideration by itself is not enough to show that we should all adopt the utilitarian formula. There are many different political, economic, and social mechanisms for addressing the great needs of the billions who are poorly nourished, susceptible to diseases and natural disasters, and victims of oppression. Many of us could do far more to address these problems than we currently do without sacrificing the well-being of others. We can recognize that this is true without having first to convince ourselves that utilitarianism is true. The question whether utilitarianism gives the correct account of how we should live our lives cannot be properly answered simply by taking note of how much suffering and misery there is in the world, and how much wasted energy could be put to better use by being redirected toward those who need assistance. Our resources are often squandered; frequently they do no good at all. One does not have to be a utilitarian to insist that they should be put to better use.

The reasons given here (and in section 4 above) for rejecting utilitarianism should be distinguished from a different sort of charge that might be made against it. It could be said that each of us is entitled to refuse to have to do anything, beyond a certain limit, for the good of others. We have that entitlement not because it is good for anyone that we have it; rather, we simply have it. Once one has fulfilled one's duty to do what is good for others—once one has reached that minimal level—one has the right to live one's life as one chooses (so long as one does not wrong others), not because it is good for one to have this right, but simply because it is one's right. Utilitarianism goes wrong, according to this line of thinking, because it overstates what is required of us. We must give to others only as much as we owe them; if we do more, we go beyond what it is our duty to do.

This way of thinking more fully abandons the utilitarian approach than I do here. It holds that in addition to justifications that appeal to what is good for someone, there are other sources of practical justification that rest on no assumptions about what is good: what we owe, what we must do because it is a duty, what we are entitled to do or refrain from doing, what we have a right to do. By contrast, the way of resisting utilitarianism proposed here adopts (for reasons offered in Chapter 4) one of the central utilitarian ideas: that all justification stems from the prospect of what is good or bad for someone. Utilitarianism does not get off the ground even when this component of it is accepted.

13. Self-Denial, Self-Love, Universal Concern

So far we have found no adequate answer to the question "Whose good should one (directly) promote?" We should not accept the egoist's answer: "Only one's own." Nor should we accept the utilitarian thesis that it is the quantity of good alone that we should attend to. The failure of these theories should feed our suspicion that perhaps the question that they try but fail to answer is not one that admits of an answer and is therefore fruitless to pursue. Why, after all, should we suppose that a question so abstract and general, so remote from the particular circumstances of any person's life, admits of an answer? When we are given certain kinds of information about an individual (he is a father, his parents are ailing, he is a doctor, he made a promise), we can no doubt say whose good he should promote; but if we are told nothing except that he is a human being, then there may simply be nothing for us to say—not because we are defective, but because the question is defective.

But perhaps it would be premature to draw that conclusion. We might consider this way of answering it: "Each person should promote his own good." That is crucially different from egoism, for that doctrine holds that one should have a direct concern for oneself *and no one else*. If we drop the emphasized words, we are left with something that seems unexceptionable: one should (indeed, must) promote one's own good. And what should (or must) one do for others? Perhaps the best reply—at any rate, one worth considering—is that it is neither the case that one should (or must) care for others, nor the case that one should (or must) *not*. Direct regard for others, in other words, is optional; but so is indifference to others. By contrast, according to this hypothesis, one should have a direct concern for one's own well-being; disregard for oneself is not an option, as disregard for others is. So there are two proposals now under consideration: the first is that one should always directly care about oneself; the second is that there is an asymmetry between self- and other-regard, in that indifference to self is unacceptable, whereas indifference to others is acceptable. Both, I believe, should be rejected.

Most people have a direct concern for their own well-being. They do not have to be talked into caring for themselves because they already have a powerful desire to do so. But consider someone who pays attention to his own good only because and to the extent that doing so allows him to care for certain other people. He does not treat the fact that some activity would be good for him as by itself a reason for him to engage in it; it is only the good of certain other people that directly motivates him. He takes excellent care of himself: he gets enough sleep, has an adequate diet, protects himself against disease—all because these are means toward his ultimate goal of caring for others. But he forgoes opportunities that would give him a great deal of enjoyment (travel, gourmet food, opera) whenever seizing them would detract from what he could do for the people to whose well-being he is devoted.[57] To make the example more

57. Suppose the selfless individual described here has a choice between providing a benefit only to S, the object of his direct concern, and providing that same benefit to S and also to himself; and suppose there is no cost to him or anyone else in choosing the second alternative. He is subject to criticism if he chooses the first option, because the second has every advantage that the first has, and more. Helping himself in such situations does not call upon him to single out his own well-being as a special object of concern. It only requires him to treat himself as someone, not as an object of love. For the same reason, if a selfless individual has an opportunity to acquire some benefit, at no cost to himself or anyone else, he should not decline it because helping someone is always to be chosen over helping no one. He will help himself in such a situation not because the person being helped without cost is *himself*, but because he fa-

concrete, we might think of a doctor who voluntarily devotes himself to the health of a destitute group of villagers and takes care of his own needs only because that enables him to live for them. We can reasonably suppose that, because of his work, he is not in the pink of condition, but that he makes this sacrifice and others because he places his patients' needs above his own.

It might be thought that there is something admirable about such a person not only because he cares for others, but also because he has freed himself from self-love. But that is not a credible thesis. Having some direct interest in one's own well-being is not in itself objectionable; it becomes so only when and to the extent that it leads one to do or feel things that one should not. And we should not assume, without argument, that any degree of direct concern with oneself will lead to that result.

It might, to the contrary, be thought that this person exhibits a defect: he has no degree of direct self-love, and, it might be said, that by itself is a fault. But that thesis is as arbitrary as its opposite; so, at any rate, I will argue. If a person's lack of direct self-love enables him to serve others better and has no objectionable consequences for them, if he imposes no burdens on other members of his social world and does for them whatever he should do, then there is no basis for criticizing it. Of course, someone who forgoes travel, gourmet food, and opera is living less well than he might (sections 36, 38, 47); but voluntarily making sacrifices for others is not by itself a defect. (Self-sacrifice will be more fully discussed in section 48.) Acts of self-sacrifice are, by definition, bad for the person who undertakes them; but that feature of them hardly makes them blameworthy. Similarly, I believe, caring for oneself only in order to care for certain others is not necessarily a defect.[58]

---

vors helping *anyone* when this is costless and the alternative does no good for anyone. As Harry Frankfurt notes, self-love, like the love of any person, is "ineluctably personal" (*The Reasons of Love*, p. 79); that is, "Someone who loves himself is devoted to his beloved as a particular individual rather than as an instance or exemplar of some general type" (ibid., p. 81).

58. Here I disagree with Frankfurt, who writes: "There are . . . some wantonly indifferent, or severely depressed, or mindlessly self-indulgent individuals who do not care at all about themselves. Cases of these sorts . . . are so discordant with our fundamental expectations concerning human nature that we generally regard them as pathological. Normal people, we suppose, . . . cannot help being powerfully inclined to love themselves" (ibid., p. 84). I take Frankfurt to be endorsing, and not merely reporting, the widely accepted idea that the absence of a direct regard for one's own good is pathological. But the fact that we *expect* people to have some direct self-concern does not by itself support the conclusion that it is pathological whenever it

Of course, there are ways of embellishing the example that would make this individual subject to criticism. Perhaps the reason he takes no direct interest in himself is that he falsely assumes that he is inferior to others in intelligence or physical appearance, or that he is undeserving of anyone's attention, including his own. If so, the falsity of those assumptions by itself provides a basis for criticism. It might be thought that whenever someone lacks a direct interest in his own good, false assumptions he harbors about himself or sheer servility must stand behind his lack of self-concern. Certainly some and perhaps many instances of self-indifference fall into this category, but it would be dogmatic to suppose that all of them must do so. If S takes no direct interest in some arbitrarily selected T, that by itself does not show that S is mistaken in some way about the qualities T has and is taking T to be inferior in some respect. So we should not suppose that whenever someone lacks a direct concern for *his own* well-being, he must be mistaken in some way about the qualities he has.

It is possible to fall into error about this matter because we rightly assume that direct self-love should become part of our psychological equipment at some stage in our development. A child who is brought up properly must be taught how to take care of herself, and it is good for her to have a direct interest in her own well-being. She must learn to see that, in appropriate circumstances, "That is good for me" can serve on its own as a powerful reason for action. For example, no one who loves a child will want her to take an interest in her own health only because she realizes that she needs to be healthy in order to care for her grandfather. That would not be a good attitude for her to have toward herself; she needs to develop a stronger ego than that. But when we become adults and have the maturity we need to make sound decisions that have long-lasting effects, we may reasonably choose a course of life in which we place the good of certain other people above our own. Over time, when a person makes emotional commitments of this sort, he may, in effect, be putting into place a motivational structure in which his self-

---

is absent. Frankfurt is surely right that wanton indifference, severe depression, and mindless self-indulgence are conditions that should be avoided and either cause or betoken an absence of self-regard. But someone who cares for himself only in order to serve others is not necessarily the victim of these conditions. For another discussion of self-love, see Michael Slote, *Morals from Motives*, p. 78; he withholds judgment on the question whether "self-assertiveness on behalf of one's own interests" is not only permissible but also a virtue.

regard plays an entirely instrumental role. By hypothesis, that kind of psyche is not the best kind to have for the person who has it; it is, after all, a self-sacrificing structure. It is not a motivational configuration that a loving parent would want her adult child to come to have—for parents want their children to have whatever is most in their children's interests. But that does not show that one ought never become this type of person, no matter what the circumstances, and no matter how much good such a person might do for others. After all, by hypothesis, the sacrifices such a person makes have a point: they promote the well-being of others who would be worse off were it not for those self-sacrifices.

If the thesis under consideration—that one must directly care for one's own good but need have no direct concern for others—has some justification, that rationale must rest on some picture of human nature. To see this, imagine a world very different from our own.[59] Suppose each human being were embodied in a way that made it impossible for him to help himself. In this world each individual has a sibling to whom he is organically attached, and that sibling is the only person he can take care of. S can feed and defend only brother T (not himself), who in turn can feed and defend only S (not himself). S and T might agree to cooperate, and their relationship might be based entirely on self-interest; but if love and sympathy were sufficiently powerful and reliable forces, there would be no need for direct self-concern. An emotional attachment of each to the other might serve each couple better than a pact based largely or entirely on self-concern. In fact, to secure the strongest bond of trust, it might be better for each individual to think only of the good of the other, and not his own; the recognition by each of the other's selfless devotion might banish all fear of neglect. In such a world it would be bad advice to tell someone that he should directly care only about himself. It would be better to tell each to care directly only about the other. Each would fare better were each to love not himself but the other.

In our world most of us, most of the time (after we emerge from the earliest stages of childhood), can succeed to some degree in helping our-

---

59. Foot conducts a similar thought experiment, imagining rational beings who "find it impossible to think calmly about *their own* future" and so invent "a kind of 'buddy system' by which each person had someone else to look out for him" (*Natural Goodness,* p. 17, n. 16, her emphasis). But her larger point is that each adult should have "a reasonable modicum of self-interest" because, as we are constructed, "we can look out for ourselves much better than anyone else can do it for us" (*Natural Goodness,* p. 17).

selves. Often the person one is in the best position to help achieve a certain good is oneself. Even so, there are situations in which it is easier to care for others than oneself. You can scratch someone else's back more easily than your own. You can often see that someone else's anger is excessive, or that he is deceiving himself, more easily than you can detect these faults in yourself. So your ability to counsel another person can surpass your ability to manage your own emotions. Why, then, must S pick out S as the one person for whom he should care? And even when one can more easily oversee one's own well-being than another's, why should the ease with which care can be delivered settle, by itself, questions about whom it is one should care for?[60]

There is another reason to reject the principle that the one person S should directly love is S. It is plausible to suppose that, in certain circumstances (particularly when resources are especially scarce), one person's good conflicts with another's. No matter who T is (whether he be a stranger or S's closest friend), circumstances might be such that S's good comes into conflict with T's. Now, on the assumption that one should love oneself, although one may (but need not) love others as well, what is one to do in such conflictual situations? There would be no inconsistency if one replied, "One should sacrifice one's good for the sake of the other person." But although there would be no inconsistency in that reply, it would be out of keeping with the thesis that self-regard is mandatory whereas altruism is merely optional. That thesis holds that one has a special normative relationship to oneself. It places the self ahead of others, in that it allows one to be indifferent to others but not to oneself. Because it assigns that kind of primacy to the self, it would be mysterious (though not inconsistent) to combine that thesis with one that insists that one should give priority to the good of another person when that person's good conflicts with one's own. The natural extension of the idea that the one person one should directly love is oneself to situations of conflict will resolve those conflicts in favor of the self. But that thesis about conflict resolution is nearly as insupportable as egoism.

---

60. Adam Smith remarks, "Every man is, no doubt, by nature, first and principally recommended to his own care; and as he is fitter to take care of himself than of any other, it is fit and right that it should be so" (*The Theory of Moral Sentiments,* part 2, sec. 2, chap. 2). He seems to be inferring, unjustifiably, from the natural prevalence of self-regard ("by nature . . . recommended") that it would be a defect not to have any; but he certainly does not make the mistake of supposing that the self is the only required object of one's regard.

(Egoism is worse, because it forbids one from caring directly for others.) There is no reason always to place oneself first in situations of conflict, or always to refrain from making large sacrifices for the good of others. Similarly, it is not necessarily a defect to love others more than oneself. We should infer that it is not necessarily a defect to have no direct concern for oneself—provided that this selflessness actually does some good for others.[61]

Since this line of thought is unpromising, we should turn to another option. Consider now the possibility that one should directly care for oneself not because one has a special normative relationship with oneself but because one should have at least some degree of concern for the good of *all*. According to this hypothesis, there is no one in whose well-being you should have no direct interest. That is why you should care for yourself: because you should care for everyone.

Those who are attracted to utilitarianism because of its unlimited scope—its exclusion of no one from our circle of concern—will certainly find this thesis, which calls upon us to care for everyone to some degree, appealing. It is also a point in its favor that it lacks one of the most disputed components of utilitarianism: it does not require the maximization of good. And it has another attractive feature: it permits one to have a greater degree of concern for some—oneself, or one's family, or one's community—than others.

But it imposes a heavy burden on us. We must care about all six billion (and counting) human beings. And there is no reason to stop there. Good and bad things happen to all animals, and to all plants too. Must we really do something for them all? The question is not whether we should answer "Yes" when we are asked, "Would it be nice if the good of every living thing could be enhanced?" Our question is "Whose good should one promote?" and this is a question not about what our idle

---

61. One sometimes hears such rhetorical questions as these: "Why should we help him if he will not help himself?" "Why should we love someone who does not love himself?" These questions make a sensible point when they are taken to mean that efforts to help others will be ineffectual, and therefore not worth undertaking, unless they cooperate with those efforts. For that is often the case: much of what can be done for a person is only a contribution to his own efforts to secure certain goods for himself. Nonetheless, it should not be inferred that S should not love T unless T has a *direct* concern for himself. If I discover that my adult son has become the sort of doctor (mentioned above) who lives only for his patients, that is no reason for me to stop loving him directly and giving him, for his sake, whatever aid he will cooperatively accept.

wishes should be, but about what we should actively desire and make some effort to bring about.[62]

It is not difficult to think of ways in which prosperous people can make some contribution to the good of a great many others. We can contribute to organizations that fight against malnourishment, torture, painful diseases, crippling poverty, and cruelty to animals. But we fall into the quantitative trap that afflicts utilitarianism if we hold that those who are not concerned with the well-being of large numbers are, for that reason alone, subject to criticism. A devoted teacher, for example, is concerned with the well-being of only a tiny portion of humankind, and what she aims at is the improvement of basic skills of literacy, not the alleviation of pain and suffering. Are we to think less of her because she is concerned only with the good of a few and not concerned at all about pain and suffering, except when it occurs to those within her small circle—her friends and family and those in her immediate environment? She falls further short than do others when she is judged according to the principle that one should do something for everyone. But that standard of judgment is absurd (though not as objectionable as utilitarianism) because it shares with utilitarianism a quantitative bias. It directs us toward projects that affect large numbers, as utilitarianism directs us to maximize the good. There is no reason to allow quantity to play that role in our practical thinking.

It is easy to agree with someone who claims that every human being— indeed, every living creature—should receive the help it needs to achieve its good. In an ideal world, whenever someone is in need of aid, that aid would be delivered by someone or other. But precisely who should deliver that aid? Who should take responsibility for overseeing the well-being of any arbitrarily selected human being or creature? It would be strange to reply, "Everyone should." There is no need for every creature to be cared for by *everyone*. That would be an oversupply of caretakers. It

---

62. The hypothesis now under consideration should be distinguished from the entirely unexceptionable view that we all have duties to help anyone, even strangers, whom we are especially well positioned to aid with minimal cost to ourselves. If a stranger asks me for directions and I can easily help him, I should. There are no human beings to whom I should be indifferent when circumstances select me as the one who can best help them and the burden of giving aid is small. But the hypothesis under consideration demands far more than this: it tells us to be an active helpmate to all human beings (or, more broadly, all creatures that can fare well or badly). Mere passive willingness to help this or that stranger in special circumstances would not be enough to meet this demand.

is enough—in fact, it is all that could be hoped for—that each human being or creature is cared for by *some*. Ideally, some division of labor should be in place so that no one's good is neglected. We are very distant from this ideal, for there are many human beings who have been abandoned by all others. Someone should help them, and there are many different ways of dividing the task of bringing this about. Having everyone care for everyone else would be one way—an extremely inefficient and ineffective way—of arranging the world so that no one is neglected. If we ever do create a world in which no one is neglected, it will not be a world in which each actively cares for all.

We have examined four ways of answering the question "Whose good should one promote?" (1) Only one's own. (2) At least one's own. (3) Everyone's, to some degree. (4) Anyone's, to the extent that doing so produces the greatest amount of good in the universe. The failure of these answers suggests that the question to which they are responses is too broad, too general, too abstract. Philosophy is in the business of posing broad, general, abstract questions; but when all the answers prove defective, it is time to ask whether we really need to work at so high a level of generality. And in fact, we do *not* need a formula that tells all people whatsoever, regardless of their circumstances, whose good they should promote. We can instead rely on common sense and recognize that the world as it is already offers countless opportunities for doing what is good. Nearly every social organization and line of work is devoted to a certain kind of good and seeks to secure it for a certain group of people. Organizations that seek to alleviate suffering and misery are not the only agents that aim at what is good. So do schools, theaters, orchestras, governments, athletic clubs, restaurants, bakeries, plumbers, farmers, police officers, and so on. Of course, not every organization that aims to do some good succeeds; some do more harm than good, or in any case the amount of damage they do is often distressing.

These are platitudes, but it is helpful to recall them in order to avoid the error of merely supposing that we will go astray if we lack a philosophical answer to the question "Whose good should one promote?" Philosophy, as we shall see, can help us clarify and improve our ideas about what is good and about the nature of goodness. But we do not need a philosophical theory to decide which of the many ways of doing good we should choose; and in any case, as we have seen, philosophy does not help us make this choice. It has not succeeded in its efforts to say once and for all, "These are the people, or this is the person, whose good one should promote."

14. Pain, Self-Love, and Altruism

When someone is in pain, that is bad, to some degree. We will see that this is an elliptical way of speaking (sections 17–18). It should be taken to mean: pain is bad, to some extent, *for* the one whose pain it is. It detracts from the well-being of the person who feels it. But let us leave that aside for now; and let us assume, with common sense, that pain is indeed bad (but see section 38.) The questions we should address are "What is the practical upshot of the fact that pain is bad? What, if anything, follows about what should be done about it?"

The answer may be "Nothing at all." There may be pains that go away most quickly if they are left to subside on their own. Because the pain is bad, it will be good when it goes away; but no one should try to make it go away.

But suppose a pain can be most quickly alleviated through intervention. Who should intervene? Not necessarily the person who feels the pain. It may require considerable medical expertise to diminish the pain, and the person who is suffering may lack that qualification.

But suppose the pain that S feels is a mere headache and will respond quickly to medication. It will soon go away if S takes an analgesic. There is aspirin in the medicine cabinet, and S, sitting only a few yards away, can easily help himself to it. Should he do so?

The only reasonable answer is that he should—provided there is no cost, to S or to anyone else, in his doing so. After all, whenever someone, S, is faced with a choice between two alternatives, and the first does some good for someone (perhaps himself, perhaps another) at no cost, whereas the second does no good at all, there is an excellent reason to choose the first. If these are the only differences between the two alternatives, the first must be chosen. So S must help himself to the analgesic, not because he should have some special ongoing concern for himself that he does not extend to anyone else, but because he should help *anyone* when doing so does not detract in any way from his ability to help himself or others. If S has a headache and is thirsty, and one of two glasses of water set before him contains an analgesic, and the other does not, he would be guilty of needlessly neglecting someone's pain if he chose the second glass.

But acts that help someone often incur some cost or other. Analgesics do not fall from heaven. They must be purchased, and the money used for that purpose might have been used for some other. When one takes two aspirin, there are two fewer aspirin in the bottle that are available for others. The time and energy expended in helping oneself often leave less time and energy for others. Because self-help is so often in competition with other goals, it would not be unreasonable for someone who is deeply committed to serving others to adopt a general policy of helping himself only to the extent that in doing so he will be better able to serve those others. His working assumption is that if an option benefits himself alone, choosing it will almost certainly detract, to some degree, from his ability to help others. And so when he has a headache, and it is mild enough not to interfere with the work he does for others, he lives with it, even though he recognizes that it is bad for him to be in pain. He takes aspirin only when and because his headache is so severe that he would be unable to work as effectively for others. That diminishes the frequency with which he needs to replenish his supply of analgesics, and the money he saves is used for the good of others.

So if someone has a headache and can, at some small cost, make it go away, it does not follow that, all things considered, he should do so, or that he exhibits a defect if he fails to draw this conclusion. He should have a direct and ongoing concern for *someone's* well-being; otherwise, he will care about nothing that is good for anyone, and he will do no good for anyone. But the person whose well-being it should be his goal to serve need not be himself.

Since promoting or safeguarding S's well-being need not be among S's goals, it is difficult to believe that doing S some good must be one of the goals of all other human beings. Nothing need be amiss, then, if there are other people besides S who are indifferent to his pain in the same way he is. Of course, S's friends and family should have a direct concern for his well-being. (That is because they are his friends and his family: these relationships, unlike self-identity, have practical significance.) So should his doctor, his colleagues, his neighbors, and the people who represent him in the political arena. These should not be purely instrumental relationships, because when they are, considerable harm is done.

And so there are many people who should not be indifferent to what is good or bad for S. Their social roles (which are good roles for them to play because of the good they do) call upon them to have some degree of direct concern for his well-being. His wife will want him to take aspirin and will fetch the bottle from the cabinet. The fact that he happens not to care directly for his well-being does not require *her* to have that same attitude toward him.

If there are many people who are already doing a satisfactory job of looking after S's well-being, there is no reason there should be more and more of them, without limit. And, of course, there are billions of people who are in no position to alleviate S's pain, or to contribute to its alleviation, or even to know about it.

Although very few can alleviate S's pain or help him in any way, everyone can adopt a certain attitude toward the suffering of each other person. Each can say to himself, "I want all the pain in the world to stop, because each person's pain is a bad thing. For any S, if S is in pain, I want that pain to stop." In that sense, we might say that everyone should want S's pain to go away.

Should we want this? That is not a question about what each of us should *do* about the world's pain, but about what each of us should *desire*. Wanting something to be the case is not a matter of answering "Yes" when one is asked, "Would it be nice if that were the case?" If you want all the pain in the world to come to an end, then in some way that desire must be a component of your psychological economy. You must devote some psychic energy to the object of your desire, even if you are not aware that you are doing so. That object must take up some space in your life, causing you to pay attention to certain things rather than others, inclining you to act in certain ways rather than others, and so on. When given the opportunity to bring about what it is that you desire, you must be at least somewhat tempted to do so—perhaps without realizing that you are.

Desires are subject to evaluation—there are good and bad desires—and that evaluation is made by considering the good or harm they do to people. Typically, when they are bad for people, that is because there is something bad about their objects. One might try to rid oneself of a desire for alcohol because of the harm drinking does to oneself. But there are other cases, less common, when having a desire is bad for someone even though the object of the desire is good. Suppose it will be good for

S if he can impress T. Even so, it might be that S should not want to impress T: doing so might make it impossible for him to succeed. Similarly, the fact that something is bad for you does not entail that you should want it to stop, even when you have a direct concern for your well-being, because the very desire to be rid of what is bad might sustain or intensify it. Certain pains might diminish more quickly if we could rid ourselves of the desire that they stop; they may increase because we focus on them and ratchet up our desire to be rid of them.

So when we ask whether each of us should want all the pain in the world to stop, we are not asking whether we should answer the question "Should the world's pain stop?" in the affirmative. The answer to that question, we are assuming, is yes. What we are asking is whether we should build into our psychological economy a desire to make all the pain that is now felt come to an end. Is this something that would do some good? Would it do any harm? A desire that does no good—either for the person who has it or for anyone else—is a desire that one is well rid of. In effect, a desire that does no good at all does harm: it expends psychic energy that could be put to better use.

As I noted earlier (section 12), the world's suffering needs more attention than it is currently getting. Resources are being wasted and opportunities lost. But to solve this problem it is not necessary that every human being build into his psychological economy a desire that the world's pain come to an end. There are more effective ways to alleviate pain and misery. If all human beings wanted all suffering to end, many of those desires would be bad desires: they would do no good and some harm.

We have arrived at two conclusions. First, the fact that S is in pain does not give everyone in the world a reason to do something about it or to want the pain to stop. Second, the fact that pain is bad for S does not require S to have a standing policy or goal of avoiding pain and alleviating it whenever it occurs. But we chose pain simply to serve as one example of what is bad. Our conclusion can be generalized to all goods and harms.

If one points out that something is good for someone, that partially builds a case for reaching the conclusion that someone has reason to undertake some action—but it is not by itself enough to bring one all the way to that conclusion. One needs something else. If a good is precisely the one that S promised to give T, then S has reason to deliver it. If S is T's parent, then facts about T's good will properly take S to conclusions about what he has reason to do. If S is T's doctor, then facts about T's pain will take S to practical conclusions. If S has a direct concern for T, that too, together with facts about what is good and bad, will lead to a practical conclusion. To act, one must answer the question "Whose good should I be serving?" and not merely "What is good?"[63] There are unlimited ways of properly answering the first of these questions, and so philosophy cannot help us here; it can help only with the second question.

15. Agent-Neutrality and Agent-Relativity

It is crucial to distinguish the mere assertion that a state of affairs should not exist, or that an event should not occur, from the stronger assertion that someone should undertake some action. It is easier to support the first sort of statement than the second. Suppose a volcano erupts: a vast number of plants are destroyed, and no living thing benefits. What happened is bad for those plants, and there are no gains that might be entered on the opposite side of the ledger. It seems reasonable to draw a conclusion: considering the losses (many) and gains (none), that was, all things considered, an unfortunate event. And unfortunate events are events that should not happen.[64] (This category is not restricted to events that are good for none; when the good done is small enough and the harm great enough, the conclusion that the event was, all things

---

63. If one puts into the category of rightness whatever considerations must be added to an argument to secure a practical conclusion, besides those that characterize some type of thing (e.g., pleasure) as good for someone, one can easily see why these—the right and the good—are the two main components of practical reasoning. The idea, in other words, would be that all good practical arguments must advert to what is good for someone, but they must also claim that it is right, in these circumstances, to do what is good for *these* individuals. But this taxonomy of concepts, whatever its merits or deficiencies, would not by itself show that considerations of rightness must all have something further in common, or that *moral* rightness (however that is to be explained) is one of the main concepts of ethics, or that rightness is prior to goodness.

64. "It should not have happened" does not merely restate, in different words, what is already said by "It was bad for them." Statements about what should happen are conclusion drawing, whereas statements about what is good for something are reason giving. That is why one cannot move from "That should not happen to those plants" to "That is bad for those plants"; the order of reasoning goes in the opposite direction. ("It should have rained weeks ago, because that would have done some good"; not "It should have rained weeks ago, and *therefore* that would have done some good.") But even though there is a movement of thought here from one statement to the other, that does not entail that the premise or the conclusion gives anyone a reason to do anything.

considered, unfortunate, can be sustained.) But although we have all the information we need to arrive at the conclusion that this event should not have happened, we cannot yet, simply with this information, support the further conclusion that someone or other has reason to do something about it. Perhaps no one cares about those plants; perhaps there is no reason anyone should care (section 56).

Similarly, when someone is in pain, we can say, on the assumption that this is a bad thing (that is, it diminishes the well-being of the person who feels it), that this should not happen. But merely to say that it ought not to go on is not to say that anyone has a reason to do anything about it or to want it to stop. As we have seen, there may in fact may be no reason at all to do anything about it. Trying to do something about it may merely make it worse. Similarly, there may be no reason at all for the person who feels the pain to want it to stop—that too may make the pain worse. Pointing to the badness of an event does not by itself take us all the way to the conclusion that someone should do something about it—that some action or desire, directed against the event, is the appropriate response to it. Even when the facts about a bad state of affairs support the conclusion that *someone* should intervene and try to stop it, the fact that it is bad does not by itself secure any conclusion about which person should intervene.

Thomas Nagel disagrees. He holds that whenever someone is in pain, the badness of that pain gives everyone in the world a reason to be concerned about it—to do something about alleviating it or at least to want it to be alleviated. Our attitude toward any and all pain, no matter whose, is "*This experience* ought not to go on, *whoever* is having it."[65] When we strive to occupy an objective and detached practical standpoint, stepping outside the self-centered perspective from which we normally deliberate about what to do, we should be able to recognize that the reason one should alleviate one's own pain is identical to the reason anyone at all should want to alleviate anyone else's pain and to take steps to do so. It is everyone's business to bring about the alleviation of pain, whoever is feeling it. Pain is something that ought not to happen and so something that everyone—not just its victim—ought to want to take steps to stop. Nagel dubs pain an "agent-neutral" reason because its badness does not give only to certain agents, but not to others, a reason to

65. Thomas Nagel, *The View from Nowhere,* p. 161, his emphasis.

seek its alleviation; it is in that sense neutral between them.[66] But he denies that all reasons are agent-neutral. If S wants to become a pianist, that gives S—not everyone—a reason to want S to take effective means to that goal.[67] This is therefore what Nagel calls an "agent-relative" reason. Each person's pain is everyone's business. Someone's learning how to play the piano is not.

Nagel is right that human beings normally can, at a certain stage in their moral development, abstract away from their quotidian preoccupations and, when prompted, will agree that pain is a bad thing, whoever is feeling it. They can occupy a detached and impersonal perspective, and when they do so, they can say to themselves, in all sincerity, that all the pain in the world should come to an end. When they occupy that perspective, so removed from the press of personal projects and everyday cares, they may also arrive at the thought (one that Nagel believes should be encouraged) that there is something amiss in the way they lead their lives, because normally when they deliberate, they do not occupy this detached perspective. They have ongoing concerns that block out many of the world's troubles. They could barely manage their lives were they not to use these filters. But every now and then, they can reflect upon that engaged and internal viewpoint and convince themselves that it is defective. As Nagel remarks, "When we take up the objective standpoint, the problem is not that values seem to disappear but that there seem to be too many of them, coming from every life and drowning out those that arise from our own."[68] From this standpoint—which Nagel calls "objective" because he believes that it makes manifest to us the real world of values that lies behind the appearances of ordinary practical reasoning—we see that the demands on our attention, stemming from the needs of others, are nearly unmanageable. The difficulty of ethical life fully reveals itself to us. Everyone is equally important, everyone's suffering matters, and one can do so little about it.

Thus Nagel. But we have seen how to avoid this conclusion. We are granting, for the sake of argument, that pain is always a bad thing for the person who feels it. When pain occurs, something is happening that should not be because of its badness. But that does not yet secure the conclusion that there is a reason for the person feeling the pain to want

66. Ibid., pp. 152–153.
67. Ibid., p. 167.
68. Ibid., p. 147.

it to stop or for him to take steps to alleviate it. Nor does it secure the conclusion that everyone should want the pain to stop. What Nagel is right about is this: it is not the case that when S is in pain, there can be only one person—S—who has reason to do something about it. (That is the egoist's error.) But he goes astray because he assumes that S must have such a reason. Having made that error, he makes another: he infers that everyone else has a reason to want S's pain to subside. For he sees no reason to delimit the class of people who have a reason to want S's pain to go away. Having felt compelled to put S in that class, he holds that there is equal reason to put everyone else in it as well.[69]

The distinction between agent-neutral and agent-relative reasons, which is now so commonly drawn by philosophers, is therefore unfruitful. Using those terms would be justified only if, from the fact that B is bad for S, it follows that someone or other, or perhaps everyone, must have a reason for wanting to put a stop to B. If everyone does, B has agent-neutral value; if instead only S, or some delimited group of people related in some way to S, has such a reason, then B has agent-relative value.[70] But the presupposition that lies behind these terms should not be accepted. Admittedly, bad things should not occur. But it does not follow that someone has reason to do something about them.

To achieve an objective conception of what we should do, we must, in some way or other, step outside of ourselves. We must assure ourselves that the way we view things is not merely the product of blind spots, biases, or other distortions in our point of view. But objectivity in that sense can be achieved by subjecting our assumptions to a critical examination that exposes them to the competing thoughts of other people, including those who live in times and places other than our own. We can examine the philosophical theories of many different periods and parts of the world and compare the best reflections of other people with our own. When we notice differences between our own views and those of others, we must be open to the possibility that we are mistaken. If we

69. Nagel often speaks of pain as a bad thing rather than as something that is bad *for* someone. That does not affect the questions we are discussing here, but we will return to this point in section 18.

70. If having agent-relative value were simply a matter of lacking agent-neutral value, then my thesis would be that whatever is good for someone (or bad) has agent-relative value. But there is more content to the notion of agent-relative value than that. The claim that a certain good (or harm) has agent-relative value must be supported by a specification of precisely who does and who does not have reason to be concerned about that good (or harm).

think that our views are correct, we must explain why other people, no less serious and capable than ourselves, are in error. A philosophical theory that can survive these tests is somewhat better than a collection of subjective impressions, and if we act in accordance with a theory that we have scrutinized in this way, we can rightly claim that we do so with some degree of objective warrant—even if what we want and seek is what is good for *these* people, and the welfare of those others never enters our minds. The proper test of a person's objectivity, in practical matters, is open-minded self-scrutiny, not an impersonal regard for the good of all.

TWO

Good, Conation, and Pleasure

16. "Good" and "Good for"

We are now ready to turn to a new set of problems. We are looking for a nonutilitarian ethical theory that nonetheless resembles utilitarianism in the way it gives supremacy, in practical reasoning, to considerations of good and harm. Whose good, and whose harm? That depends on the circumstances. No simple formula has survived as an adequate answer to that question. There is no reason to pick out only oneself as the person whose good one should aim at. There is no reason to suppose that nothing less than the good of all must be the object of our concern. Some devote themselves to the good of a handful of people, whereas others serve vast numbers. So be it; there is no reason to be disturbed by *that* difference. That many are not receiving from anyone the help they urgently need is a distressing practical problem, one that is best addressed collectively by groups with large resources, and most especially by the governments that are best situated to give such aid.[1] But it is also important that we not act with a misguided conception of what is good, because if we do so, all our efforts may go for naught. Perhaps we can do good even if we do not really know what is good. But it is better to avoid such blindness if we can.

The use of "good" that we have assumed to be most important for practical reasoning is relativized: it is what fills in for G, when we say

1. Further discussion of this issue can be found in Garrett Cullity, *The Moral Demands of Affluence*; Tim Mulgan, *The Demands of Consequentialism*; and Liam Murphy, *Moral Demands in Nonideal Theory*. I accept Cullity's thesis that affluent individuals ought to contribute a fair share of what they should be collectively doing for those in dire need (*The Moral Demands of Affluence*, p. 9).

that G is good for S. That assumption must now be put to the test. Why not think, instead, that the key to practical reasoning is what is good "absolutely"—that is, good not for someone, but just plain good, good "sans phrase," as W. D. Ross puts it?[2]

That might seem to be an academic puzzle, one that has no implications for the practical problem of how one should live one's life. But we cannot understand what is good for people without knowing how to interpret the preposition "for" that occurs in "good for." What is it about S that we must know to determine what is good *for* S? What do we mean to convey when we say that some G is good, not absolutely or "sans phrase," but for some S? Mistaken answers to these questions can lead to defects not only in philosophical theories but in everyday practices. We must understand why "good" by itself, unsupplemented by "for," does not give us the tool we need for practical reasoning.

17. "Good for" and Advantage

Suppose someone says about something or someone: "S is good." So far, we understand almost nothing of what he is saying about this unspecified subject. For what he has said so far is compatible with his adding: "S is bad." The bare assertion that something is good is practically useless.

How can one and the same thing be good and bad? There is no mystery here. When someone says, "He is good," his statement, though grammatically complete, is elliptical, because we do not yet know enough about what he means to convey.[3] He might mean to be saying of

---

2. Ross, *The Right and the Good*, p. 102.

3. Here, with some hesitation, I use "elliptical" not in the technical sense discussed, for example, by H. W. Fowler, *A Dictionary of Modern English Usage*, s.v. "ellipsis," but in an extension of this sense. His first example well illustrates the word's technical meaning: "The ringleader was hanged and his followers imprisoned." We supply "were" so naturally between "followers" and "imprisoned" that we are hardly aware of doing so. (That is why such an ellipsis is acceptable usage.) A part of the sentence has been omitted, but our knowledge of grammar would be enough to guide us to its restoration—if such restoration were necessary. But speaking more broadly, any sort of omission from a sentence might be counted as an ellipsis, and perhaps there is no reason to confine this word only to the use discussed in Fowler's entry. The important point is that to claim that a sentence is elliptical in this nongrammatical sense is to engage in a philosophical search for clarity of meaning—a matter that is inevitably more delicate and open to debate than is the claim that a sentence is elliptical in the strict sense. I am grateful to Judith Thomson for calling my attention to Fowler's discussion.

someone that he is a good poet. Or a good spy. Or a good person.[4] "He is a good spy" is a fuller specification of what is meant by "He is good," not a justification of a statement whose truth can be assessed on its own. If someone says, "He is good," and insists that we enter into a discussion of whether his statement is true but refuses to tell us whether he means to be saying that he is a good spy, or a good cook, or a good person, then he is telling us too little, and we may wonder whether he really means to convey anything at all.[5] His statement is not yet complete as an object whose truth or falsity can be evaluated.

Someone can be a good spy and a bad poet. That is why "S is good" is compatible with "S is bad." In fact, it is possible for someone to be both a good K (member of kind K) and a bad K! Suppose he is a child, and we say that he is a good writer. What we have in mind, presumably, is that he is a good writer in comparison with other children his age. We do not intend to compare him with the very best writers who have ever set pen

4. What of the statement "God is good"? Must that too be construed elliptically and, if so, what is omitted? Religious philosophies should not hesitate to treat this as an incomplete statement, though they may differ in the substantive phrases they use to fill the ellipsis. For many, God is a good *person*—in fact, the best person possible, by virtue of infinite wisdom, justice, mercy, and so on. An ethical and metaphysically ambitious religion might claim, in addition, that God is the supreme *substance,* by having such attributes as timelessness, simplicity, incorporeality, etc.

5. Someone who insists that "He is good" leaves no gap would have to analyze "He is a good poet" as the predication of two attributes: being good and being a poet. That way trouble lies: "He is not a good spy," said of the same person, would mean that he is a spy and that he is not good. So he is both good and not good. And since we are being asked to construe these as complete statements, they are contradictory. (I am grateful to David Reeve for this point.) "He is a good poet" is therefore not to be interpreted in the same way that we treat such statements as "He is a living poet," for the latter *can* be decomposed into "He is living" and "He is a poet." This feature of "good" was brought to the attention of philosophers by P. T. Geach in "Good and Evil," pp. 64–65. As he points out, "a good car" and "a red car" are to be understood along different lines. But he inferred, unjustifiably, that speaking of what is good of a kind is the only legitimate way of using "good": "There is no such thing as being just good or bad, there is only being a good or bad so-and-so" (ibid., p. 65). He therefore dismissed as worthless the attempts made by G. E. Moore and W. D. Ross to show that the uses of "good" that are philosophically most fundamental are those in which we say of certain things—pleasure, friendship, knowledge, and so on—that they are good. Geach is followed by Philippa Foot in *Natural Goodness,* pp. 2–3; his criticism of Moore leads her to propose that good actions, good qualities of the will (virtues), and defective qualities of the will (vices) are "fundamental to moral philosophy" (ibid., p. 3). She nonetheless also proposes that "a genuine virtue would have to be such as to fit an individual for his own good" (ibid., p. 112): that can only mean that a quality of someone's will should be counted a virtue only if it is good *for* him that he have that quality. So she does not banish from moral philosophy the question of what is to count as a benefit (ibid., pp. 41–42, 51, 93–94).

to paper. To be a good K is to stand high on some scale or other, and it is always in order for someone who talks about a good K to be asked what standard he means to be using.

As we noted from the start (section 1), the statement form "S is good" can be an elliptical expression of two different sorts of claims. It can be short for ". . . is a good K," but also for "G is good for S." If one says, "Regular practice is good," what one probably has in mind is that it is good for those who practice—for musicians, for example. Similarly, when one says, "Sunlight is good," what probably lies in the background is the thought that sunlight is good *for* someone or something.

But some philosophers have put forward theories of goodness that entirely ignore or deny the importance of "good for." Pleasure, they would say, is good. Knowledge is good. Pain is bad. Ignorance is bad. These statements, they insist, are not to be relativized. "Pleasure is good" is not to be treated as an elliptical expression—a grammatically complete but shortened form of "pleasure is good for S." G. E. Moore insists that pleasure is good "absolutely."[6] Ross, following Moore's lead, holds that certain states of affairs are good "sans phrase" and argues that the elementary building blocks of such states are pleasure, knowledge, virtue, and the proper apportionment of pleasure to the virtuous.[7]

Moore and Ross cannot easily be dismissed. On their behalf, one can draw the following contrast. On the one hand, as we have seen, the statement "S is a good K" is compatible with "S is a bad L" (and also with "S is a bad K"). We do not know enough about what is being said about someone when we are told that he is a good K but do not yet know which K the speaker has in mind. George is good—but a good what? (And as measured by what standard?) On the other hand, we do *not* seem to be at a loss when we are told that pleasure is good, knowledge is good, pain is bad, ignorance is bad. There *seems* to be no reason to expand these into statements about what is good or bad for some person or group.[8]

6. G. E. Moore, *Principia Ethica*, p. 150.

7. Ross, *The Right and the Good*, pp. 102 (for the phrase "sans phrase") and 134–141 (for the list of the elements of what is good "sans phrase").

8. Judith Thomson argues that "all goodness . . . is goodness in a way" (*Goodness and Advice*, p. 19), and so she would insist that "knowledge is good" cannot be understood until the way in which it is good is specified. I am indebted to her discussion. My reasons for agreeing with her that "G is good" is incomplete will be presented in section 18. But I will claim, as she does not, that this incompleteness can be remedied by means of a "that" clause.

Moore goes further. He does not merely believe that there is no need to fill out the statement that pleasure is good—to regard it as an ellipsis for the statement that pleasure is good for human beings, or for whoever it is that feels pleasure. He claims we are talking nonsense when we talk about what is good for someone. He holds that "good for someone" makes no more sense than "exists for someone."[9] Of course, pleasure is experienced by someone. But that does not mean it is good for someone. The goodness of pleasure, Moore insists, is not relative to someone. It is good absolutely that you enjoy pleasure, not good relative to you that you enjoy it (whatever that would mean). (We will turn to the expression "good that" in the next section.) In Moore's own words, "The only reason I can have for aiming at 'my own good,' is that it is *good absolutely* that what I so call should belong to me."[10]

Moore is of course right that talk of what "exists for someone" makes no sense. Suppose one person believes that a certain object exists, and someone else believes that this same object does not exist. We do not infer that it exists for the first and not for the second. We say instead that, according to one person, it exists; according to the other, it does not. Both of them cannot be right. But to see how weak Moore's position is, compare the way we think about statements made with "good for." If someone asserts that a certain kind of food is good for S and not good for T, we do not reply, "It cannot be both good and not good, and so one part or the other of your assertion must be rejected." We let stand both the assertion that something is good and that it is bad—provided we can interpret this to mean that it is good for one person and bad for another. By contrast, we do not let stand the assertion that something exists and does not exist; and we do not regard "It exists, according to him" as a

9. Moore asks in the opening sentence of a paragraph: "What, then, is meant by 'my own good'? In what sense can a thing be good *for me*?" (*Principia Ethica*, p. 150, his emphasis). The rest of the paragraph focuses on the proper interpretation of such expressions as "a good that is mine," "my own good," and "my good"; "good for me" and other phrases that contain "good *for*" do not recur. Nonetheless, the position he is attacking is Henry Sidgwick's egoism—or, more generally, any theory that claims that one's ultimate aim should be what is good *for oneself*, not good "absolutely." He thinks he can refute egoism by showing that if my good or what is good for me is not understood as my having what is good absolutely, then aiming at it is as nonsensical as affirming that something exists for me. His target is not the more restricted thesis that when it is said of *pleasure* that *it* is good, this should be taken to mean that it is good *for* someone (namely, the person who feels it). One might well have doubts about that idea; I address them in section 19.

10. Ibid., his emphasis.

way of saying that it exists for him. There simply is no need to talk about or to make sense of what exists *for* someone. But talking about what is good *for* someone is ubiquitous and necessary, despite Moore's claim to the contrary. Without such relativization, one and the same thing will be simply good and simply not good.

There is another reason to reject Moore's position: a philosopher who denies that his topic is what is good for anyone is bypassing a question that other philosophers have long been interested in, a question that there is every reason for them to ask. If one refuses to ask about what is good for us, one will have nothing to say about what is in our interest to desire, pursue, and attain. One will have nothing to say about what it is for someone to be well-off. That is the question posed by Socrates, Plato, Aristotle, and the whole tradition of moral philosophy they initiated. They ask: "When we seek what is good—that is, what is beneficial—*for* our children or our fellow citizens, and when we look for the resources they will need to lead a life in which they are well-off, at what should we be aiming?" There is no such thing as being advantageous, but advantageous for no one—just as there is no such thing as being to the left of, but to the left of nothing. Their question about good, being a question about what is beneficial or advantageous, is necessarily about what is good *for* someone.

In fact, we may wonder why we should allow ourselves to be attracted by something if it has no place in a life that is good to live—good *for* the person living it. Why set one's sights on acquiring knowledge or disseminating it, why set one's sights on *anything*, if the goodness that is claimed for it is not one that is in the interest of anyone? There is no point in having a good knife, merely to have something that is good. There would similarly be no point in knowing something, if all one could say about knowledge is that it is good, but not good *for* anyone.

18. "Good that" and "Bad that"

Sometimes, when we say that it is good (or a good thing) that some action was undertaken, or that some event came to pass, we do not mean that it was good *for* someone or other. Consider someone who thinks that lawbreakers should be punished because they deserve to suffer, and for no other reason. He may express this idea by saying, "It is by itself good *that* criminals get what they deserve." That should not be taken to mean that punishment is good *for* criminals, or that it is good for anyone else. This statement about what is good is not meant to rest on any notion of what is advantageous, but is supported by appealing to different ideas—ideas about what is owed, or due, or just. Of course, "It is good that P" or "It is a good thing that P" (where "P" is a placeholder for some proposition) does not *mean* that when P obtains, a debt has been paid, or justice has been done. When someone simply says that it is good that P, his assertion does not give any backing to the claim that it is good that P. He may go on to say that when P obtains, justice is done: that is *why* it is good that P. But there are indefinitely many ways of supporting the assertion that it is good that P.

If a philosopher thinks that people should have some pleasure in their lives because that makes them to some extent better-off—because, in other words, it adds to their well-being—he can express this claim by saying, "Pleasure is good *for* human beings." And, speaking elliptically, he can say, "Pleasure is good," standing ready, whenever clarification is needed, to expand on his statement by referring to those for whom pleasure is good. That same philosopher might, speaking elliptically, also say that punishment is good—meaning by this that it is good *that* certain people are punished. To say of something like pleasure or punishment that it is good is not by itself a sufficiently clear expression of a philosophical idea. "G is good" might be short for "G is good for (advantageous to) someone," or short for "It is good that P."[11]

Let us return now to Nagel's thoughts about pain (section 15). He thinks it is a bad thing. He says, "The objective badness of pain . . . is not some mysterious further property that all pains have, but just the fact that there is reason for anyone capable of viewing the world objectively to want it to stop."[12] He does not say here that pain should stop be-

---

11. It might be suggested that "It is good that P" is in turn short for something else, but I would not agree. Admittedly, someone who says, "It is good that P," has not thereby specified *why* it is good that P. But we should not say that a statement is elliptical merely because it is unsupported. The meaning of "It is good that P" is clear enough: as I will say, this locates P on the credit (positive, favorable) side of the ledger of practical reasoning; there is something (not yet specified) to be said in favor of P's being the case. By contrast, statements of the form "G is good" do not by themselves permit us to understand what is being claimed about G: this is a problem about how to construe the statement, not about how to support it. (Similarly, it would be a mistake to suppose that "G is good for S" is elliptical whenever it is unsupported or whenever no conclusion is drawn from it.)

12. Nagel, *The View from Nowhere*, p. 144.

cause it is bad *for* the person who feels it.[13] Instead, he says that there is a reason pain should not happen. What is that reason? His reply is simply that the badness of pain is precisely the reason it should not occur.[14] He takes "bad," when said of pain, both to indicate that there is some reason pain should stop and to specify what that reason is: its badness. Note how different his use of "bad" is from the ones we have surveyed. One can say that it is bad that criminals escape punishment and then specify the reason it is bad: it is unjust. One can say that pain is bad and treat this as an abbreviated way of saying that it is bad for the person who feels it. One can say that it is bad that people feel pain, and then support that claim by saying that it is bad for them. But Nagel believes that calling pain bad is already specifying the reason pain should not happen. He thinks that one should not kick someone in the head because the pain it would cause is a bad thing: that by itself is all the reason that need be given against doing so. There is no need to go further, according to Nagel, by saying that the reason it is bad for someone to be kicked in the head is that it is bad *for* him.[15]

It is crucial to distinguish the different roles played by the expressions "good for" and "good that." To assert that it is good that P (that some

13. At one point (ibid., p. 158) Nagel says that what we intensely like or dislike is good or bad *"for us"* (his emphasis), meaning by this, I believe, not that these things are personally advantageous or disadvantageous, but that if we have normal human sensory powers, it is good or bad that they happen to us.

14. "There's a reason for me to be given morphine which is independent of the fact that the pain is mine—namely that it's awful" (ibid., p. 162). I take this to mean that the reason pain should be avoided and stopped is that it is bad ("awful" being a stronger way of saying "bad"). Nagel speaks of the immediate impression of one who feels intense pain that it is in itself a bad thing—an impression that he (Nagel) regards as impossible to explain away as an illusion (ibid., pp. 145–146, 157–158). That is, he assumes that the sufferer does not merely assume that there is *some* reason—though he may not know what it is—to put a stop to his pain; rather, the sufferer knows precisely what that reason is: he immediately apprehends the badness of pain (ibid., p. 161). I think Nagel would have done better to drop the idea that the badness of pain is immediately apprehended and to say instead that the reason pain should be avoided (when it should be avoided) lies in something that every sufferer does apprehend: the quality of the experience, barely possible to describe, that we have when we are in pain. (In fact, one might take him to be grounding pain's badness in its phenomenology when he says the reason to be given morphine is the awfulness of the pain. Perhaps "awful" gestures at the way the pain feels and is not merely an emphatic reference to its badness.) I return to these issues in section 38.

15. Compare this to Ross's way of talking about pain (and everything else he takes to be intrinsically bad): we can recognize its badness by adopting a "commanding standpoint" from which we see that it is "a thing for whose occurrence the world is the worse." See *The Right and the Good*, p. 103.

state of affairs obtains, or some event occurs, or some action is undertaken) is to say that P should be located on the credit (positive, favorable) side of the ledger when we take P into account in practical reasoning. If one remarks that it is good that P, one would undermine that remark if one then added that the goodness of P should count against undertaking some course of action. (Of course, the ledger may contain other facts, entered on the negative side, that outweigh P. Furthermore, there may be features of the situation that give us decisive reason not to enter P onto the ledger or to remove it. Even so, if it is good that P, then if P is to be taken into account at all, it counts positively.)

By contrast, "good for" is suited to play a more concrete justificatory role in our practical reasoning: it can be used to support the claim that it is good *that* P. When we learn that a course of action under consideration would make someone feel pain, that fact about it is generally regarded as a bad thing. Why so? It might be replied: because it is bad for S, the person who feels the pain; it is, in other words, contrary to S's interests. That reply proposes that the occurrence or prospect of S's pain, because it is bad for S, be placed on the debit side of the ledger in our practical calculations. But someone who hates S might reject the suggestion that, because pain is bad for S, it is bad that he be made to feel pain. He might say, on the contrary, that the fact that pain is bad for S shows that causing him pain is a good thing, not a bad one. It is a substantive ethical claim, not a point about language, that if a state of affairs P is bad for S, that never counts in favor but always against promoting P. It is also a substantive ethical claim, not a point about language, that one should do only that which is good for someone or other. It is a point about language, however, that if it is bad that P, that counts against P and never in favor of it. It is empty to say that everything we have reason to do is something it is good that we do.[16]

The hypothesis we are exploring in this study is that all good practical

16. To use T. M. Scanlon's terminology (*What We Owe to Each Other,* pp. 11, 97), "It is good that P" should be given a buck-passing analysis. "It is good that P" does not state the reason that P should occur, but it indicates that there are such reasons. By contrast, to say that G is good for S is to offer a premise that can be used, when conjoined with other premises, to make a case in favor of acting in a certain way. Scanlon implies that all assertions about what is good should be given a buck-passing analysis, but I believe this overlooks the most important use of "good." He uses "good" and "valuable" interchangeably, but being good for someone is a specific way of being valuable. The term "valuable," I suspect, is too generic, too thin in content, to play a useful role in ethical reflection or theory (section 69).

arguments rest on claims about what is good or bad *for* someone. If pain really is a bad thing, if it really should always be placed on the debit side of the ledger, then there must be a reason for placing it there, and that reason must consist in the badness of pain for someone or other (and surely that is the person who feels it). To hold that pain is bad, but not bad for anyone—not even the person whose pain it is—would be to make the badness of pain a mystery. Pain would, in that case, make no one worse-off, would be contrary to no one's interests, would detract from the quality of no one's life—and yet it would, somehow, be a bad thing.[17]

One might be leery of saying that pain is bad *for* the person who feels it, if one assumes (mistakenly) that this form of expression carries with it the implication that it is only the person who feels it who has reason to do something about it. If a pain is bad for you, then, it might be thought, it is precisely you, not someone else, who should want to stop it. The desire to avoid that implication is precisely what motivates Moore's hostility toward talking about what is good for someone. He says, "If it is *good absolutely* that I should have [something], then everyone else has as much reason for aiming at *my* having it, as I have myself."[18] What Moore says here implies that if something was good *for* me to have, then it would be I alone who has reason for wanting it and pursuing it. But we have seen that this is not so (section 15). When we say that something is good for someone, that statement leaves entirely open the question not only *who* should do or want something, but whether anyone has a reason to do or want anything.

Our discussion of Moore and Nagel should lend further support to the conclusion we reached earlier in this section: statements such as "Pain is bad" and "Pleasure is good" are as much in need of completion as statements of the form "He is good." The last is a shortened version of the statement that he is a good K or he is good at V-ing. The earlier statements might mean simply that whenever a pain occurs it is bad that

17. To take a different example: whenever there is an unjust inequality among people, it can be said that it is bad that there is such inequality. According to my hypothesis, it can be bad *that* there is such inequality only if there are some people *for* whom the elimination of such inequality would be good. Surely it is reasonable to say that there are if injustice has to do with the maldistribution of what is good for people. It would be good for those who unjustly have less than others to have as much as those others. The connections between justice and well-being will be more fully explored in sections 58–60.

18. Moore, *Principia Ethica*, p. 150, his emphasis.

there is that pain, and whenever pleasure occurs it is good that there is that pleasure. So construed, "Pleasure is good" merely says that the pleasure that some event or action brings counts in its favor. Alternatively, "Pleasure is good" can mean that pleasure is good *for* whoever experiences it; it is part of anyone's well-being, something whose presence makes anyone, to some degree, better off. So construed, "Pleasure is good" specifies what it is about pleasure that grounds its character as an item on the credit side of the ledger of practical reasoning: it puts pleasure into the same category as every other component of well-being (although it says nothing about how large or small a component it is).

But if someone insists that pleasure is good, and he then goes on to say that by this he does not mean that that pleasure is good for anyone, or that "it is good that there is pleasure," or to make any other statement of the form "It is good that . . . ," then we have no idea what he means to say about pleasure. We cannot begin to examine whether his statement about pleasure is true because we do not yet know what he is saying about it. We are just as much in the dark as we are when confronted with the statement that George is good but are not told whether he is a good poet, or a good spy, or a good person, or good at chess.

The difference between "good for" and "good that" explains why I have chosen the former as the focus of this study. When we say that "S should, all things considered, do V," we draw a conclusion that needs to be supported by argument. What can do this job? If we reply, "S's doing V is by itself a good thing," or (equivalently) "It is good that S will do V," but cannot back this up with anything further—if we cannot point to anyone for whom it is good and do not propose any other reason that S should do V—then we have offered no defense of our assertion. We are simply asking our audience to agree that S should do V.

But when we say, "If S does V, that will be good *for* T," we have gone at least some way down the road toward supporting our conclusion. If V is merely of instrumental value, we will want to know what it leads to: what further thing will V bring about, and is that further thing good for T? But if V can be shown to be noninstrumentally good for T, then our search for justification may be at an end. That S's doing V is good for T can serve, all by itself, as a justification for doing V.[19] If S is to do some-

---

19. Recall, however (section 2), that some beings (e.g., plants) for which some things are good and others bad are not beings whose good we have any reason to promote or care about.

thing that will have an effect on T, then what could speak more in favor of the way it affects T than that it does what is best *for* T? And if S's doing V does no good for anyone at all, that casts a pall on it: we must wonder how such an action can be justified.

19. Pleasure and Advantage

An objection may be raised at this point: we have been saying that "Pleasure is good" needs elucidation, and that one way of clarifying what this statement means is to expand it, so that it reads, "Pleasure is good for the person who feels it." Similarly for pain. "Pain is bad" should normally be taken to mean that pain is bad for the person who feels it. But, it may be said, we have now transformed eminently plausible assertions into statements that are questionable. "Pleasure is good" is a claim with which nearly everyone would agree. "Pleasure is good for us" sounds like something that would be said by someone who has the wrong attitude toward pleasure. Surely pleasures should be welcomed because they are good—not because they are good for anyone. They are not a means to a further end, but that is what we would be taken to be saying about them were we to insist that "pleasure is good" not be accepted as it stands but complemented by "for us." (So too for pain: "Pain is bad for the person who feels it" might be taken to mean that pain is to be avoided because of its bad consequences, not because it is, in itself, a bad thing.)

If someone says, "Pleasure pays," we would take this to be a wrongheaded endorsement of pleasure as a means to a further end. To say that it pays for S to V is to say that V-ing brings advantages to S, and that those advantages outweigh any disadvantages. The sentence form "G is good for S" is most frequently used, in everyday discourse, to assert that G is instrumentally advantageous for S. In our workaday negotiations with each other, we usually do not question each other's ultimate ends,

---

So the mere fact that an act would do some good (for no matter what individual) is never, by itself, enough to support a conclusion about what should be done (section 56). Statements of the form "If S does V, that will be good for T" will justify doing V when T is a being who is at or above the level that merits S's concern. Statements of this sort can justify actions and, for properly selected substitutions for "S" and "T," they do so. Recall too what was said in section 4: sound practical reasoning always has to do with someone's good—"but *who* that someone is, and not just what kind of good that good is . . . makes a great difference."

but we look for ways in which each person can get at least some of what he seeks. When one is not negotiating with others, but simply deliberating on one's own about what to do, one does not usually reach down to one's basic values in order to question them. Rather, one takes one's goals to be a settled matter and asks, "What is best for me to do?"—meaning, "What will be the best way for me to accomplish my goals?" The things we consciously reflect on as items that are good for us are means rather than ends. That is why "Pleasure is good for you" sounds strange: we are accustomed to using "good for you" to refer to what is instrumentally valuable.

Nonetheless, it is undeniable that if you lose your capacity for all enjoyment, if life becomes stale and flat, that is bad news: bad news *for you,* because you are worse-off, in this respect, than you once were. The kind of life that one should want to live, for one's own good, is a life that has, to a certain degree, specific kinds of pleasures in it (section 32). When one enjoys oneself in those ways, that is to one's advantage, that is in one's interests, that is a benefit, that is a blessing. Pleasures (of certain kinds) are not advantageous; they do not have advantages; they are not productive of advantages.[20] Rather, they themselves are among the advantages we can have; they are experiences the production of which makes other things advantageous. If we did not speak in these terms, we could not make sense of our ordinary attitudes. When only one wonderful piece of cake remains, and both S and T (each trim, healthy, and hungry) would enjoy it, it is contrary to S's interests if T eats it all. That is because certain pleasures are good—good for someone, namely the person who feels them.

"Pleasure is good" carries with it no implication that pleasure is good as a means. When it is expanded into "Pleasure is good for the person who feels it," it can be misunderstood as an endorsement of pleasure as a means to a further end. The proper reaction to this, however, is not to insist that "Pleasure is good" is a statement that needs no elucidation or supplementation. Rather, it is to expand it by relativizing it—and then to be careful not to misconstrue that expansion.

---

20. I do not mean to deny that the pleasantness of an experience can ever have instrumental value. For example, we seek some pleasant amusements as a form of relaxation, and we welcome relaxation partly because of its instrumental benefits. But there are many other pleasures that lack instrumental value or at any rate are not sought even partly for their advantages.

20. Good for S That P

When we say "G is good for S," what takes the place of G can come in many forms. In place of G we can insert a noun or various verbal phrases: "knowledge," "walking" "being loved," "to swim." But it can also be good for you that something is the case. For example: "It is good for you that there will be a full moon tonight." In fact, all claims about what is good for someone can be recast in such a way that they take the form "It is good for S that P." Knowledge is good for us: that means that it is good for us that we have knowledge. Swimming is good for us: that is, it is good for us that we swim. Being loved is good for us: in other words, it is good for us that we are loved. What is good for someone, then, is a certain state of affairs. When we do something for the good of some person, we try to bring about or perpetuate some state of affairs. When we talk about someone having or possessing a good—health, love, a friend—we do not mean that there is some object to which he is related; we mean it is good that he is healthy, that he loves and is loved, that he has a relationship with someone that qualifies as a friendship. If he is not healthy, it is bad that he is unhealthy; and if he becomes healthy, it will be good that he is healthy. Simple statements such as "Pleasure is good" must therefore be doubly expanded: "It is good for a person who feels pleasure that he feels pleasure."

Not only is it *possible* to understand all claims about what is good by means of a "that" clause; it is sometimes *necessary* in order to reveal and sort out an ambiguity. Suppose I tell you, "It is good for you to sleep in the same room as your children." Am I saying that something good accrues to you? Or rather to your children? Or both? What I have in mind can be more clearly conveyed if I alter the form of my assertion. I can say instead, "It is good for your children that you are sleeping in their room." Similarly, if a philosopher says, "It is good for every human being to love some other human being," that can mean that it is good either for the one who loves or for the one who is loved. We can again sort this out by means of "that" clauses: what might be meant is that it is good for someone who loves that he loves, or that it is good for the person who is loved that he is loved. Speaking in this cumbersome way serves a purpose: it forces us to be clear about whether "for S" is meant to pick out the person whose good is served or is rather to be taken with the other words that pick out the state of affairs that is alleged to be good for someone. In what follows we will sometimes use these "that" clauses, but when there is no danger of ambiguity or misunderstanding, we will continue to use the simpler expression, "G is good for S." Nonetheless, we should always bear in mind that statements of the form "It is good for S to V" are not necessarily assertions about what is good for S.

There is another kind of ambiguity, noticed earlier (section 17), that can lurk in statements about what is good for someone. All talk about what is good for someone, like all talk about a good individual of some kind (a good poet, a good watch), presupposes some comparison class and some standard for making a comparison. (The members of the comparison class need not actually exist: all existing watches might be good watches, but even so, they are better than the defective watches that would be produced if the manufacture of them went awry.) Since we can vary the class with which we compare an individual we call good, we can say that someone is a good writer and that he is not a good writer: we mean that, in comparison with one group, he deserves a high grade; when compared with another, a low grade. To be a good K is to stand high on some scale or other, and it is always in order for someone who talks about a good K to be asked what standard he means to be using. Similarly, when it is said that G is good for S, it is always in order to ask: "Good for S in comparison with what?"

So if it is good for you to learn solid geometry, then it is—by comparison with something else—good for you that you do so. But there may be something (in fact many things) that is better for you than learning solid geometry. Learning this subject may be good for you when that activity is compared with certain alternatives, but bad for you when compared with others. And although it would be good for you (compared with something else), it may be that when you consider *all* the alternatives available to you, it would be best for you that you not study this subject, because there are so many other things that are better for you to do.

Similarly, a person's desires might be both good and bad for him to satisfy. It may be better for him that those desires are satisfied than that they remain unsatisfied; but at the same time he would be far better off if he did not have those desires. Certain pleasures may likewise be good and bad: better to have that pleasure than no pleasure at all, but worse than many other kinds of pleasure that one could have. Some goods may be small goods—too small to bother with—in that they are inferior to so many others; and others may be so great that they are always worth striving for. A study of what is good for us should shed some light on how we are to make these distinctions. We must ask (sections 33, 35, and 44), what standard of comparison should we be using?

21. The "for" of "Good for"

What work is done by "for" when we say that G is good for S? The question may strike us as baffling, perhaps even absurd. For precisely what is being asked? How else can we reply, except to say, unhelpfully, that "for" indicates that G is good *in relation to* S? Although the words "in relation to" are unexceptionable, they tell us nothing about what kind of relationship this is. But is there anything to say about it? Perhaps we simply have to rely on synonyms: by placing "for" after "good," we indicate that we are talking about what benefits someone, or is advantageous for him, or is in his interests.

We will see, nonetheless, that something helpful *can* be said about the sort of relationship that holds between G and S when G is good for S. We can easily fall into serious philosophical error by misconstruing what that relationship is—indeed, we have already seen how this can happen. For one way to understand the statement that G is good for S is to take "for S" to be picking out the person who has reason to do something about G—to retain, desire, or pursue it. So construed, "good for S" is a tool for laying out an argument acceptable to S; the "for" of "good for" says who it is that has reason to take up a favorable attitude toward a certain thing because of the goodness of that thing. We have seen that this is a misreading of the "for" of "good for." To say that G is good for S is not to say that someone, S, or anyone else, has a reason to want or seek G. The questions "Is G good for S?" and "Who, if anyone, should want S to have G, or help S to have G?" are entirely separable.

The are two other ways of misreading the "for" of "good for." Seeing what they are, and seeing why they are mistaken, will help us discover what kind of relationship this is.

One possibility is that the only work done by "for" in "G is good for S" is to locate the good in question at a certain place in the world. Just as colors do not float freely around the universe, unattached to things that have the capacity to take on coloration, so goodness is always possessed by someone: it always has an address, and the job of "for" in "good for" might be to specify that address. According to this suggestion, when we say that it is good for S that P, "for S" picks out the place where that state of affairs obtains. To say, for example, that it is good for S that he enjoys playing chess is to say that a certain kind of good can be found at a certain place in the world—namely, the place where the enjoyment occurs. That pleasure is S's pleasure, and since that pleasure is good, there is a good thing located where he is.

Another possibility is that the word "for" in "good for" means "according to" or "from the perspective of."[21] That is certainly what it means in many of its occurrences. "For me, blue is a warm color." "For me, a five-mile walk is a long walk." "For me, he is a boring speaker." "For Berkeley, material objects are composed of ideas." By relativizing statements in this way, we indicate that the statement that follows "for me" is not one we expect others to accept without qualification, or perhaps to accept at all. I do not claim that blue is a warm color—period. But for me, it is. Perhaps material objects are not composed of ideas, but for Berkeley—that is, according to Berkeley—they are.

When the "for" of "good for" is read in this way, what is good for someone is a matter that is to be settled by the opinion or perspective of the person in question. To say that it is good for S to learn mathematics would be to say that it is the perspective of S—something about his state of mind, his attitude toward learning mathematics—that makes it true that doing so is good for him.

Perhaps the fact that the "for" of "good for" can be interpreted in this perspectival way explains why certain philosophers deny that the question "What is good for someone?" has practical or philosophical significance. They think that what is good *for* someone is a matter to be settled by that person's point of view, but since that point of view can be riddled with errors and confusions, we should pay no attention to what is good for him. Why should ethical truth depend on the way things appear to someone?

Ross hints that this is how he regards the "for" of "good for." He says

---

21. According to L. W. Sumner, when we talk about what is good for someone, we are saying that his life has a "peculiar perspectival kind of value" (*Welfare, Happiness, and Ethics*, p. 20). He later adds: "You are the proprietor . . . of a set of attitudes . . . towards the conditions of your life. It is these attitudes which constitute the standpoint from which these conditions can be assessed as good or bad *for you.* . . . Prudential value is . . . perspectival because it literally takes the point of view of the subject" (ibid., p. 43, his emphasis). Scanlon also identifies well-being with an assessment that is made "from the point of view of the person whose life it is" (*What We Owe to Each Other*, p. 111).

that according to Meinong, goods are in a sense "unpersonal," in that they are "not essentially *for* a subject at all, though they are *in* a subject" (emphasis added). That, Ross adds, "is exactly the position I wish to establish."[22] He thinks, in other words, that we must choose: either we must say that G is good *for* S, meaning that G, viewed from the perspective of S, is good, or that something that is good "sans phrase" is located *in* someone. Since the first alternative is merely a statement about appearances, and ethics, like all philosophy, is a search for what is the case, not what seems to be the case, we must choose the second alternative. According to Ross, what is good can be located somewhere—it is *in* something—because all good things are in states of mind. "Contemplate any imaginary universe from which you suppose mind entirely absent, and you will fail to find anything in it that you can call good in itself."[23] A mindless universe would be devoid of the individuals who feel pleasure, acquire knowledge, and exercise virtue, and so in such a world there would be nothing for goodness to be in. But Ross rejects the idea that judgments about what is good depend for their truth on the attitudes of some mind. He thinks that "good for" means "good from the perspective of" or "good according to," and so banishes these phrases from his ethical theory.

Ross is right to think that an ethical theory should not make the truth of statements about what is good depend entirely on the perspective or authority of this or that person. We are about to examine that approach and to see its weaknesses. But he is wrong to infer that, for this reason, ethical theory should avoid talking about what is good *for* someone.[24] The "for" of "good for" can easily be interpreted in a way that does not make the truth about what is good for someone depend solely on that person's point of view.

In fact, Ross's way of thinking about goodness accords, in an important respect, with the hypothesis that when we talk about what is good for a person, we are locating a good at a certain place. He rejects this way of understanding the phrase "good for"—but that is merely a point

22. Ross, *The Right and the Good*, p. 104, n. 1.
23. Ibid., p. 140, and compare with p. 122.
24. Ross himself occasionally uses "good" and "bad" as incomplete expressions that are to be completed by "for." For example, in discussing our prima facie duty to return good for good, he speaks as though this enjoins us to "bring about advantages for our benefactors" (ibid., p. 31). But an advantage is necessarily an advantage for someone; "advantageous for" and "good for" are interchangeable.

about how a word is to be interpreted. What is more significant is his idea that the things that are good—pleasure, knowledge, virtue, and the proper apportionment of pleasure to the virtuous—have their goodness because of their own features, and not because of any features of the minds that feel pleasure, possess knowledge, and exercise virtue. This is what he means when he says, "That which is good owes its goodness not to being possessed by one person or by another, but to its nature."[25] According to Ross, pleasure, knowledge, virtue, and the proper apportionment of pleasure to the virtuous are inherently good: they do not need to be a proper match, in some way, for the minds that possess them in order to be good. They do not have their goodness in relation to something else—for then they would not be inherently good; rather, they would be good in relation to certain things, but not in relation to others.

In effect, then, Ross has a locative way of thinking about what it means for goodness to be present in the world. In a mindless world there would be no goodness, for there would be no places in the universe for the things that are good to reside. That is why he talks about the things that are good as being "in a subject." Those subjects—the minds that receive pleasure, knowledge, and virtue—are the repositories of what is good, places where these good things are stored. But those good things are good because of what they are, not because of any features of those who receive them. Ross would not have altered his theory of goodness in any important way had he decided to speak of pleasure, knowledge, and virtue as being good *for* those who possess them. He need only have insisted that we take "for" to play a locative role.

Our normal ways of using the phase "good for" should not be dismissed out of hand. As we noted from the start, it is one of the fundamental terms we use when we make decisions. An ethical theory that says nothing about what this relationship is—the relationship that holds between G and S when G is good for S—is ignoring one of the fundamental features of our evaluative practices. Ross's refusal to propose a theory about what is in a person's interests—what it is for something to be an advantage or benefit for someone—is a serious omission. We should see whether that gap in his thinking can easily be filled simply by offering him a locative reading of "for." His theory, altered in this way, would claim that pleasure, knowledge, and virtue are good for anyone

25. Ibid., p. 151, and compare with p. 103.

who possesses them. But the "for" of "good for" would simply be a device for saying where the things that are good are located.

But that way of construing "for" simply will not work. We use "good for" in the same way we use any relative term. Whether X is heavier than Y, for example, depends just as much on the weight of Y as it does on the weight of X. Both relata are equally contributory to the holding of the relation. That is precisely how we normally use "good for." It is the name of a relation. Nothing is inherently good for, just as nothing is inherently heavier than.

What is good for a beginning student? That depends on the needs of the beginner. What is good for a beginning student may be quite bad for an advanced student or an expert. Examples can be multiplied easily and indefinitely. It is good for philosophers to mull over arguments with care but not necessarily with speed; by contrast, it is good for corporate lawyers to think fast: the needs of their profession are quite different from those of philosophy. What is good for poets is (of course) to make poems; not so for lawyers. And so on. When we assess whether G is good for S, we must assess both G and S to see whether they are properly matched to each other. That leaves open the possibility that some things are always good, wherever they occur, because wherever they are they are suitable to their subjects. It is possible, for example, that it is good for every creature capable of feeling pleasure that it do so. But if that is the case, it does not follow that we can explain why pleasure is good wherever it occurs without saying anything about the nature of those who experience it.[26]

---

26. As we will see (section 33), there are bad pleasures—more precisely, kinds of pleasures that it is bad for a human being to experience. Any human being would do better to avoid them altogether, and to choose others in their place. That thesis depends for its plausibility on facts about human beings, namely, what they are capable of achieving. So the human pleasures that are good (for those who experience them) owe their goodness to the nature of those who experience them. The point can, I believe, be generalized to all other creatures that can feel pleasure: some pleasures are good for them and others are not (for example, addictive pleasure that undermine their health). In these cases too, an explanation of the goodness of pleasures (when they are in fact good) requires some reference to the nature of the living organism that experiences them. But even if all pleasures of every type were good for those who feel them, an explanation of that truth would have to appeal to something about the way in which pleasure is part of the psychological economy of the creatures who feel it. Pleasures would owe their goodness to the various appetites, needs, desires, and so on, of certain living forms; so even in this case the goodness of pleasure for someone or something would be based not only on the nature of pleasure but also on the nature of the creature that experiences it.

An analogy should help. There is a point on earth that is to the north of all other points. But what makes one point north of another is the location of both points, not just one of them. Similarly, anything that is a gift is a gift for someone. Nothing is just a gift, plain and simple. But there may be some gifts that are so versatile and varied in their uses that they are good gifts for all people, regardless of the peculiar shape of their needs. Those gifts suit the needs of all. In the same way, it may be that some goods—pleasure, for example—are good, no matter who or what experiences them. If that is so, it remains the case that pleasure "owes its goodness" (to use Ross's terms) to certain facts about the subjects who experience it.

Ross is right to say that pleasure owes its goodness "not to being possessed by one person or by another, but to its nature."[27] It makes no sense to say that my possessing pleasure or your possessing pleasure is one of the factors that makes it true that pleasure is good for all those who experience it. But what does make sense is to think of everything that is good for S as being like a good gift for S, in this respect: it is only by looking on the one hand to what is presented as a gift, or what is said to be good, and on the other hand to the one for whom it is a gift, or for whom it is good, and seeing a match between them that we can be assured that it is a good gift, or something good for the one who receives it. In fact, it is not strained to think of all the things that are good for us as gifts, in some way or other: either they flow, to some degree, from the intentional actions of others, or they are gifts of nature or of fortune. And it makes sense to cultivate an attitude of thankfulness not only for the gifts, strictly so called, that we receive on gift-giving occasions, but for all that comes our way for our good. But, in any case, whether goods are like gifts in these respects or not, they are like gifts in that they are always for someone or other. "This book is a gift" is grammatically complete, but with a moment's thought we recognize that nothing is a gift all by itself; gifts are made to be gifts by their being one element in a gift relationship. Just so with the things that are often called goods. "Pleasure is good" is grammatically complete, but there must always be a "for" in the background, and the one for whom it is good makes no less a contribution to its goodness than does pleasure itself.

According to the hypothesis under consideration, the "for" in "G is

27. Ross, *The Right and the Good,* p. 151.

good for S" is best taken to indicate that G has a certain kind of suitability to S: their properties are so matched to each other that G serves S well. That is a better way of thinking of the "for" in "good for" than the way proposed by the locative interpretation, and we will see that this approach is also superior to the one that takes "for" to be perspectival. "Suitable for" is the sense of "good for" in which boots are good for walking, spoons are good for stirring, watches are good for telling time. When a material object is such that it can serve a certain purpose or goal, it is good for the achievement of that goal. Artifacts can be spoken of as goods (sheets, towels, curtains as "dry goods") because they are designed to support some human activity or purpose; they are goods because they are good for something that someone does. But "good for" does not differ in meaning as applied to final ends and as applied to means. Just as boots serve us well in certain conditions, so a poet is served well by the use he makes of his linguistic powers; the boots serve well as means to the end for which they are designed, and the exercise of literary imagination, being an activity suitable to the craft of poetry, serves a poet well and is good for him. If certain kinds of enjoyment are good for all human beings, that is because those sorts of pleasures and certain elements in the psychological composition of all human beings are well matched to each other. The pleasures of sociability, for example, are good for us because companionship, friendship, and love correspond to and do well at serving other-directed drives that are present in us all.

"For" is the word by which suitability of some sort is conveyed not only when it follows "good" but also when it follows "right." "That sweater is right for you" means that you are the sort of person on whom the sweater looks good. An action might also be said to be right for you, rather than right without qualification. That would mean that in light of facts about you or your situation, this is the action you should perform. And by relativizing—by saying not "right" full stop, but "right for you"—we imply that someone else, whose circumstances, personality, or character is different from yours, should not make the same kind of choice that you should.

Ross has no interest in either "right for" or "good for." But what he says about the things that are good can be modified in an obvious way, and nothing said here would undermine such a modification of his theory. He says that pleasure, knowledge, virtue, and the proper apportionment of pleasure to the virtuous are good "sans phrase." What he should have said is that they are good *for* all those who possess them. His ideas, thus transformed, will occupy us later (sections 32, 42, 52, 59).

22. Plants, Animals, Humans

Another way to bring out what is missing from Ross's approach to ethics (and from Moore's as well) is to remind ourselves of the elementary point that human beings are not the only sorts of individuals for whom some things are good and others bad. We talk about and care about what is good or bad for animals and plants. Whatever stunts their growth or threatens their lives is bad for them. They are the sorts of things that can be healthy or diseased, and it is good for them to be healthy, bad to be diseased, to be stunted, to die before they mature. To determine what is good for some living S, we need to know what sort of thing S is— whether it is a human being, a horse, or a tree. If there are things that are good for all human beings, their goodness must be grounded not only in the properties of those things, but also in the properties of human beings.

Yet when one reads Ross, one finds no recognition of these elementary points and no awareness of their significance. (An exception will be noted in the next section.) He does not ask Aristotle's question "What is the *human* good?"[28] That is no mere oversight; it is the outcome of his assumption that goodness is not relational. Pleasure, knowledge, and virtue—the things he takes to be good—do not have their goodness in relation to human beings. According to his way of thinking, the thesis that knowledge is good does not have to be grounded in the propensities or needs of human nature. The thesis that courage is good can be recognized to be true without being supported by facts about fear, self-control, and risk. He holds that knowledge is good "sans phrase," not good for human beings, because the capacity human beings have for acquiring knowledge has nothing to do with the goodness of knowledge. It is not a condition for the goodness of knowledge, but merely a place where that good thing, knowledge, can be present in the world. Our cognitive capacities make it possible for us to receive that good, but the goodness of knowledge is not grounded in a peculiarly human need for knowledge or in any empirical facts about human psychology. Similarly for the

28. Aristotle *Nicomachean Ethics* 1.2–7.

goodness of virtue: we are supposed to see, quite simply, that it is something that is good or would be good for anything to have. Courage, conscientiousness, and honesty are taken to be good, but not good for human beings; the role these virtues play in human relationships and in the management of our emotions is of no importance to ethics, because ethical inquiry need take no account of the circumstances of human life or the psychology of human beings.

Ross's way of thinking prevents him from acknowledging the elementary truth that some things are good and others are bad for plants, despite the fact that they cannot feel pleasure, acquire knowledge, or exercise virtue. Nor can he acknowledge the elementary truth that when we think about the good of animals, our thoughts vary according to the kind of animal we have in mind. We must ask what is good *for* a member of this species or that, and the answer to that question will not necessarily be uniform across all species. Unimpeded flying is good—that is, good for birds. Although pleasure is good for every animal capable of feeling it, the kinds of pleasure that are good for an animal will depend on the kind of animal it is. And the stimulation of the pleasure centers of an animal's brain may, on balance, be very bad for it if it prevents the animal from getting what it needs and engaging in the kinds of behavior that constitute a healthy life for a member of its kind. If Ross had recognized that our thinking about what is good in connection with plants and animals must be relativized—must be about what is good *for* them, and therefore responsive to facts *about* them—he would have seen that the same approach must be taken *whenever* we reflect on what is good.

When we ask how the lives of human beings can be improved, we must not overlook the fact that they are members of a certain kind—they are human beings. That does not mean that their well-being is affected by their membership in this group and no other. For we are not only human beings. By virtue of our choices and traditions, we place ourselves in many other categories as well: we are cooks, teachers, farmers, engineers, and so on. An adequate answer to the question "What is good for a farmer?" obviously must cater to the needs, goals, and circumstances of a farmer; it will differ radically from an answer to the question "What is good for a doctor?" Questions about what is good for a particular human being can be answered only by paying attention to the fact that he is a human being, but the social roles he fills will also figure in our answers (section 36).

The mistake philosophers sometimes make about good—their failure to think in terms of "good for"—would never be made about health. Which foods are healthy depends not only on the nature of those foods, but on whose health we have in mind. What is healthy for a horse to eat can be quite unhealthy for a human being to eat. And since the questions "What is healthy?" and "What is good?" are not so far apart, the importance of relativizing the first question suggests that we should relativize the second as well. For most living things, to flourish is simply to be healthy—to be an organism that is unimpeded in its healthy functioning. That holds true for human beings as well, but in our case flourishing consists not only in the healthy functioning of our bodies, but in psychological health as well. Truths about what is good, when they are made about human beings, are truths about what is good *for* us—just as facts about our health are facts about what is healthy *for* us—and must therefore be grounded in facts about our physical and psychological functioning. A theory about what is good that is applicable to human life must rest on ideas about the healthy development and exercise of the human mind (section 35).

That is why the rules that regulate our interaction with each other must in some way be responsive to our peculiar psychology. When we ask, for example, whether rules regarding sexual activity are to be taken seriously, and what it is for such rules to be good rules, it would be mad to ignore facts about human sexuality—not only facts about our sexual organs, but about the drives, instincts, and proclivities that are inherent in our psychology. The question "Is promiscuity bad for a child?" would be absurd if it were a question about any young member of any species whatsoever. It may be bad for human beings but good for bonobos, just as high humidity suits certain kinds of plants but not others (sections 43, 44).

This leaves open the possibility that there may be little or nothing that can be truly said about what is good for all human beings. Human sexuality, to take this example again, might be so variable that no simple and uniform set of rules regulating the sexuality of all human beings could be good for everyone. Men might have a somewhat different psychological profile from women because of the influence of different genes and hormones, and this might make it true that what is good for many men does not apply as broadly to women. Regardless of the empirical deficiencies or strengths of such a hypothesis, it illustrates an important philosophical point: however much diversity or uniformity there is among human beings, a theory of well-being must attend to the generic properties of the individual S for which G is said to be good. If certain things are good for all human beings, at all times and places, then that fact must be grounded in properties that all human beings have at all times and places. Skepticism about that kind of universalism is by no means ruled out at this point. But neither should we rule out the possibility that all human beings at all times and places share certain features, and that, because of this, some statements of the form "G is good for S" apply to every human subject.

Certainly that *seems* to be the case. It is good for any human being to have some pleasure and some knowledge. When we attend to the peculiar features of our own time and place, we may be able to say more. For many millennia it has been the case that the failure of a child to learn any language has been very bad for that child. That was not always true of human children, but it is true now and will continue to be true for as far into the future as we can imagine. Human nature, human society, human needs—all these things may change, and so what is good for us may change. A theory of well-being that has been and will be applicable to all human beings for ages and ages, but perhaps will no longer apply millions of years from now, is nonetheless a theory worth having.

23. Ross on Human Nature

I must now acknowledge an exception and make amends. *For the most part,* Ross's theory about what is good has no connection with anything that might be called a conception of human nature. It rests on no psychological claims, paints no picture of the human soul. But at one point he does enter into this terrain, and it is significant that when he does so, he enhances the plausibility of his theory. The four goods, he claims, are pleasure, knowledge, virtue, and the proper apportionment of pleasure to the virtuous.[29] The statement that these four types of thing are good, he thinks, is self-evident. That is, when we carefully reflect on that statement and consider whether it is true, we find that it is inherently credible and does not need to be justified by tracing a relationship between it and any other statement. But at one point he adds that although his list

---

29. Ross, *The Right and the Good*, pp. 134–141.

of goods has been arrived at "on its own merits, by reflection on what we really think to be good, it perhaps derives some support from the fact that it harmonizes with a widely accepted classification of the elements in the life of the soul."[30] What he has in mind is this. Human psychology has three compartments: we cognize, we feel, we aim. Within each of these spheres we can achieve an ideal state. The ideal state of cognition is knowledge, the ideal state of feeling is pleasure, the ideal state of conation is virtue, and the ideal relation between feeling and aiming is the proper apportionment of pleasure to virtue.

Here Ross recognizes that a theory of what is good can receive some support from reflection on the sort of being whose good is being talked about. His idea, perhaps, is that we should not be surprised that his list of goods contains precisely these items—pleasure, knowledge, virtue— because each corresponds to one of the major aspects of human life. We are feeling creatures, and so we can do well or poorly, in the way of feeling; to feel pleasure is to do well here, to feel pain to do poorly. And so on. We no longer have a mere list of goods; instead, we have an explanation for why we have precisely this list, and that explanation is based upon a division of the human psyche into general faculties.

But Ross does not think his theory of what is good needs any such support. His "classification of the elements of the life of the soul" is an afterthought, and he arrives at it only after he has engaged in "reflection on what we really think to be good." His readers, he hopes, can be brought to agree that pleasure, knowledge, virtue, and the proper apportionment of pleasure to the virtuous are self-evidently good, and that no justification of the statement that they are good is needed because their goodness is grounded in what they are, not in any facts about the subjects in which they reside. That is where he goes wrong.

24. The Perspectival Reading of "Good for"

Our hypothesis (section 21) is that the "for" in "G is good for S" conveys the suitability or conformability of G to S: it indicates that G serves S well. But there is another possibility, mentioned earlier (section 21), and we should examine it now. The preposition "for" is often used to convey the point of view, perspective, or outlook that someone has. Recall the

30. Ibid., p. 140.

examples used above: "For me, blue is a warm color." "For me, a five-mile walk is a long walk." "For me, he is a boring speaker." "For Berkeley, material objects are composed of ideas." If this is how "for" operates in "good for," then to say that G is good for S is to say that, from the standpoint of S, G is good.

Does that shed light on "good for" or cover it in darkness? To begin with, notice this difficulty: we saw earlier (sections 17, 18) that although "G is good" is grammatically complete, it always requires elucidation before it can be understood and evaluated. Are we being told that the subject of the sentence is a good something or other—and if so, a good what? A good father? A good spy? Or are we being told that the subject of the sentence is to be placed on the credit side of the ledger of practical deliberation—as when, for example, someone says that punishing criminals is good? Or are we being told that the subject of the sentence is good *for* someone?—and if so, for whom? If it is agreed that "G is good," taken in isolation, is obscure because its truth cannot be evaluated until it is completed in one of several different ways, then it looks as though the perspectival reading of the "for" of "good for" is committed to saying that we cannot understand what is even meant by the fuller statement that G is *good for* S, all by itself. The perspectival reading takes the "for" of "G is good for S" to mean that from the perspective of S, G is good. But now we are entitled to ask, good in what way? From the standpoint of S, is G a good something or other? Or a consideration in favor of a practical conclusion? Or good *for* someone? And if the last, how, from the perspective of S, is "for" to be interpreted?

How are these questions to be answered? By asking S? But suppose S has no answer and has not even thought of these questions. It looks as though this perspectival way of thinking about "good for" turns that expression into a mystery.

A perspectival reading can solve this problem in the following way. The perspective of S that determines whether G is good for S is not constituted by S's thoughts about whether G is good. (For in that case, we would have to understand the meaning of those thoughts, and the difficulty just raised would remain unsolved.) Rather, what determines whether G is good for S depends on S's conation: if he plans to pursue G, or desires G, or wants to continue to have G, or has other such positive attitudes toward G (if he likes G, enjoys it, finds it appealing), then G is good for him. S does not have to think of G as good, and he does not even have to possess the concept of goodness; but if S pursues G, or would be upset if G were taken away from him, and the like—if he has this favorable orientation toward G and his actions are informed by this orientation—then G is good for him. According to the perspectival interpretation of the "for" of "good for," something is good for someone by being the object of certain attitudes, desires, plans, and the like. It is that individual's orientation or perspective on the world—the world that is the object of his conation—that makes it true that certain things are good *for* him, that is, from his point of view.

But the perspectival reading of "good for" cannot be right. What is good for a plant is not a matter of what is good from the perspective of the plant, because it has no perspective, no outlook on the world, no goals, plans, or desires. That point by itself shows that the "for" of "good for S" is not perspectival when S is a plant. But it also shows that the "for" of "good for S" is never perspectival, for "good for S" does not have one meaning when S is a plant, and another when S is an animal or a human being. It makes sense to say about certain conditions that they are good for plants but bad for humans, and when we say this we are talking about one and the same relationship: what we mean is that a single thing bears that good-for relationship to plants but does not bear that same good-for relationship to humans. When we finish talking about the good of plants and turn next to a discussion of the good of human beings, what changes is that which is good for each; different things are good for these two groups, because the nature of the members of these groups differs. But the meaning of the expression "good for" does not alter. The relata are different; the relationship is the same.

25. The Conative Approach to Well-Being

We have arrived at this conclusion: the "for" of "G is good for S" does not say who has reason to do or want something, does not locate where goodness is, and does not refer to the orientation of S; rather, it refers to the conformability or suitability of G to S. It indicates that G is well suited to S and that G serves S well. That does not mean that these expressions—"well suited," "serves . . . well"—give us better ways of communicating with each other, in the ordinary circumstances of human life, than "good for." If, in the course of normal conversation, someone asks us what we mean by something's being "good for" someone, the best initial reply is to appeal to such equivalent expressions as "to the advantage of," "beneficial for," and "in the interest of." There is no better way than this to make one's meaning evident. And if these substitutions do not succeed in conveying our meaning, "well suited" and "serves well" are not going to help either. Nonetheless, it is important, when we are looking for a philosophical account of what advantageousness is and which things are advantageous, not to start off on the wrong foot by being misled by the "for" of "good for." It is at this point that it is useful to recognize that the "for" of "G is good for S" caters to some conformability and suitability between G and S, and that it plays *this* sort of role, rather than one of the other roles for which "for" can be used.

This way of construing "good for" does not, all by itself, tell us which things are good for this person or that. Nor does it tell us, all by itself, whether all the things that are good for someone share a common nature. A reading of "good for" cannot perform either of these tasks. Nonetheless, a defensible reading of "good for" is worth having. It helps us see why Ross is wrong to think that goods are in subjects but not good for subjects. And it also can play a role in our assessment of a widely accepted approach to well-being—the "conative" approach that we considered in the preceding section. For although we have rejected a perspectival interpretation of "good for," it is possible that conation holds the key to understanding not what "good for" means, but what is good for anyone and what all such goods have in common. The basic idea behind the conative approach is extremely simple, though it will need development: to find out what is good for someone, look at what he wants, or plans to get, or pursues.[31] If he is well on his way toward getting it, or his plan is successfully executed, or his desire fulfilled, then it is good for him that this is so. It is good for S that P if and only if S wants that P and P occurs, or S plans to bring it about that P and is on

31. These—wanting, planning, pursuing—are of course different kinds of psychological states. A conative theory, as I conceive it, is any approach that defines human well-being in terms of one or more of these states. (More about this in section 28.) I shall assume throughout that wanting to do something is not merely a matter of having some "pro attitude" toward it (that would include believing oneself morally required to do it); more specifically, it involves some yearning, or appetite, or urge, or longing thoughts, or a disposition to choose to do it gladly. See Kraut, "Desire and the Human Good," and *Aristotle: Political Philosophy,* pp. 20–49, for my earlier thoughts on this approach. I accept Watson's thesis ("Free Agency," pp. 19–27) that it is not part of the nature of desire that an individual who has a desire thereby places some positive value on pursuing or achieving its object; as Watson notes, this helps explain the possibility of weakness of will.

his way toward doing so. What do all the things that are good for us have in common? They are all the objects of successful conation. What makes one thing better for us than another? In our plans, preferences, and desires, we place one ahead of the other.[32]

It might be thought that something like this idea has to be correct, because the very phrase "good for" must be understood perspectivally; the "for" of "G is good for S" seems to suggest that it is the outlook or orientation of S that determines what G is. But we have just seen that the conative theory of well-being cannot be defended in that way. If it is defensible, it must be construed as a theory about what it is for S and G to match each other in such a way that G serves S well. It holds that what makes them a good match for each other is the fact that S wants or seeks or plans to get G; G answers to something in S, namely S's desires and plans. For example, is it good for S that he has won a gold medal? Yes, because his goal was to win a gold medal, and he succeeded. Winning the medal is a match for his desires.

But this idea is too simple, and so the theory must be supplemented if it is to remain viable. Suppose S plans on cooking and eating a certain mushroom—one that he takes, with justified confidence, to be healthy

---

32. The conative approach, or something closely resembling it, is adopted by Sidgwick (*The Methods of Ethics*, pp. 109–112), Rawls (*A Theory of Justice*, pp. 358–372), Griffin, (*Well-Being*, pp. 7–39), and many others. It is what Sumner (*Welfare, Happiness, and Ethics*) calls "the desire theory" (pp. 113–137), and he notes: "Versions of the desire theory now define the orthodox view of the nature of welfare, at least in the Anglo-American philosophical world. In the theory of rational choice the equation of well-being with utility (preference satisfaction) has achieved the status of an unquestioned axiom" (p. 122). Some elements of it are accepted by Sumner (ibid., pp. 138–183). Although Scanlon holds that one component of well-being is success in the achievement of one's rational aims (*What We Owe to Each Other*, pp. 118–119), his term "rational" is intended to allow for "substantive criticism of aims" (p. 119); he later adds that one's aims must be "worth pursuing" (pp. 121, 124) or "worthwhile" (p. 124). (So too Joseph Raz, *The Morality of Freedom*, pp. 298–299.) That conception of rational aims protects his theory against many of the objections I make to the conative approach (but see section 28). Nonetheless, it is unclear why S's achievement of a goal that is worthwhile should be counted as good *for S*. Perhaps calling a goal "worthwhile" is simply a way of saying that it is good for someone that he attain it, but if so, we are moving in a small circle: what is good for someone is (among other things) the achievement of a worthwhile goal, and in turn the worthwhileness of a goal consists in its being good for someone to achieve. On the other hand, if what makes a goal worthwhile to achieve is independent of its being good for someone to attain it, what entitles us to infer that because it is worth pursuing it is not only good that it be achieved, but also good for the one who attains it that it be attained? The account of flourishing proposed in Chapter 3 is an attempt to say which aims are "worth pursuing" or "worthwhile" insofar as it is good for someone that he pursue them.

and delicious. But even though he is the world's leading authority on mushrooms, he is mistaken about this one: with one bite, he dies. As it turns out, it was not good for him to eat the mushroom; it would have been far better for him had he not. But he got what he wanted; his plan was executed.

Something must be added to the conative account—but what? The man in our example was extremely well informed about the mushroom that killed him. But he did not know that eating it would frustrate one of his deepest desires—his desire to continue living. He wanted to live more than he wanted to eat that mushroom, and had he known that the mushroom would frustrate his will to live, he would have chosen not to eat it. What is good for us, then, is the satisfaction of the desires we have and would continue to have even if we knew what effect their satisfaction would have on our chances of satisfying our other desires. More briefly, what is good is the satisfaction of our properly informed desires. (I use "properly" because we do not need to know everything about the objects of our desires; we need to know only the ways in which those objects will affect our other desires.)[33]

There is another kind of complication: we can have and satisfy desires that we wish we did not have; we can pursue courses of action that we believe we should abandon, even as we carry them out. Someone can wish he did not crave drink but plan to spend the day drinking. These are forms of practical irrationality, cases in which one sets oneself against oneself in one's actions. The self is opposed to some action, but something in the self refuses to be governed by it and sets out, sometimes with careful and calm thoughtfulness, to act nonetheless. When a plan or desire is irrational in this way, its satisfaction or execution is not good for the agent. So the conative approach to well-being must say that what is good for someone is the satisfaction of his properly informed and rational desires.[34]

Another problem arises: suppose someone achieves what he has been aiming at but gets no satisfaction at all from doing so. In one sense of

33. This is a variation on a theme explored by Griffin in *Well-Being*, pp. 11–17.

34. Here "rational" is used in the narrow way adopted by Scanlon (*What We Owe to Each Other*, pp. 25–30); this differs markedly from the broader way in which he uses the term when he presents his theory of well-being (ibid., pp. 113–126). Rawls "suppose[s] with utilitarianism that the good is defined as the satisfaction of *rational* desire" (*A Theory of Justice*, p. 27, my emphasis; compare with p. 80). One may well ask why it might not sometimes (or often) be better for one to act irrationally than rationally, but I will not pursue that question.

"satisfied," his desire has been satisfied: he wanted to do V, and now he is doing V or has done it. But he discovers that he does not enjoy V in the slightest. His desire has been satisfied, but *he* is not satisfied.

Should we modify the conative theory once again? Should we say that what is good for someone is the *enjoyment* of the satisfaction of his properly informed and rational desires? It could be argued that this further modification is unnecessary and ill advised. For there are times when we pursue our plans and succeed in executing them, but we have no expectation that we will get any satisfaction from doing so. S insists upon going to the dinner party tonight, an event that he knows will offer no satisfaction; but he just wants to be there. Should we say that it is good for him to go, simply because this is what he wants?[35]

The conative theory can be developed in either of two ways at this point, but neither of them is appealing. Suppose it rejects the proposed modification. In that case, it is no longer clear that it is good for someone to satisfy his desires—even his properly informed and rational desires. Would it not be better for him to suppress and, if possible, eliminate those among his desires whose fulfillment will not bring him the slightest satisfaction? Should he not instead cultivate an interest in doing things that he will enjoy? The life of a person who gets what he wants but feels not even the slightest satisfaction in getting what he wants is hollow, futile, meaningless. That is because each desire whose fulfillment brings not even the slightest sense of satisfaction is empty.

Suppose, on the other hand, that the conative theory accepts the proposed modification: it holds that only desires whose satisfaction is satisfying are good to satisfy. So modified, the conative theory makes a distinction between, on the one hand, desires and plans that are good for someone to have and, on the other, desires and plans that are bad to have; and it makes this distinction by affirming the goodness of pleasure. It says: pleasure is good for you, whether you realize it or not, and so if you have a choice between satisfying a desire that will bring no pleasure and another desire that will, you should choose the latter. But on what grounds does the conative theory affirm that pleasure is good for someone to feel? It cannot reply that pleasure is good for S if and only if S seeks it or wants it. For that reply would force it to admit that

---

35. In his discussion of what he calls the "informed-desire account" of well-being, Griffin writes, "A desire is 'fulfilled' in the sense in which a clause in a contract is fulfilled: namely, what was agreed (desired) comes about" (*Well-Being*, p. 14).

there is no reason someone should give greater weight to his pleasure-giving desires than to those that bring no pleasure. So the conative theory must instead reply that the pleasure of a fulfilled desire is one of the things that we *should* want because it is good for us to experience. But in saying that, the conative theory abandons its root idea, which is that nothing is good except that wanting or planning makes it so. It must therefore hold that if pleasure is good for us to feel, that is because we want to feel it; if one believes that the order of explanation goes the other way—that we should want pleasure because it is good—one is no longer working with a *wholly* conative approach to well-being. (We will examine in section 31 the thesis that one type of good, though not the only one, is successful conation. Even that less ambitious idea cannot be sustained.)

We started our examination of the conative theory with the simple idea that what is good for someone is his getting what he wants. That has now been modified to read: what is good for someone is the satisfaction of his properly informed and rational desires. That version, if left unmodified, leaves us wondering: what is so good about satisfying such desires, if doing so brings no felt satisfaction? But if we add that getting what one wants must bring some pleasure if it is to be good, we have moved away from the conative theory. What to do?

The proper response is to look for an alternative theory, and then to ask whether it does a better job than the conative approach. But before we do that (in Chapter 3), we should recognize, more fully, how odd and inadequate that approach is.

26. Abstracting from the Content of Desires and Plans

A remarkable feature of the conative approach to well-being is that it proposes to assess the value of our psychological attitudes without paying attention to their content. Its basic idea is that it is good for us satisfy our desires or to carry out our plans, and that it does not matter at all what it is that we want or what we plan to do. Provided that we show no internal inconsistency and are properly informed about the consequences of the satisfaction of our desires and the fulfillment of our plans, getting what we want or pursue will be good for us, whatever it is that we want or pursue.

We would not say any such thing about our beliefs. Beliefs, we think, are fit subjects for assessment and criticism. When we assess someone's belief that P, we ask whether P is true or whether it is good for him to believe that P—and we do not assume that his believing P by itself assures us that P is true or that it is good for him to believe P. Why should we not take a similar attitude toward the assessment of desires and plans?[36] Someone wants to V. We ask, is it good for him to have that desire and to satisfy it? How strange it is to think that we can answer that question without being told what V is! "Good" is a term that we use to evaluate everything under the sun—hotels, food, friends, no less than desires and plans—but to do so we must be told what it is we are evaluating. If someone says to us, "S has a desire, but you cannot know what it is a desire for; now tell me whether it is good for him to satisfy it," why should we not make the obvious response? Why suppose that it is not *what* we want that matters, but merely our wanting it?

The conative theory admits that desires and plans are fit objects for the kind of criticism that looks to the good of the person who has them. It is bad for S that S satisfies a desire or achieves an aim that is irrational or misinformed. But it is arbitrary to assume that these are the only grounds on which we can assess whether it is good for someone to have and satisfy a desire or carry out a plan. Human beings have many more psychological features than desires and plans; they also have capacities, powers, skills, and talents. A desire or plan might be bad not only because it interferes with some other desire or plan, but because it makes it difficult or impossible for someone to exercise a capacity, skill, or talent it is good for him to have. A desire or plan might be bad because it un-

---

36. Michael Smith, in *The Moral Problem*, pp. 111–112, cites the following passage from Mark Platts's *Ways of Meaning*, pp. 256–257 (here Platts takes himself to be describing the difference between desires and beliefs, according to G. E. M. Anscombe in *Intention*): "The distinction is in terms of the direction of fit of mental states with the world. Beliefs aim at the true, and their being true is their fitting the world. . . . Beliefs should be changed to fit with the world, not *vice versa*. Desires aim at realisation, and their realisation is the world fitting with them; the fact that the indicative content of a desire is not realised in the world is not yet a failing in the desire, and not yet any reason to discard the desire; the world, crudely, should be changed to fit with our desires, not *vice versa*." The idea here is that because a desire is not subject to criticism merely for not yet having been realized, there can be no basis at all for criticizing it. But it is more plausible to suppose that desires should be suppressed when something is amiss in their objects; there is *something* that they must be made to fit, though it is unhelpful to call that something "the world." Anscombe would not disagree. She says, "Goodness is ascribed to wanting in virtue of the goodness (not the actualisation) of what is wanted" (*Intention*, p. 76).

dermines one's mental health and diminishes the likelihood that one will flourish. By focusing solely on conation as that which determines where our well-being lies, the conative theory proposes too limited a conception of the aspects of the human mind that have a bearing on what is good or bad for us. There is nothing special about plans and desires that makes them stand out as the sole or preeminent features of the world that determine what it is for G to be good for S.[37] Plants lack them entirely; animals do little or no planning. Desires, intentions and goals are among the motor forces that propel us into our environment, but there is more to us than conation, and therefore more to consider when we think about our well-being.

27. The Faulty Mechanisms of Desire Formation

If we consider some of the common ways in which desires come into existence or plans are laid down, that should make us ever more doubtful that fulfilling them is good for those who have them, provided only that they are rational and properly informed.

When children reach a certain age, they are capable of making and executing complex plans, but they are also quite vulnerable to manipulation and exploitation. Under the right circumstances, a powerful and attractive adult can instill desires in them and set them to work on plans that, by any standard of common sense, are utterly destructive to those children. For example, an adult might be able to induce pyromania in a child. Most children love fires, and it would not take much to turn them into accomplished, dedicated arsonists. They can want to spend all their time lighting fires and take considerable pleasure in their success. But someone who turns a child into an arsonist has done him no favor. Of what possible value can a settled desire to light fires be to a child? He

---

37. Plans can nonetheless have *some* bearing on the constitution of what is good for a human being. Suppose many different careers or hobbies are good for someone to pursue, because he will flourish in whichever of them he adopts. When he has chosen one of them and is faring well in his pursuit of it, these facts give him reason to continue with this activity rather than turn back to an alternative that was once on his menu and would have been no worse a choice for him. Furthermore, when what we choose to do is a reflection of what we would most enjoy doing, that too has a bearing on our well-being because of the close connection between enjoyment and what is good for us (sections 30, 33). I am grateful to Jon Garthoff for discussion of these points.

needs to develop in all sorts of ways that will be of use to him later in life, and pyromania will impede his psychological growth.

A healthy but easily manipulated child can even be talked into committing suicide. He can be made to want to die. But that would be an act of great cruelty: that he wants to die does not make us doubt in the least that it would be terrible for him to satisfy his desire. There are many things that a child can be made to want that it would be bad, from the point of view of his well-being, for him to want. And the same point applies to adults, although they are usually less easily manipulated than children. But it can be done; they too can be led to love lighting fires or to cut short their lives prematurely out of a longing for death.

If these examples have force against the conative theory, that is because it is a matter of common sense that certain things are good for people and other things are bad for them, whether they want them or not; and others are neither good nor bad, even if they have a desire for them. Lighting a fire and watching something burn is not something that is, in itself, good or bad. But it fascinates us, and so it is not mysterious that someone could spend a great deal of his time doing this. For a healthy child or adult to die when his future is bright is, we all assume, bad for him. If he develops a desire to do so, that is a bad desire for him to have because of its content. But we know that, in certain conditions, suicide can be made to seem appealing.

There are many other mechanisms by which bad desires and plans can take shape in us. We are mimetic creatures: what we see others doing we imitate. A child can set his heart on wearing a certain kind of ring and devote himself to saving enough money to buy it because all the other children he knows already wear one. Is it good for him to have that desire and execute that plan? Is it good for the other children, who already have their rings, to own and wear them? If none of these children wanted a ring, we would not be tempted to suppose that we should induce such a desire in them. For a child to wear a ring is not, by itself, something that is good, or bad, for him. It is a matter of indifference, and it does not become a good thing for a child simply by virtue of his desire. Here, too, the mechanism of desire formation that plays such a powerful role among children is often at work among adults.

Another example: when we take ourselves to have been injured or insulted by another person, we want to strike back. Our aim, then, is to inflict harm on a certain person, or on those close to him, merely for the sake of making him worse off. In fact, we can devote our lives to taking revenge. Is it good for the person who satisfies such a desire that his enemy has been made worse-off? One person's being worse-off is not identical to another person's being better-off. The desire for revenge propels us into a course of action that is single-mindedly devoted to causing harm, and has nothing to do with our own good. That project may in fact carry a terrible price, absorbing all our resources and resulting in the loss of much that we love. We don't care; it is enough for us that someone else is worse-off (section 51).

Destructive urges and plans can be directed inward. Much of what one does to an enemy can be done to oneself. Psychopathology is a reality: we can seek to humiliate and humble ourselves, to make ourselves suffer, to deprive ourselves of enjoyments, to torture our bodies, to diminish our capacities. Someone who puts these plans into effect need not believe that, in doing so, he is promoting his well-being; it is far more likely that his goal is to inflict upon himself the punishment he thinks he deserves. But obviously the successful execution of such plans as these—rational and properly informed though they are—is not good.[38] We can do what is bad for ourselves, wanting what is bad for ourselves and convinced that it is bad for ourselves—just as we can do these things to others. We should not accept the conative theory out of a naïve assumption that people are always guided by self-love, or that their attitude toward their own well-being is that it should always be increased rather than decreased.

---

38. It is reasonable to ask: how can it be rational to harm oneself deliberately—for example, by torturing one's own body? The answer is that the word "rational" is often used, by philosophers at any rate, to assess an action or other mental state solely in terms of its coherence with the other elements of an agent's psychology, and therefore without reference to a standard external to that agent (for example, his well-being). This is the narrow use of "rational" that typically plays a role in conative approaches to well-being (section 25). Such approaches cannot make what is rational for S depend on what is good for S: taking rational conation to be constitutive of goodness, they cannot (on pain of circularity) also take rationality to be even partly constituted by what is good for a person. If a person bent on harming himself is entirely of one mind about doing so, then his policy and action will be counted as rational in this narrow sense. That is certainly not the only possible way to use the word. For an alternative that defines rationality in terms of harm, see Bernard Gert, *Morality: Its Nature and Justification*, pp. 29–55.

28. Infants and Adults

Our description of the conative approach to well-being has given it wide latitude: it is a theory that, in some way, constructs what is good for an individual out of the material provided by successful conation. What is good for someone is the satisfaction of his desires, or the fulfillment of his plans, or the attainment of his goals.

Some philosophers find it difficult to believe that the satisfaction of someone's desires—rational and properly informed desires—is always good for him. For those desires can be directed at what seems to be the good of someone else, not the person whose desires they are. A sports fan watching his favorite team wants it to win. If it does, is that good for *him?* Is *he* better off? A newspaper reader follows a story about an attempt to rescue mine workers: when the rescue effort fails, and his desire that they be saved is frustrated, is that bad for *him?*[39] The conative theorist might feel some discomfort because of these questions. One way to protect the theory against such objections is to insist that goals and plans, not desires, are the materials from which our good is constructed. What is good for someone, according to this version of the theory, is only the successful execution of his plans, not the satisfaction of his desires.

The conative theory does not have the ambition of explaining what is good for all living things (plants are not conative beings); by formulating the theory in terms of plans rather than desires, it further narrows its scope, for fewer animals have plans than have desires. But at the very least we can expect the conative approach to well-being to offer a theory about what is good for all human beings. It will not do to have one conception of what it is for something to be good for an adult human being and a different conception of what it is for something to be good for a human infant. Of course, some things that are good for adults are not good for babies. But the conative theory is an attempt to say what all the things that are good for someone—at any rate, someone who is a human being—have in common. They are all the objects of successful conation. What makes it true that it is good for S that P is this: S plans that P, and P occurs. That is a general theory that is meant to apply to all human beings—children no less than adults.

---

39. The problem is raised, using a different example, by Derek Parfit in *Reasons and Persons,* p. 494. Scanlon's conception of well-being is expressed in terms of rational aims rather than rational desires in order to avoid the problem (*What We Owe to Each Other,* pp. 115, 120).

But the conative theory, so formulated, faces another insuperable obstacle: infants do not make plans. They think. They are intelligent. But they do not yet have the mental equipment that is needed to engage in the complex thought processes that count as planning, deliberating, and making decisions.[40]

They do, however, have wants and preferences. And so, if the conative theory seeks to explain what it is for G to be good for S when S is an infant, it should do so in terms of an infant's desires. Its general theory of what is good for human beings should be broadly formulated: what is good for us is the execution of our plans *or* the satisfaction of our desires. That disjunctive formulation gives it the flexibility it needs to account for the well-being of children and adults.

In fact, however, there is no plausibility in the idea that a baby's good can be constructed out of what she wants. Babies must, for their own good, be nurtured in a way that gives them certain competencies and brings them into certain human relationships; but the states of affairs that are good for them are not already present to them as the content of their desires. They do not know what is good for them and cannot know. So the conative approach to well-being has no resources for accounting for the good of infants. They do not make plans or decisions; and although they do have desires and preferences, these are not robust and complex enough to provide an adequate account of what is good for them. The conative theory has, at best, a limited domain: it must leave aside all plants, many animals, and all human beings at the earliest stages of life. (And, as we have seen, it does not give a satisfactory account even in the one case to which it is applied: adult human beings.) We of course expect it to be the case that different things are good for plants, animals, children, and adults. There are all manner of differences among human beings—political and social, no less than psychological and biological—and some things that are good for some might not be

40. Scanlon (*What We Owe to Each Other,* p. 124) holds that "well-being depends to a large extent on a person's degree of success in achieving his or her main ends in life, provided that these are worth pursuing." Since infants lack such ends, Scanlon must assess their well-being in terms of the other component of well-being that his theory recognizes: "experiential states (such as various forms of satisfaction and enjoyment" (ibid., p. 124). But that seems too narrow; we make judgments about what is good for children and how well they are doing by appealing to other factors beyond their experiential states. The same limitation is present in the accounts of well-being proposed by Rawls (*A Theory of Justice,* pp. 358–372) and Raz (*The Morality of Freedom,* pp. 288–320).

good for others. But we want to know not only what is good, but what it is to say about something that it is good for someone. An answer to that question that limits itself to saying what it is for something to be good for an adult human being is arbitrary. There is no reason to pick out that peculiar group—or any other peculiar group—of individuals and to propose an account of what makes something good that applies only to that group.

Can there be any doubt that the conative theory fails when it is taken as a general account of what it is for G to be good for any S, even when S is an infant? Healthy babies of course do have appetites, desires, tendencies, drives, and the like. Notice that we say that this is what *healthy* babies have: that is already to acknowledge that what is good for babies does not rest on their conation. Conation is itself rightly considered to be good for a certain type of creature, and its absence a great misfortune. And it would be implausible to suppose that conation is good for a creature because it is desired by that creature. No baby wants to be a conative being—they are incapable of possessing that concept. If a baby lacks all conation (she will not live for long), that is a great misfortune—bad for that baby—even though, by hypothesis, this condition does not frustrate any of her desires.

Consider, then, a healthy baby filled with all the desires of a normal child her age. The conative theory holds that what is good for the baby is the satisfaction of those desires, and that *only* those things are good for it. Later, the baby will be a small child. She will have other desires; the satisfaction of those new desires will be good for her, and *only* those things will be good for her. And so on, as she grows toward adolescence and adulthood.

According to the conative theory, something is (or will be) *bad* for a baby only if it prevents her from getting what she wants (or will want). But that is highly implausible. It will be good for her to start learning a language as soon as she is able to do so. But although a baby babbles, that is not because she has a desire to learn a language. Nor is it inevitable that at some later time she will want to learn a language. If we are not responsive to her vocalizations, she will lose all interest in verbal interaction with others, and nothing she does will count as evidence that speaking a language is what she wants. If a child comes to have a desire to improve her skills as a language user, that is because we instill that desire in her, for her good. A desire to speak well is a good desire for a child to have, but not because it is a desire that the child wants to have.

A child who fails to develop normal linguistic skills has limited access to the wide range of social, cognitive, and affective interactions with other human beings that have become prevalent among human beings. Before the linguistic age—the age when we became language users—it was no defect for a human being to fail to have a language. Now it is. But it would be a mistake to think of a language as a tool we use to get only those things we would want even in the absence of language. Our linguistic interactions transform our social world, making certain types of activity good for us, not as mere means to other ends but in themselves. Someone (and not only a poet or writer) can enjoy using language skillfully and for its own sake and sharing that activity with others; that, we will see (sections 42, 47), is one component of flourishing. Someone who lives in a language-using community, but because of an innate deficiency cannot learn a language and so cannot enjoy its use, is worse off than he otherwise would be. Adults who can correct such a deficiency would do so without hesitation for the good of that child. But that is not because this is something the child wants, or solely because the learning of a language is a means to what the child already wants or will inevitably come to want. The learning of a language will transform what a child will want, and the plans she will make, in ways that are good for the child.

The point can be generalized and does not apply to language learning alone. When parents nurture a young child, they shape her desires, goals, and plans, and they do so for her good. They do not assume that, however they treat their child, she will come to have certain goals they would like her to have, for her good (to have friends, to work at satisfying projects, to learn, to enjoy music, to have sexual pleasure, etc.). On the contrary, if they treat their child badly enough, she may want none of these things. Parents take for granted a developmental story about how it is best for the lives of their children to go as they grow up (section 35). They do not take the present desires of their child to be fixed, as psychological mechanisms that will remain unaltered and permanent; nor do they take her future desires to be fixed, as inevitable onslaughts that will arrive, regardless of their interactions with her. Rather, they assume that their child must be transformed for her own good—a matter that is not determined by her present desires. She does not have a desire to grow mentally and emotionally; still less does she plan to do so or aim to do so. She has a capacity, perhaps even a tendency, to do so. And we recognize that these capacities and tendencies are good for a child to have because of what they are capacities and tendencies to do. It is not because a child has a capacity or tendency to become a language user that doing so is good for her; rather, it is because it is good for human beings to be language users (when all other members of their social world do so) that it is good for children to have that capacity.

Because the conative theory abstracts away from the content of plans, goals, and desires, it gives each individual a peculiar kind of authority over the question of what is good for him. It is not *what* you desire that matters, but the fact that *you* desire it (provided that you are rational and properly informed). You might not know your own mind very well; you might think you want something, even though your actions (your failure ever to take steps easily available to you) and your mental life (the absence of any signs that you have this hankering) show that you do not. You can be mistaken in your ascriptions of desires to yourself, but if you are not, then you know what is noninstrumentally good for yourself because it is precisely those desires that make it the case that it is good for you to get those things. In that sense, you have authority over what is good and what is bad for you.[41]

That is why one of the weaknesses of the conative theory is brought out by its failure to give a plausible account of what makes things good for children. It is certainly not what *they* want that matters, because they are not yet in a position to know this. Adults must guide them to an understanding of their good, and in doing so they must rely on their own ideas (certainly not their children's) about what is good for them. If all goes well, children, as they develop, come to recognize where their good lies and need to rely less on others for guidance. But it makes no sense to suppose that, at some point in the development of an individual, it becomes the case that the very fact that he wants something or plans to get something makes it the case that the object of his conation is good for him. It takes some doing to arrive at true beliefs about what is good for oneself, or for anyone. There is no mantle of authority that descends upon one, at a certain age, giving one the magical power of making something good for oneself simply by wanting it.

41. Thus Sumner, *Welfare, Happiness, and Ethics*, p. 171: "On a subjective theory, individuals are the ultimate authorities concerning their own welfare." A conative approach is subjective in the sense Sumner assigns to that term: it "make[s] your well-being depend on your own concerns: the things you care about, attach importance to, regard as mattering, and so on" (ibid., p. 42).

A theory about what is good for human beings should be tested in part by seeing whether it plausibly explains what makes something good for an individual when he is a young child. Barring misfortune, that is when we human beings are more plantlike and animal-like than we will ever be. During that brief period we have no plans and make no decisions; our capacities have not developed, and we are likely to be mentally simpler than we are ever to be again. Of course, at a certain level of specificity, the things that are good for the youngest human beings are vastly different from those that are good for other species. (Would it do any good for an animal to learn a language, even if it has this capacity?) But at a high level of generality, there is something that the good of a human child and that of young members of other kinds of species have in common: it is good for them to grow, to develop, to be healthy, and to flourish.

29. The Conation of an Ideal Self

Will the conative approach to well-being become more appealing if it drops the idea that it is the satisfaction of all and only our *actual* desires (save those that are not rational or properly informed) that is good for us ? What would the theory look like if it proposed that well-being consists in the satisfaction of desires we *would* have under certain conditions?[42] One reason for altering the theory in this way stems from the familiar psychological observation that reflection on the causal mechanisms that account for the origin and strength of our desires can lead to

42. Sidgwick's theory (*The Methods of Ethics*, pp. 111–112) has this feature, and Rawls (*A Theory of Justice*, pp. 365–372) follows his lead. The idea is more fully developed by Richard Brandt (*A Theory of the Good and the Right*, pp. 70–129). My discussion in this section addresses a problem about desire formation discussed by Brandt (ibid., pp. 100–102), though not by Sidgwick or Rawls. Note too Peter Railton's definition: "An individual's good consists in what he would want himself to want, or to pursue, were he to contemplate his present situation from a standpoint fully and vividly informed about himself and his circumstances, and entirely free of cognitive error or lapses of instrumental rationality" ("Facts and Values," p. 54). For reasons presented in this section, I believe that this definition is too broad to capture the notion of what is beneficial for or advantageous to someone; for some of what we want, or would want under cognitively enhanced conditions, is desired for the sake of others. A similar point is noted by Scanlon (*What We Owe to Each Other*, pp. 133 and 387–388, n. 27). See too section 48. Note also that if one seeks—as philosophers should—a theory of goodness substantial enough to serve as a practical guide, a characterization like Railton's will not help (nor is it intended to do so).

their alteration. When we learn about the circumstances in which our desires first came into existence, we sometimes lose our confidence that they are worth satisfying; we may abandon goals long taken for granted after we consider the forces that drove us to adopt them and still drive us to pursue them. Someone can come to realize, for example, that his desire to go to medical school is merely his response to parental pressure, or his way of showing his superiority to them, or a form of sibling rivalry, or a mere imitation of a friend. If someone becomes convinced that these are the psychological forces that are driving him, he may decide that he has no good reason to become a doctor. After some soul-searching, he may abandon his project. Of course, that is not the only possibility: he might decide that pleasing his parents, or showing them up, or besting his brother, or being like his friend is precisely what he wants to use his medical training for.

The conative theory does not and cannot take a stand about which of these would be the right course of action. Its basic idea is that what is good for someone is a matter to be determined by an act of will—by someone's decision, or plan, or desire—and not by the content and character of what is willed. It is up to you—or rather, an improved version of you—to decide what is good for you. When the conative theory is formulated in terms of a hypothetical rather than a real will, it is not the desires and plans you happen to have whose fulfillment is good for you; rather, it is the desires and plans that you would be left with after you scrutinized them all and decided whether, in light of the factors that lie behind their formation and current force, you wish to continue to have them and act upon them. The conative theory so formulated holds that it is not the conation of S that determines where the good of S lies, but, rather, the conation of someone very much like S—a more reflective S. Whether S reflects upon his desires or not, those among his desires are good for him to fulfill that a more reflective version of S would affirm.

The conative theory so formulated is no more acceptable than the version we have been considering, which holds that the fulfillment of actual, not hypothetical plans or desires is good. But before we come to that point, we should recognize that the example of the medical student contains an elementary but important insight—one that the conative theory, on either formulation, fails to properly appreciate and exploit.

The insight is this: suppose we ask which premises will provide a good argument for the conclusion that it is good for a particular individual, S, that he become a doctor.[43] We must keep in mind that our question is whether it will be *noninstrumentally* good for him to live his life in that way. There will indeed be some premises that support that conclusion, but this is not one of them: "He will give pleasure to his father by living the life of a doctor." That S's activity gives pleasure to someone other than S is no reason at all for inferring that this activity is good for S. Someone who goes to medical school and becomes a doctor as a way of pleasing his father may be doing a great deal of good—by giving pleasure to his father, if for no other reason. But pointing to the good he does for others is not a way of establishing that he is doing something that is good for himself. Therefore, if the only justification someone can give for his living the life of a doctor is the good that he does for his father or others by living such a life, then he does not have any reason for thinking that such a life is good for *him*. There may be such a reason; it may in fact be good for him to live such a life. But he is not aware of this if the only reasons he can find for living such a life have to do with the effect he has on others.

Neither of the two versions of the conative theory recognizes this point. According to one version, we can infer from the fact that the medical student has a rational and properly informed desire to be a doctor that it is noninstrumentally good for him that he do so. According to the other, we cannot yet make this inference; we can accept that conclusion only if the medical student's desire would survive a process of reflection; if, but only if, it would survive, then it would be good for him that he lead the life of a doctor.

But if we say of someone that it is good *for him* that he is living the life of a doctor, there must be some suitability between him and that life, some match between them that makes it the case that such a life serves *him* well. That, as we have seen (section 21), is what is conveyed by the meaning of "good for." And there are many ways of supporting the idea that there is some such suitability: he may thoroughly enjoy his job because he is a talented doctor who is intellectually stimulated by the problems he addresses and emotionally satisfied by his work with patients. He may, in other words, be flourishing as a doctor. That is

---

43. Careful thinking about these issues must always keep in mind the point made in section 20: In sentences like "It is good for you to live the life of a doctor," it is unclear whether "for you" picks out the person whose good is served or is meant only to be part of the state of affairs that is alleged to be good for someone.

the sort of answer we expect when we ask whether his doctoring is noninstrumentally good for him and not only for others. It is no answer to our question to be told that by living the life of a doctor, he is successfully carrying out his plans.

People do sometimes reconsider their undertakings when they come to recognize that their pursuits are mere reactions to the expectations or preferences of others. They think that there is too little reason to continue if they can find nothing about their activity that makes it good for *them* and not merely for others. A conative theory that is formulated in terms of actual desires and plans overlooks this common phenomenon. Its central idea—that if you want or plan to do something, that makes it good for you—is insensitive to a distinction we ordinarily make when we ask: should I want to do this simply because doing so is good for others, or is there also some reason to think that doing so is good for me? A conative theory formulated in terms of hypothetical willing has at least this merit: it recognizes that one cannot infer that it is good for someone that he engage in an activity simply on the grounds that he has a rational, properly informed desire to do so. But then it fails to do justice to this point. It supposes that if someone would reaffirm his desire to become a doctor after reflecting upon it, that shows that he, and not just his father or his patients, is one of the people whose good is served by his being a doctor.

One further point should be made about the version of the conative theory that constructs one's good out of hypothetical desires: although it recognizes that more desires need to be excluded from the set whose satisfaction is good for us than merely those that are irrational or not properly informed, it must, in addition, recognize the possibility that someone can benefit by cultivating and fulfilling desires and plans that he does not yet have.[44] Our experience and imagination can be more limited than they should be for our own good; these deficiencies may prevent us from cultivating interests, forming desires, and making plans that it would be good for us to have. It might be best for someone that he study medicine because he would flourish as a doctor; he might have the temperament and talents that would make a medical career the best career for him. And yet this possibility may never have entered his mind.

---

44. See section 46 for discussion of Rawls's attempt to accommodate this point in a formal manner—that is, without attending to the content of the new plans that should be cultivated.

We say: this is something he should want and should pursue *because* it would be good for him that he do so—and of course, good for others as well. Notice the order of explanation: the fact that it would be good for him is what stands behind the claim that he should cultivate a desire for this project. All conative theories, both those that construct well-being out of real desires and those that construct it out of hypothetical desires, mistakenly move in the opposite direction. They say: he has rational and properly informed desires for this, and so it is good for him that he should get it; or he would reaffirm these desires, upon reflection, and so he should fulfill them. That gets the order of explanation the wrong way around.

For example, consider again the point that it is good for children to enter the linguistic community. An infant has no desire or plan to do so. But could one say, in defense of the conative theory, that if the child were older and a language user, she would be glad that she had acquired this skill? Is that what makes it true that it is good for her to enter the linguistic world? Not at all. When we reflect on the good fortune we had to emerge from childhood as fully functioning adults, we do not take our gladness to be a necessary condition of our good fortune. Rather, we take our emotional response to be justified because the process of growth that took place was part of what it is for a human being to live well.

30. The Appeal of the Conative Theory

Having noted so many difficulties for the conative approach to well-being, we may wonder why anyone should be attracted to it. Can it have no appeal or merit at all? If not, why is it that people—both those new to philosophy and masters of the subject—are often inclined to suppose that when we are looking for an account of what is good for a human being, we should start with what a person wants, not as a means to something else, but for itself? Careful thought reveals that it is not the satisfaction of every such desire that is good, and so some desires are dropped from this set of good-making mental attitudes. But why choose someone's motivation as the place to start when we look for what is good for him?

It is doubtful that all those who are attracted to the conative theory have the same reasons for finding it plausible. But we should be able to

point to the mistakes that could easily lead *some* people to accept a conative approach to well-being, even though not everyone who adopts such
an approach has made or would commit each of these errors.

To begin with, it is often the case that a person's preferences deserve to
play an important and even decisive role in any judgment we make
about what is good for him. Suppose a young child wants to learn a sport
and strongly prefers baseball to basketball. Surely it is better for him to
play a sport he likes than one he does not. If someone is choosing between two careers, and doing so not on the basis of their instrumental
benefits—the money, status, or power they bring—then it is better for
him to work at the job that he has a greater desire to do. When someone
decides how to fill his leisure time, it is best for him to do something that
he really wants to do. All this is true. But these examples bring out the
important role that pleasure rightly plays in the decisions we make
about what is good for us (section 33). We reasonably use our preferences as a rough guide to what we will enjoy, and often they are an accurate guide. When they are not, we say that we made a mistake: the child
preferred baseball, but when he learned the game, he hated it, and in fact
his talents and temperament would have made basketball the sport that
he most enjoyed. Nonetheless, desires and preferences properly play a
leading role in the way we think about what is good for us, and that
gives a conative theory some initial appeal. Perhaps the fact that we talk
about the *satisfaction* of desires and the *fulfillment* of plans increases the
theory's appeal. It can easily be forgotten that the satisfaction of a desire—the occurrence of the state of affairs that is desired—might bring
no felt satisfaction.

A conative theory can also be found appealing because, as we have
seen (section 28), it gives a person a special role to play in the determination of what is good for him. It is not what your parents want or what
your community wants that figures in your well-being, but what *you*
want; and this is something that you have a way of creating and discov-
ering that no one else has. By making up your mind about what to
choose and what to do, you have, according to the conative theory, a
starring role to play in the construction of what is good for you: *your* desires are the desires that are good for you to satisfy. That flatters us and
caters to our individualism. One can think, "What I owe to others may
not be up to me alone, but in the realm of what is good for me, I am the
only one whose attitudes matter." The conative theory would not have
this kind of appeal in a society that inculcates deference to authorities. If

you are in the habit of letting other people make all the most important decisions about what is good for you, you may find it bizarre to suppose that for there to be such a thing as your good, you must have preferences and set goals for yourself.

It is true, of course, that what is good for you depends crucially upon something about you. We have rejected the locative way of reading the "for" of "good for" (section 21). But it is easy, though mistaken, to suppose that what it is about you that matters, in the construction of your good, is your conation. That is certainly not the case at the earliest stages of life. And as we will see (section 35), even in the case of adults, powers, skills, and talents—not merely desires and plans—play an important role in our thinking about where someone's good lies.

There is another social fact that may help explain why the conative theory seems attractive. In the ordinary business of life, we must learn how to cooperate, negotiate, bargain, compromise, compete, and fight. When we do so, we use the language of "good" and "bad," "advantage" and "disadvantage," "benefit" and "burden." We seek solutions that are good for all parties; or we offer to sacrifice our own good to some degree; or we complain that others are getting too large an allotment of what is good and failing to share in burdens; or we propose to harm certain people in order to benefit others. To be successful in these discussions, one does not need to reflect philosophically about what is good for people and what it is for something to be good. The press of business encourages us to take people's preferences and ends as fixed, unchallengeable, and the determinants of what is good or bad for them. We can try to persuade other parties that what they seek is really contrary to their interests, but in doing so we take their interests to be determined by their basic preferences and ends. That is a far more practical approach than appealing to some philosophical theory about what is good for people whether they realize it or not. This quotidian conception of good and bad is not something we should expect people to leave behind when they leave the marketplace and engage in a philosophical discussion of what is good. In philosophy a good working hypothesis is one that we employ all the time in our everyday activities. That is why it is important to give a careful hearing to the conative approach to well-being.

Even when we start to reflect on what is good, it is difficult to detect the errors that lead from undeniable premises to a conative conception of well-being. One can easily think: "(1) Since I want to do V, that is a reason in favor of my doing V. (2) Since there is a reason in favor my doing V, it is good for me to do V. (3) Therefore, whenever I want to do V, it is good for me to do V." Suppose we accept the first premise, for the sake of argument. For reasons we have discovered (section 18), the second premise is acceptable only if "good" is used, as it sometimes is, to place a consideration on the positive side of the ledger of practical reasoning. So construed, the second premise is trivial. But "good for," as we have seen, can also be used to pick out a special kind of reason for putting some-thing on the positive side of the ledger: the fact that an action is bene-ficial, and good for someone in that sense, provides a reason that action should be undertaken. In this sense of "good for," from the fact that there is a reason in favor of my doing V, we cannot infer that it is good *for me* that I do V. That should be obvious: the reason in favor of my action might consist in the advantages *you* will have because of what I do. (Having seen this much, we might also question the first premise: If I want to do V, but doing so is not good for me or anyone else, why sup-pose that my wanting to do V is a reason for me to do V?)

Other philosophical errors and questionable philosophical programs can also make the conative conception of well-being seem attractive. The "for" of "good for S" can be taken to mean that it is the perspective of S that provides the materials from which S's good is to be constructed (section 24). Or it might seem, as it does to many philosophers, that there can be no value in a world devoid of minds (section 3). Although acceptance of that idea by no means leads inevitably to a conative theory (it did not move Ross in this direction; section 21), such a theory is one way in which the philosophical program that makes all value dependent on mind can be carried forward. One can defend the thesis that there is no goodness without mind by proposing that whenever G is good for S, that is because S has some desire for G or takes G as a goal.

The conative theory is built partly on truths, partly on social habits, partly on philosophical error, and partly on the role it can play in an am-bitious philosophical program. But there is one other explanation for its widespread acceptance: the alternatives to the theory do not seem plau-sible. The conative theory will and should be set aside only if we find some other way of making sense of our ideas about well-being.

31. Conation Hybridized

We will soon move away from the conative approach to well-being in or-der to find a more plausible alternative. (Hedonism will be our next topic and then, in Chapter 3, the theory I will call "developmentalism.") But before we abandon the conative theory, let us see whether it can succeed if it lowers its sights and proposes a less ambitious thesis—a thesis about one kind of good, not about all that is good, or about the nature of goodness. We have been investigating the hypothesis that it is good for S that P if *but only if* S wants that P and P occurs, or S plans to bring it about that P and is on his way toward doing so. If that were true, then all the things that are good for us would have something in common: they would all be objects of successful conation. If we are troubled by the objections to this theory, we might nonetheless continue to believe that successful conation is *one* good among others. That is, we might hold that if S wants that P and P occurs, then it is good for S that P. Other things, we might say, are also good; we might adapt Ross's ideas about goodness, for example, and propose that pleasure, knowledge, virtue, the satisfaction of desire—and only these things—are good for us.[45] That would be a mere list of goods; we would no longer have any answer to the question "What do all of the things that are good for us have in common?" But perhaps there simply is no commonality here. (We would also have a list of things that are bad for us: pain, ignorance, vice, and unsatisfied desires. Here, too, no common features can be found.)

We need not concern ourselves at this point with the other items that we have tentatively placed on our list of the types of things that are good (pleasure, knowledge, virtue). At this point they are merely serving as placeholders; we will soon (Chapter 3) ask what should occupy those places. The question we want to ask now is this: should successful conation (the satisfaction of desires, or rational and properly informed desires, and so on) be *one* of the items on our list?

That question needs further refinement. We do not quite mean to be asking whether all the things that people desire or pursue (rationally, with proper information, and reflectively) are good for them to have. For it might be the case that the reason those things are good has nothing to do with the fact that they are objects of conation. They might be the other things on our list—pleasure, or knowledge, or virtue. If those things are good, and they are the only things that are ever wanted, then it will be true that all that is pursued is good to have. But the explanation for that truth will simply be that we human beings are always wise: we train our conation on things that are worthy of being desired because

45. Ross, *The Right and the Good*, pp. 134–141.

they are good to have. So the question we want to ask is whether successful conation *creates* goodness—not whether all successful conation
is good. More precisely: is it the case that whenever S wants (rationally,
with proper information, and reflectively) P to occur, and P does occur,
that is good for S simply *because* it is something he wants in that way? If
so, successful conation is one type of good. That would be an important
component of a theory of well-being—if it were true.

It should be kept in mind that according to this hybrid theory, some
things should be desired because their goodness for the person who acquires them makes them worth wanting. The order of explanation sometimes is: that is good, and that is why you should want it. But, according
to the hybrid theory, the order is sometimes the other way around: you
want this, and that is why it is good for you to get it. The hybrid theory
says that in some cases our desires should reach out to objects because
they are good for us to have; but in other cases our desires just happen to
reach out to objects that are not in themselves worth wanting, and when
they motivate us to acquire those objects, that is good for us.

But if it is good for us to acquire knowledge, become virtuous, and enjoy pleasure, then should we not cultivate our desires so that they reach
out precisely to these objects and none others? Why should we allow
ourselves to form intentions and make plans that have as their objects
items that are not the sorts of things that are worth wanting? If some
things are worth wanting (because they are good for us to have, and
wanting them will help us get them), other things worth avoiding (for
the opposite reasons), and still other things neutral in value (deserving
neither desire nor aversion), why should we not organize our conation
so that we pursue things in the first category, avoid things in the second,
and maintain an attitude of indifference toward those in the third?

The hybrid theory can reply that this is not the only possible or reasonable way to shape our psyches. We can simply let desires arise in us
as they will, provided that they are not desires for what is bad for us
(pain, ignorance, vice). We need not cultivate desires that have as their
objects the things that are on our list of what is worth wanting. For
when we come to possess something that is not on our lists of good
things and bad things, it will be good for us to have it. Nothing about
those objects made them merit our wanting them; nonetheless, in getting them, we satisfy our desire for them, and that is why it is good for us
to get them.

Notice how weak the hybrid theorist's position has become. Most of us would say that if someone reaches for a stick on the ground and picks it up, that action in itself is not good for him. (It may of course be instrumentally good: that may be precisely the exercise he needs, or the stick may have posed a hazard, or it might be needed for his art project.) And of course we can go on giving such examples. There is no end of actions we can perform that are neither good nor bad. We do not engage in them (for themselves), and are not tempted in the slightest to do them, for an obvious reason: that would be pointless. But the hybrid theorist is forced to say that if we were to do them, that would be good for us, precisely because it is good for desires to achieve their objects (provided those objects are not bad).

The fact that we sometimes feel pleasure when our desires are satisfied or our plans successfully executed is of no help to the hybrid theory. We can agree, for the sake of argument, that such pleasure is good. But the hybrid theory holds that getting what one wants is a distinct item that must be included on a list of goods, even if that list already has pleasure on it. That theory maintains that satisfying a desire is good even when it brings no pleasure: if someone picks up a stick because that is what he wanted to do, it does not matter whether this gives him pleasure—it is good for him. That is not a plausible proposal.

We should also bear in mind that people are often attracted to courses of action simply because of the good or harm that they will do to others. We can want to aid our ailing parents, or injure our enemies, even when we see no way in which we ourselves will benefit from doing so. These actions can bring us great pleasure if we see that our goals have been achieved; and we are, for the moment, assuming that pleasure is on the hybrid theory's list of things that are good. But leaving aside the pleasure it brings, is it good for you to help your ailing parents simply because that is something you want to do? Is it good for you to have harmed your enemies, simply because you successfully executed your plan to do so? The example used in the preceding paragraph—picking up a stick—shows how implausible it is to suppose that an action can be made good simply by virtue of its being what someone wanted to do. What these new examples—helping or harming another person—show is that we can easily form desires to perform actions that are like picking up a stick in that they are neutral when considered in terms of what is good or bad for the agent. Going to the hospital to see a friend can be good for people in all sorts of ways: it can speed along a sick person's recovery, and it can give pleasure to the visitor. But there is not, in addition to these goods, a further good that consists in the accomplishment of what someone aims to do.

We should conclude that the conative approach to well-being is not even one element of a satisfactory theory. It is plausible to suppose that there are many different kinds of things that are good for us, but successful conation—the execution of a rational plan, regardless of its content—is not one of them.[46]

32. Strict Hedonism

But is what I have just said—that many different types of things are good for us—really true? Of course, we can name many goods: houses are good for us (they keep us warm in winter), food is good for us (it gives us energy), and so on. But these are trivialities and not what we are investigating: we are talking about noninstrumental goodness. We want to know whether it is really true that there are many different components of well-being.

That is certainly a widely accepted idea. I have, for example, referred

---

46. Some desires and plans are expressions of an independent mind—the mind of a person who does his own thinking and makes judgments for himself. That kind of autonomy is a good quality for a person to develop, possess, and express (section 53), even though it can issue in decisions that harm the decision maker and others. Someone who enjoys thinking things through for himself has a good (something good *for himself*) that is not possessed by someone who merely imitates or unreflectively obeys others. And so, when the execution of a plan or the satisfaction of a desire puts into action this quality of mind, there is something to be said in its favor, even aside from the content of the plan or desire: it is good for someone that he is able to express this independence of mind. But that does not show that it is good, even slightly good, for him to plan or desire to do precisely what he did—that the content of his plan or desire passes muster, and that it is good for his plan to succeed or for his desire to be satisfied. What someone plans to do on a particular occasion may be entirely misguided, even though it is better for him to arrive at his plans with some independence of mind than to lack this quality. Similarly, it is better for someone that he can get from place to place by moving his legs than by being transported there by others; in doing so, he is exercising his own powers. But he may be walking to all the wrong places. It is better for him that he is walking than disabled, but there may be nothing to be said in favor of his walking *there* rather than somewhere else. Conative approaches to well-being lack the resources for saying why independence of mind is noninstrumentally good and for subjecting the content of our plans and desires to criticism. (Typically, they construct well-being out of *rational* plans or desires, not the conation of an independent-minded agent, of whom there may be very few.) They do not say why we should move on our own, or where we should go.

several times to Ross's thesis that there are precisely four types of good: pleasure, knowledge, virtue, and the proper apportionment of pleasure to the virtuous. He insists that these are good "sans phrase,"[47] but when his theory is transformed (section 21) and turned into a proposal about which things are benefits, or components of well-being, it will claim that these four items, and these alone, are good for us.

Some would go much further: human life, they would say, is teeming with goodness; there are more types of good than one can name. But other philosophers (Bentham and Mill, for example) move in the opposite direction: Ross's list, they would say, is too large, because only one type of thing is good: pleasure. All pleasure is good, and all that is good is pleasure; that is one way to formulate a doctrine that, following common philosophical parlance, goes by the name of "hedonism." We will see that neither half of this doctrine can be easily dismissed or easily accepted. Hedonism, so defined, should not be rejected outright; properly understood, it is compatible with the seemingly opposite idea that life is teeming with a great variety of goods things. Before we can see the truth in hedonism, we need clarification of what it is saying. (I leave aside, for now, the other side of hedonism: its doctrine that all and only pain is bad. We will see that not all pain is bad in section 38, and that much that is bad is not painful in sections 38–43.)

We earlier (sections 17–18) arrived at the conclusion that "G is good" is always an abbreviation for some longer formulation. When it is construed as a statement about well-being, it should be taken to mean "It is good for S that P." So, to understand hedonism, we should express its thesis by fitting it into this schema. It holds that all pleasure is good. That is best taken to mean: whenever S is pleased, that is good for S. It also holds that only pleasure is good; that is, all that is good is pleasure. That is best taken to mean: whenever it is good for S that some state of affairs occurs, that state of affairs is one in which S is pleased.

But that still does not fully capture what some philosophical devotees of pleasure say about its importance. To see what is missing from this formulation, recall what we said in the previous section (31) about the conative theory of well-being: it does not merely claim that whenever S's desire is satisfied, that is good for S; rather, it holds that whenever S's desire is satisfied, that is good for S precisely because, and only because, of

47. Ross, *The Right and the Good*, p. 102.

that satisfaction. It is not because we desire wisely—because the objects we desire are worthy of being desired—that the satisfaction of desires is good for us; rather, the idea behind the conative theory is that when we get what we want, that is good for us simply by virtue of our wanting and getting it.

Similarly, hedonism, strictly speaking, should be taken to mean that whenever it is good for S that some state of affairs occurs, that occurrence is good for S simply and only by virtue of his being pleased; and whenever S is pleased, that is good for S simply and only by virtue of his being pleased. More simply put: pleasure alone makes something good. If someone enjoys swimming, for example, that is good for him, not by virtue of the fact that he is swimming, but by virtue of the fact that he is enjoying himself. His swimming is the cause and the object of his pleasure, but the explanation of why it is good for him to swim appeals only to the pleasure he gets from it.

These terms—the causes and objects of pleasure—perhaps need some explanation. Some pleasures have no objects, although they have causes. When a dog's stomach is scratched, that gives it pleasure, but it is not pleased *that* its stomach is being scratched. It experiences sensations that it likes when it is being scratched, but it does not reflect with pleasure on what it is feeling. It can like running, but it cannot be glad that it is running. It can be pleased by its owner, but it cannot be pleased with its owner. Human beings, by contrast, can experience pleasure not only through pleasant sensations but by taking up attitudes that they put into words. We can be pleased that yesterday's headache is gone. The dissipation of pain does not by itself cause any pleasure, but by taking cognizance of it, we can be glad that we are rid of it. Many of the pleasures of human beings are cases of being pleased that something is so. But many are not. When we enjoy swimming, that is not a matter of our being pleased that we are swimming. Someone recovering from an illness may be glad that he is swimming again, but his ability to swim may still be too limited to allow him to enjoy this activity. Conversely, we can enjoy certain activities without realizing that we are engaged in them, and so without being pleased that we are undertaking them. Someone might enjoy belittling a colleague, for example, without being pleased that he is doing so, and without realizing that he is doing so.

Human pleasures run the gamut. They include sensations that have no objects (the rush induced by a drug, the soothing of an itch), enjoyments that have activities as their objects (swimming, sailing), and being pleased that something is the case. The hedonist embraces them all: each and every one of them is good for the person whose pleasures they are, and no state of affairs from which pleasure is entirely absent is good for anyone precisely because of the absence of pleasure. The objects of the pleasures, if they have objects, have no bearing on what is good for us because it is the pleasure, not the object, that makes being pleased or taking pleasure good. If someone likes swimming, that is good for him because he gets some enjoyment from something; what it is that he enjoys does not matter. If someone is pleased that P, that is good for him, no matter what the content of P is.

Does the hedonist believe that there is any basis for choosing one pleasure over another? If S is choosing between two activities of equal duration and has as good a chance of performing one as the other, but will enjoy one much more than the other, the hedonist will of course have to say that the more-enjoyed activity will be better for S. The basis for his decision must be quantitative because, as we have just seen, his theory of well-being abstracts away from the object of the pleasure and looks solely to pleasure itself as that which makes an act worth choosing. If he enjoys doing V and doing W, it is not to V and W that he must look in order to choose between them, but to the enjoying of them. And if he enjoys one more than the other, that must be decisive.

Mill, as we noted earlier (section 4), distinguishes the quantity of a pleasure from its quality, and he insists that the latter has no less an important role to play in our choices than the former. For him, when S is choosing between doing V and doing W on the basis of how good each is for himself, S should ask whether it is better for him to take pleasure in doing V or in doing W, and not only how much he will enjoy each. It might be the case, Mill thinks, that even though S enjoys doing V more than doing W, it is better for him to W because his enjoyment of W is better for him than his enjoyment of V. Philosophizing, for example, might be a better activity for S to enjoy than bowling, though he enjoys bowling more; since it is better for him to philosophize than to bowl, the enjoyment of the former is of higher quality than the enjoyment of the latter. That, at any rate, is the way in which Mill thinks we should make these comparisons: an activity of higher quality is better for us and provides a pleasure of higher quality. We should ask ourselves not only how much we will enjoy two competing activities, but also what the qualitative difference is between their objects.

It should be evident that Mill is not a strict hedonist, as we are using that term. A hedonist of the strict sort holds that it is pleasure alone, not the object of pleasure, that should figure in our decision making. Saying that Mill does not count as that type of hedonist is of course no criticism of him. He did well to steer clear of it—though that does not show that his own brand of hedonism is defensible. As we are about to see, strict hedonism is utterly implausible.

To begin with, strict hedonism goes astray merely by virtue of its assumption that whenever it is good for S that P, P involves some pleasure that S feels. Obviously, that is not true, since plants feel no pleasure, and yet, as we noted from the start (section 2), it is good for a plant to grow and flourish. In this regard, strict hedonism commits the same error as the conative theory of well-being. It is an attempt to say, for any S about whom it makes sense to say that G is good for it, what it is that makes G good for S. It does not set out merely to say what is good for men, or for Americans, or for human beings—for these would be artificially restricted groups; rather, it includes animals within its purview because it strives for complete generality. It holds that *whenever* it is good for S that some state of affairs occurs, that occurrence is good for S simply and only by virtue of S's being pleased; and whenever S is pleased, that is good for S, simply and only by virtue of S's being pleased. But when S is a plant, this analysis fails.

At best, hedonism is a theory about what makes something good for human beings and animals. It must acknowledge that some other account is needed to explain what makes something good for a plant. But it can give no reason to suppose that not only are the things that are good for plants different from those that are good for other things, but also what makes something good for a plant has nothing in common with what makes something good for other living things.

Second, as we have seen, hedonism, strictly so called, abstracts away from the objects of pleasure. It holds that when S enjoys V-ing, or is pleased that P, what makes this good for S has nothing to do with V-ing or P. In this respect, too, it resembles the conative theory. That theory holds that whenever S satisfies a desire or executes a plan, that is good for S, regardless of the content of the desire or plan (section 26). The very fact that a desire has been satisfied or a plan carried out is what is good for S. But one of the weaknesses of the conative theory is that it offers no reason to believe that we can properly decide whether a desire or plan is good to fulfill in the absence of any information about its object.

Hedonism is implausible in the same way. If the hedonist dogmatically insists that the object of a pleasure plays no role in determining whether it is good for someone to feel that pleasure, we have been offered no reason to agree. It simply asserts that all pleasures are to receive positive evaluations—it deems them all good for the person who feels them—without explaining why these evaluations should be made without considering the objects of those pleasures. Having rejected a similar idea advanced by the conative theory of well-being, we have no reason to accept its analogue in hedonism.

Third, hedonism, as we have seen, holds that when we make decisions about someone's well-being, a greater pleasure should always be preferred to a smaller one. That makes intensity of feeling the sole guide to judgments about well-being, and that is a guide that has no plausibility. A high induced by a drug might be one of the most intense pleasures a human being can experience. Suppose it were possible to administer such a drug to a human being soon after her birth, and to keep that child alive but dysfunctional in every way for the normal span of a human life. She would lie in her hospital bed, fed by a tube through which drugs flow, and would remain in that state of truncated development for the remainder of her existence. The pleasure felt in such a life is, by hypothesis, intense, uninterrupted, certain, and long-lasting. Even so, this is not an option any sane parent would choose for a child if she could instead live a life in which her faculties grow and mature and the less intense satisfactions of a normal and happy life, albeit accompanied by some measure of disappointment, sorrow, and pain, are available to her. Mill was right: quantity of pleasure is not and should not be our guide. (It does not follow, of course, that it is something else about *pleasure*—its peculiar phenomenological quality—that should always be our guide.)

Since we are capable of choosing, for the good of our children, a less intensely pleasant life than the drugged life that might be made available to them, the hedonist who thinks that we should opt to have the drug administered must say why this is so. The hedonist must admit that what is good for S always has some kind of suitability to S; as we saw (section 21), the "for" of "G is good for S" conveys the idea that there is a relationship of conformability between G and S, one in which G, given the nature of S, serves S well. But the nature of a child is not that of a mere seeker of pleasure from no matter what source. The psychology of a normal child, and of course of a normal adult, is a far more complex matter than that. A child who is totally unresponsive to her environment, and whose only enjoyments are drug-induced sensations, has suffered a crippling blow, since she cannot develop the powers—cognitive, social, and emotional—of a healthy, flourishing person. Why should all those aspects of the mind be ignored? Why assume that the only human equipment to be cultivated is our receptivity to intensely pleasant sensations?[48]

33. Hedonism Diluted

None of these objections to strict hedonism poses a problem for two theses that the hedonist endorses: all pleasures are good, and whatever is good for a human being is a pleasure. What are we to make of these two claims? Can we accept one of them, or even both, without committing ourselves to the strict hedonism that is so problematic?

Begin with the idea that all pleasures are good. We can state this more strictly: whenever S is pleased, that is good for S. For example, S enjoys swimming, and so it is good for S that he enjoys swimming. Why so? Because of the enjoyment. But should we say, *solely* because of the enjoyment? Is what S enjoys—the swimming—irrelevant to the goodness of his enjoyment of that activity? If we make it irrelevant, we will be led down the path to strict hedonism and all its troubles. For we will then find no reason to reject the idea that when we choose among pleasures of equal duration, those that are more intense are better. And intensity is

---

48. Robert Nozick's well-known thought experiment (*Anarchy, State, and Utopia*, pp. 42–45), in which one spends an entire life attached to a machine that simulates experiences of one's choosing, vividly makes a point similar to the one I convey with the less fanciful thought of a life that contains nothing but a drug-induced high: there is more to what is good for a person than the kind of consciousness he has. Nozick's example, though well known, has evidently not convinced social scientists to set aside pleasure, or subjective reports of happiness and well-being, as the sole basis for theorizing about what is good for people. See, for example, Richard Layard, *Happiness*, pp. 114–115; he complains that Nozick's unrealistic thought experiment makes a "weak test case" against his thesis that "the greatest happiness is the right guide to public policy" (ibid., p. 115). For other surveys of empirical research on subjective well-being, see Haidt, *The Happiness Hypothesis*; Daniel Kahneman, Ed Diener, and Norbert Schwarz, eds., *Well-Being*; and Bruno Frey and Alois Stutzer, *Happiness and Economics*. Such studies are of considerable interest, since there is no doubt that pleasure and, more generally, positive affect (section 39) play an important role in a flourishing human life. But there is also a philosophical and therefore nonempirical dimension to the understanding of human well-being; indeed, these empirical studies presuppose this. It is therefore at most a half truth to say, as Haidt does, that Aristotle's question "What is the human good?" is properly treated as "a question of fact that can be examined by scientific means" (*The Happiness Hypothesis*, pp. 218–219).

a poor guide to choice. So, to be plausible, a diluted form of hedonism should hold that whenever S is pleased, that is good for S because of the pleasure; but it should not say, *only* because of the pleasure. That will allow it to say that when we compare the enjoyment of swimming with some other enjoyable activity, the differences between what is enjoyed, and not only in the enjoying of them, can be taken into account in an assessment of what is good for us.

Hedonists also hold that whenever it is good for a human being that some state of affairs occurs, that state of affairs is one in which he is pleased. Further, its occurrence is good *because* he is pleased. But *only* because of that? Again, if we say so, the extremism of strict hedonism will be unavoidable. If we want to borrow something from hedonism and accept a moderate form of it, we should therefore say: if it is good for S to swim, that is because he enjoys it. But we should not add that it is good for him *only* because of his enjoyment—that *what* is enjoyed is irrelevant to goodness.

The diluted form of hedonism that affirms both these principles is free to embrace the idea that there are many different types of things that are good for human beings. All of them must be enjoyments, but the objects of these pleasures (when they have objects) might be indefinitely large. What moderate hedonism cannot allow is that the other items on a list of goods—for example, on Ross's list—are good even when they are not enjoyed. The mere possession of a piece of knowledge, according to moderate hedonism, cannot be good if it is not the object of enjoyment. Nor can the mere possession of a virtue. But moderate hedonism leaves open the possibility that the acquisition or deployment of knowledge, when enjoyed, is good. It merely insists that these are good only if enjoyed, and partly because enjoyed.

This component of moderate hedonism has great plausibility and will be accepted as a plausible working hypothesis in the remainder of this study.[49] We are, after all, talking about what is *noninstrumentally* good for someone. Swimming may certainly be a good way for us to get across

---

49. Other recent attempts to accommodate hedonism—that is, to give pleasure a larger role in well-being than merely being one of its components—are those of Sumner (*Welfare, Happiness, and Ethics*, pp. 138–183) and Adams (*Finite and Infinite Goods*, pp. 83–101). The versions of hedonism defended by Fred Feldman in *Pleasure and the Good Life* are compatible with my conception of well-being, since, like Mill's hedonism, they assess the goodness of pleasures by appealing to a nonhedonic standard. Samuel Fleischacker, drawing upon Aristotelian insights, emphasizes the importance of a conception of "proper pleasures" for political theory (*A Third Concept of Liberty*, pp. 91–119).

the lake, it may burn calories, it may maintain muscle tone; these are all good reasons for thinking that it is good for the swimmer as a means to further ends. But can it be good for him apart from these results? If we have some temptation to answer affirmatively, that temptation will certainly be strongest when we think of someone who loves swimming—who, in other words, enjoys it. For when we think of someone swimming but deriving not the least bit of pleasure from doing so, it is difficult to believe that this could be good for him for any reason other than the good consequences of his activity.

This aspect of moderate hedonism—its thesis that something can be noninstrumentally good for a human being only if it is enjoyed by him—is silent about what, besides pleasure, explains the goodness of states of affairs. It holds back from saying that it is only pleasure that explains what is good for us, and thus it permits the objects in which we take pleasure to play an essential role in that explanation. But it offers no ideas about what those objects are. It admits that there may be much more to what is good for human beings than pleasure alone, but it insists that pleasure enters into the explanation of the goodness of every state of affairs that is good. What it insists upon we will accept. That leaves a large question before us: which objects of enjoyment is it good for someone to have?

The other half of diluted hedonism proposes an answer to that question: each and every pleasure is good for the person who has it. In that sense, it does not matter what the objects of enjoyment are (if they have objects): all of them are good. But moderate hedonism does not hold that all of them are equally good, or that the only test for their comparative value is their intensity as pleasures. (If it made that second claim, it would be as objectionable as strict hedonism.) It allows the objects of pleasure to play an explanatory role in their comparative goodness. It insists that every enjoyed activity has something to be said in its favor—it is, because of the pleasure, good for the person who enjoys it—even though some have more to be said in their favor than others because of differences between the objects that are enjoyed.

This component of diluted hedonism is not worth discussing because it has no practical importance. We should recall the point (sections 17 and 20) that all talk about what is good for someone, like all talk about who is a good writer, presupposes a comparison class, and so we can say both that something is good for someone (when it is compared with one class) and bad for him (when compared with another). So it is not clear what one would be committed to, were one to agree that every pleasure, because it is a pleasure, is good regardless of its object. One would of course be committed to saying that each pleasure is better for the person who feels it than a great many other things—namely, all the things that are bad for him, as well as all the things that are neither good nor bad for him. But one would not be committed to saying that the pleasure is so good for him that he should pursue it, since even something that is good for someone is inferior—perhaps by far—to however many things are better than it, and superior enjoyments may leave no time for the pursuit of a minimally good pleasure. A small good can be at the bottom of the list of goods; it may qualify as good only because of its superiority to all that is bad or neither good nor bad. And that position may make it too small a good to deserve a place in one's life. In that respect, it can be plausibly said that it is no good at all; the comparison class we use, when we make that judgment, is all the goods that are good enough to be worth pursuing. Both judgments—that it is good and that it is not—can be correct. But here what matters is how one acts, not what one says. For *practical* purposes, what is important is whether each pleasure is good enough for the person who feels it to be worth feeling. If it is not, the fact that it can be called good for him (in relation to some comparison class) has no practical significance.

We can therefore sensibly describe certain pleasures as bad pleasures—bad for the person who feels them—even if we assume (as we have) that everything that is good for someone is good for him only on condition that he enjoy it. Their designation as bad pleasures has real practical import, since it entails that we should not desire or pursue them, and that anyone who enjoys them should stop doing so and seek better pleasures in their place. It is entirely plausible to believe that there are such things as pleasures that are not good for someone to have, even if he wants to have them; for surely not everything that can possibly be enjoyed will fit into a single life. We have not yet discussed the question of how one is to decide *which* pleasures are bad, but we have every reason to expect that there will be some. (Some examples are given in sections 43, 49, 50, and 51.)

We should therefore reject one of the components of moderate hedonism; it is not the case that whenever someone is pleased, that is good for him. We should agree, or at least accept as a working hypothesis, that

nothing can be noninstrumentally good for someone if he does not enjoy it. That leaves us free to say that many different kinds of things are
good for human beings—provided that they are enjoyments. But we are
still in need of a theory that helps us understand what those things are.
The conative approach to well-being has given us no help. Strict hedonism and one component of a diluted hedonism have been rejected. To
make progress, we should turn to the idea that human well-being, like
the good of any living thing, consists in flourishing.[50]

50. The three alternative theories of well-being that we are examining, in this chapter and
the next, correspond to those discussed by Parfit (*Reasons and Persons*, pp. 493–502): hedonis-
tic theories, "desire-fulfillment theories," and "objective list theories" (to use his terms). Even
so, "objective list theory" is not the most apt name for the approach I will be defending. If it
must have a name, I would choose "developmentalism" (section 35). See too Raymond Geuss's
discussion of three conceptions of happiness (which do not fully correspond to Parfit's
trichotomy) in "Happiness and Politics," pp. 102–107.

THREE

Prolegomenon to Flourishing

34. Development and Flourishing: The General Theory

A good theory of well-being should be built on a root idea that is obvious, widely recognized, and rich in implications. Clearly, flourishing is a good thing—good for what is flourishing. We can talk about a flourishing or thriving business or legal practice, but flourishing is primarily a biological phenomenon: "flower" and "flourish" are cognates. Above all, it is plants, animals, and human beings that flourish when conditions are favorable. They do so by developing properly and fully, that is, by growing, maturing, making full use of the potentialities, capacities, and faculties that (under favorable conditions) they naturally have at an early stage of their existence. Anything that impedes that development or the exercise of those mature faculties—disease, the sapping of vigor and strength, injuries, the loss of organs—is bad for them.[1]

1. If S is flourishing, there is always some kind to which S belongs, and S is flourishing as a member of that kind. So "George is flourishing" is an elliptical or incomplete expression (section 17). The thesis that I will be defending is that what is good for human beings is to flourish as human beings (just as what is good for the member of some other biological species is to flourish as a member of that species). We can also locate individual human beings in other categories—they are entrepreneurs, poets, farmers, and so on—and affirm that they are flourishing as members of those kinds. Since we can speak of a business as flourishing, we can also speak of someone who is a businessman as a flourishing businessman; he is flourishing as a businessman precisely because his business is flourishing. But it may not do him the least bit of good for his business to flourish. Similarly, when someone's skills are developing well or are in their full flowering, we can say he is flourishing as a practitioner of some sort—as a poet or painter, for example. But if it is good for someone to be a flourishing poet or painter, that is to be explained by the ways in which these activities make use of capacities that it is good for any *human being* to have; so, at any rate, I shall argue (section 47). It is, in other words, not the case that it is always good for an individual to flourish as a member of a kind, regardless of the kind.

131

Living things are not the only things for which some things are good and other things bad. Some things are good for a car, other things bad. But truths about what is good for a car depend on truths about the ways in which they serve the good of human beings. They are designed to improve conditions for living beings. So we can say: everything that is good for S, whether S is living or not, either promotes or is part of flourishing. What is good for an artifact like a car is what promotes flourishing—not the flourishing of the car, of course (since there is no such thing), but the flourishing of human beings. Other artifacts promote the flourishing of animals or plants: an animal shelter, a greenhouse. By contrast, what is good for a living being, as opposed to an artifact, is what promotes or is part of the flourishing of that same living thing. The good of an artifact looks to the good of something beyond it. Not so for living things: in their case, what is good for S is the flourishing of S, or what leads to it.[2]

To say that something or someone is flourishing is both to evaluate and to describe it. "S is flourishing" entails "S is doing well"; and when S is a living thing, "S is doing well" entails "S is flourishing." But "flourish" has rich empirical implications that are absent from the more ab-

---

By contrast, it is always good to flourish as a human being. If one is a businessman but fails to flourish as a businessman, one might nonetheless be a flourishing human being, and if one's failure to flourish as a businessman does not in any way detract from one's flourishing as a human being, then it is not bad. I am grateful to David Reeve for raising these issues.

2. Here I set myself against the idea, found in many philosophical authors, that the good of an animal, like that of an artifact, cannot by itself be an adequate justification for action. Kant, for example, seems to have something like this in mind when he says: "Beings whose existence depends not on our will but on nature still have only a relative value as means and are therefore called *things,* if they lack reason. Rational beings, on the other hand, are called *persons* because their nature already marks them out as ends in themselves" (*Groundwork for the Metaphysics of Morals,* 4:428, Kant's emphasis, Zweig trans., p. 229). See too his *Lectures on Ethics,* 27:458–459: "Since all animals exist only as means, and not for their own sakes, in that they have no self-consciousness, whereas man is the end . . . it follows that we have no immediate duties to animals; our duties to them are indirect duties to humanity" (Heath trans., p. 212). Kant's framework contains a fundamental division: merely conditional value is possessed by artifacts and nonhuman species on one side, and absolute value by all rational natures or persons on the other. But it is doubtful that anything is gained by speaking of the unconditional value of rational nature; we need not do so, at any rate, merely to find an alternative to utilitarianism. Ethical theory can be good centered without being committed to the maximization of good, and therefore without treating each person's well-being as fungible and each person, therefore, as thinglike. A person's good is not worth promoting only insofar as it is a component of the maximal amount of good in the universe—but neither is an animal's. Brutes are not to be grouped with artifacts, mere things the good of which cannot itself justify action.

stract and nonbiological term "doing well."[3] If you say that S is flourishing, your statement is put into grave doubt if it is then pointed out to you that S is sick, weak, mutilated, injured, stunted. Nothing so seriously impeded is flourishing. And therefore nothing so seriously impeded is doing well.

These statements, at any rate, are unexceptionable when they are made about nonhuman beings. Do they become doubtful, however, in the human case? Consider someone who is *physically* sick, weak, mutilated, injured, stunted; he might nonetheless be in the full possession of his *psychological* powers. And in that case, his physical condition need not prevent us from saying that, on balance, he is flourishing and doing well, despite his physical debilities.

But that point does not undermine the thesis that there is always a tight connection between a living being's use of its powers, its flourishing, and its doing well—whether that living thing is human or not. To accommodate it, we need only acknowledge another piece of conventional wisdom: if you say of a human being that he is flourishing, your statement is thrown into doubt if he is correctly described either as *psychologically* or as *physically* unhealthy, weak, damaged, and stunted. Certainly, if he suffers from both kinds of disabilities, the claim that he is flourishing, or that he is doing well, is impossible to sustain. For human beings, no less than other living things, it is always good to flourish; and if a human being is flourishing in all ways, both physical and psychological, he is doing very well indeed.

---

3. Flourishing therefore should be counted as what Bernard Williams calls a "thick" ethical concept. These (his examples are treachery, promises, brutality, and courage) "seem to express a union of fact and value. The way these notions are applied is determined by what the world is like (for instance, by how someone has behaved), and yet, at the same time, their application usually involves a certain valuation of the situation, of persons or actions" (*Ethics and the Limits of Philosophy*, p. 129). Noticing that flourishing is a thick ethical concept should lead to the recognition that so too are the concepts of benefit and harm. And the concept of benefit is that of G being good for S. We must be careful, then, not to count all uses of "good" as the expression of a thin ethical concept, although they are often so treated. (See for example Dancy, *Ethics without Principles*, p. 84; compare with pp. 16–17. His list includes right, wrong, good, bad, duty, obligation, and ought.) Counting the concept of being good for someone as thick by no means casts doubt on the validity and value of the thick-thin contrast. Williams rightly opposes any program in moral philosophy that seeks to reduce thick ethical concepts to thin ones. See his "Modernity and the Substance of Ethical Life," pp. 49–50. I hope the present study shows that an inquiry into goodness need not be the reductive enterprise that he rejects. Moral philosophy would lose its bearings if it assumed, mistakenly, that benefits and harms are too thin to reward investigation.

If, as we have agreed, it is always good for a living thing that it flourish, that is because the things in which flourishing consists are good for that living thing. For some plants, flourishing may consist in attaining a certain height and producing an abundance of flowers. Those are the *components* of its flourishing—not means to it, or resources for it. Good soil conditions, proper nutrients, adequate light and moisture: these are some of the conditions that lead to its flourishing. But they are not what its flourishing consists in. The distinction applies, of course, to human beings as well. Having access to a dwelling that protects one from extreme cold is a resource that any human being needs in order to stay alive, and so it is a necessary condition for human flourishing. But that access is not itself a component of flourishing. It is good because it is a means to an end, and only for that reason.

So, whatever is a component of a human being's flourishing is good for him. But should we also accept the converse: that whatever is good for someone is a component of his flourishing? The same sort of question can be asked about what is *bad* for a human being. It is unobjectionable to say that everything that interferes with some component of a human being's flourishing, by making it more difficult or impossible for him to flourish, is bad for him. But is it also reasonable to affirm the converse statement: that everything that is bad for a human being makes it more difficult or impossible for him to flourish?

We would not hesitate to accept these converse statements when they are made about other sorts of living beings. What else could be good for a plant, except its flourishing and what promotes it? What else could be bad for it, except what impedes its flourishing? But, it may be objected, human beings are different: the components of flourishing are only some of the things that are good for us, and the impediments to it are only some of the things that are bad for us.

One might be tempted to propose this objection if one assumes that when we successfully pursue our plans—or, at any rate, our rational, carefully considered, well-informed plans—then that is good for us; and when these plans go awry, that is bad for us. That is, if we accept the conative theory as a correct account of *one* way in which something can be good for a human being, that will prevent us from agreeing that whatever is good for someone is a component of his flourishing. For some of the things we want and acquire would not be properly described as components of flourishing because they have nothing to do with growth, development, or the deployment of our physical or psychological powers. If, for example, someone plans to kill his enemy and successfully executes that plan, we would not normally use his success as a reason to describe him as flourishing. That way of speaking would sever the connection we normally make between flourishing and the healthy development and exercise of a thing's faculties and powers. And the conative theory of well-being does not need to appeal to any ideas about flourishing or to affirm that a successful killer is a flourishing human being. What it claims is that killing can be good for us, if it is something we want to do. It would not enhance the plausibility of the conative theory if it were to claim that when someone plans and executes a murder, that is the analogue, among human beings, to a plant's growing to its full height and thriving by setting out an abundance of flowers.

The conative theory—or at least a hybrid version of it—is, as we have seen (section 30), something we can easily be led to accept. We normally take people's ends to be the determinants, or among the determinants, of what is good for them. We easily assume that our desires give us reasons for action, and that when we have a reason to do something, then it is a good thing, to some degree, for us that we do it. If we make these mistakes, we will deny that flourishing is all that there is to what is good for human beings—however true it may be that it is all there is to what is good for every other species. But since we have rejected the conative theory and a hybridized form of it (section 31), we have no reason to deny this. And why should we deny something that seems so reasonable? If someone is flourishing in every way, both physically and psychologically, how could it be the case that his life can nonetheless be improved—that it would be better for him if certain other states of affairs were to obtain?

35. Development and Flourishing: The Human Case

The preceding argument operates at a high level of abstraction. It does not try to say, about this species or that, what flourishing actually consists in. To give it greater specificity would require knowing something about the constitution of a particular species. Knowing what the flourishing of orchids consists in would require some knowledge of orchids.

To test the developmental theory of well-being (so we will call it—or "developmentalism"[4] for short), we should of course consider the kind of living beings in whom we are most interested: human beings. What is good for them is determined by what it is for them to flourish—not what the means to their flourishing are, but what constitutes their flourishing, that is, what its components are. To know what constitutes their flourishing, we must know something about human beings in general. We

4. The term "perfectionism," which some philosophers may be tempted to apply to the theory I defend here, seems to me less apt, for several reasons. Nothing can be perfect (full stop); whatever is perfect is a perfect thing of a kind. Presumably, then, a perfectionist ethical theory is one that holds at least this much: that we should strive to make either ourselves or others perfect human beings or perfect persons. (It might go further and urge us to become perfect in many other respects: perfect cooks, perfect musicians, perfect philosophers, and so on.) But it is not clear whether becoming a perfect human being is an intelligible ideal. Just as there are too many different kinds of good novels for it to make sense to speak of a perfect novel, so there are too many different ways of being a good human being for it to make sense to strive to become a perfect person. (Only rather simple things admit of perfection: for example, a perfect score in bowling, perfect summer weather.) It is, furthermore, naïve and perhaps even arrogant—and therefore a flaw or worse—to suppose that anyone can achieve or even come close to perfection as a human being. (It would be silly even to strive to become a *flawless* human being; and being flawless is a lesser ideal than having every good quality to the highest degree.) Another point is that the theory I am presenting here makes "good for" the central tool of practical thought—not "a good human being" or "a good K" (let alone "a perfect human being" or "a perfect K"). The label "perfectionism," when applied to a theory, implies that the theory is guided by the concept of the highest possible excellence as a member of a kind. There is also the point that in common parlance "perfectionist," when applied to a person, can be used with pejorative force. It does not serve a theory well to give it a name that can serve as a term of criticism. The term that I prefer, "developmentalism," is certainly far from ideal, but it does have the advantage that it belongs to the same family of terms as "powers, capacities, growth, flourishing" and the like; and these, I am suggesting, lie at the heart of what is good for living things. The central thesis for which I am arguing is that when we consider the good of any living thing, we should look to the process of growth and development that best suits things of its kind; and since the assumptions we make about proper development play such an important role in this way of thinking, labeling it a "developmentalist" theory has some justification. The currency of the term "perfectionism" for one approach to well-being owes something to Henry Sidgwick, who views "Happiness and Perfection or Excellence of human nature" as "*prima facie* the only two ends which have a strongly and widely supported claim to be regarded as rational ultimate ends" (*The Methods of Ethics*, p. 9). It is, however, John Rawls (*A Theory of Justice*, pp. 285–292), who is most responsible for putting "perfectionism" into general circulation as a term of moral philosophy. As I note below (section 47), he uses it as the name of a political doctrine, whereas I use "developmentalism" to designate a theory of well-being. It is worth recalling how often John Stuart Mill uses "development" and related terms in defense of liberty (see especially Chapter 3 of *On Liberty*). A typical example: "Human nature is not a machine to be built after a model, and set to do exactly the work prescribed for it, but a tree, which requires to grow and develope itself on all sides, according to the tendency of the inward forces which make it a living thing" (p. 263).

noted, in the previous section, that their flourishing requires the development not merely of physical powers, but of psychological powers as well. Which powers? Using the categories of common sense, we can say at least this much: a flourishing human being is one who possesses, develops, and enjoys the exercise of cognitive, affective, sensory, and social powers (no less than physical powers).[5] Those, in broadest outline and roughly speaking, are the components of well-being.

Ross, it should be recalled (section 23), seeks to give his conception of what is good further support by appealing to a "widely accepted classification of the elements in the life of the soul."[6] We cognize, we feel, we aim; and Ross suggests that each of three items he takes to be good "sans phrase" is an ideal state of one of these faculties: of cognition, it is knowledge; of feeling, pleasure; of conation, virtue. We, however, are not claiming that these three—knowledge, pleasure, and virtue—are good for human beings, and our broad classificatory framework does not fully match Ross's. Nonetheless, we are working with a "widely accepted classification of the elements . . . of the soul." Ross believes that he needs no such classification: his list of items that are good is meant to stand on its own merits, since it is a list of what is good "sans phrase"— not good *for* anyone. Our approach has a greater affinity to the one adopted by Plato and Aristotle:[7] both are eager to determine what is really in the interests of human beings, and they rely heavily—far more so than Ross—on a schematic picture of the human soul as a grounding for their theories of well-being.[8]

5. There is nothing sacrosanct about this rough and crude list of human powers. It accords with common sense, but common sense is subject to correction and change. We may be able to achieve a more refined and illuminating map of human powers with the help of the empirical sciences or the insights of the arts. For present purposes, it is enough to note that the flourishing of a human being consists in the development and exercise not of some single power, but of many, and that the terms we use to name them—reasoning, emotion, sensation—are part of our everyday vocabulary. Our discussion of human flourishing in this chapter will become more concrete when we ask ourselves what it is to flourish along these various dimensions (sections 38–39, 41–43, 47, 52–53).

6. Ross, *The Right and the Good,* p. 140.

7. Plato *Republic* 4 and Aristotle *Nicomachean Ethics* 1.7.

8. From Aristotle I borrow the identification of human well-being with the actualization of powers of thought, emotion, and sociality inherent in human nature; the centrality of the process of socialization through which these powers emerge; and the goodness of pleasure when (but only when) it takes as its object the activities that express these powers. The methodology of the present study, which searches for ways to refine and systematize the opinions of the many (common sense) and the wise (philosophers) and seeks the resolution of disagreements

We can also give greater content to our conception of human well-being by bringing to mind a widely accepted framework for thinking about normal human development. We take for granted not only a static classification of the faculties that are good for each human being to have, but also a dynamic and normative story about how a human life should go, from its earliest days through maturity and into old age, when it is a life that is good for the person who is living it. (These are platitudes—which is precisely what we want, because a conception of well-being is not easily dismissed if it is built upon obvious and widely accepted truths.) It is good for us to receive loving attention as children, to acquire linguistic competence and the ability to communicate with others, to grow physically and make use of our sensory capacities, to mature sexually, to learn the complex social skills of adulthood, to enrich and develop greater mastery over our emotions, to learn how to assess reasons and deliberate with an independent and open mind, and thus to interact with others as full members of the community. It is good for our powers of perception, natural curiosity about our environment, and receptivity to beauty to grow. Rather than maintain total indifference to other human beings or sheer, blind hatred of the members of our social world, it is better for us when we are children to develop the ability to form bonds of friendship, to enjoy the company of others, and to devote ourselves to the good of others. Total and lifelong isolation from other human beings would disfigure us.

It is also part of our picture of the broad contours of human life that our powers decline as we age, and that this is a loss of well-being. A life that continues beyond a certain point will start to become worse for the person living it. If we go on long enough, we will endure physical enfeeblement, loss of memory, and the constriction of social and intellectual skills. The desires of an old person who has declined in this way might

---

within and between these groups, is also indebted to Aristotle. See my "How to Justify Ethical Propositions: Aristotle's Method." But there is much in Aristotle that I leave aside: for example, his thesis that human beings have an essence, that all human goods are hierarchically ordered (with theoretical thought at the pinnacle), that the well-being of all species can be ordered on a scale and divine life is to be ranked first, and that without ethical virtue nothing can be good for a human being. I do not deny any of these Aristotelian claims, but neither do I defend them. The one to which I am most sympathetic is the thesis that in favorable circumstances human beings have better lives than do other living things. Note too that Aristotle never admits, whereas I insist, that one must be prepared sometimes to sacrifice one's own good for the sake of others.

be rational, properly informed, and fully satisfied; nonetheless, the quality of his life has diminished, and to explain why we make this judgment we must appeal to a concrete conception of the powers we take it to be good for a person to exercise (and therefore bad to lose).[9]

This narrative and normative schema does not and is not intended to answer the deliberative questions we normally have to answer about the major turning points in our lives—which career to pursue, whether to marry, whether to have children, what our ideals should be, and so on. But it is the proper starting point from which to develop a more concrete

9. If we assume that when someone dies, the powers that were good for him to exercise while he was alive and fully functioning are irreversibly lost, we arrive at the unsurprising conclusion that death is bad. More precisely, it is better that one's mature powers be fully exercised than for them to atrophy or be lost, and the longer they function well, the better (when the external conditions for their successful operation continue to be favorable). It is better for the life of a fully functioning individual who is faring well to endure than for it to be cut short; death is bad when and because it permanently makes this continuation impossible. I assume that after the point of death, one's well-being cannot increase or diminish. Nothing that happens at any later point is good or bad for one. (Were that not the case, death might not be bad, or so bad, after all.) Of course, the projects to which someone had devoted his life might come to naught after he dies; the posthumous failure of one's plans is not something anyone wants. But unless the conative conception of well-being can be defended, we should not believe that posthumous failure detracts from the well-being of a life. If a bridge collapses after the death of the architect who supervised its construction, that is bad for many people, but not for the architect. The desire he had (the endurance of his bridge) was not fulfilled, but his good is constituted by the enjoyed activation of his powers, not the satisfaction of his desires. We can say that his life, or part of it, was less successful because his bridge was destroyed, but that is simply another way to express the point that what he aimed at was not achieved. Contrast this with Thomas Nagel, who writes: "A man is the subject of good and evil as much because he has hopes which may or may not be fulfilled . . . as because of his capacity to suffer and enjoy" ("Death," pp. 6–7). He uses this conative conception of good and evil to explain why a deathbed promise should be kept: "It is an injury to the dead man" (ibid., p. 6). I would say, instead, that deathbed promises retain their force because the obligation one incurs to deliver the promised good to the individual designated in the promise does not diminish in force because of the promisee's death. The reason I should promise you to complete your manuscript and see to its publication after your death is that it will be good for people to read it, and, I having made the promise, your death creates no reason for me to fail to honor my promise. I have no less reason to keep the promise after you die than I had before. But I do not increase your well-being by fulfilling my promise, and would not injure you were I to renege. (See section 57 for a fuller discussion of promises.) The topic of posthumous harm is briefly treated by Aristotle (*Nicomachean Ethics* 1.10–11), who goes astray, I believe, because he holds that it is good for a good person to be honored, whether he knows of the honor or not; so even when the honor comes after the point of death, that is good. He has to assume that this can be only a small good to preserve his conclusion that what happens after death cannot falsify the judgment that someone's life was well lived. For other discussions of the badness of death and of posthumous harm, see Joel Feinberg, *Harm to Others*, pp. 79–83; and F. M. Kamm, *Morality, Mortality*, vol. 1, pp. 13–66.

conception of what is good for a particular person, whether oneself or another. In order to fill in the details, we must come to an understanding of who we are: what our allegiances should be, what our competencies and predilections are, what we yearn for, what our temperament is, and so on. And then that self-knowledge, together with our conception of the many things that are good for us, must be applied to particular circumstances. Speaking in the broadest possible terms, there is one kind of life that is best for all human beings—a life of flourishing, one that follows a pattern of psychological and physical growth, filled with enjoyment. But it is no less true that the concrete realization of such a pattern differs enormously from one person to another. It is not only the conative theory and hedonism that have the resources to cater to human differences—to recognize that what flourishing consists in, most specifically, for each person, varies from case to case and from one generation to another.

Our narrative about the proper course of human life stands behind assumptions we intuitively make about which course of action is better, for one's own good, than another. We will not taste a strawberry, no matter how sweet it is, if we know that it will make us blind. Why not? Because the exercise of sight, our enjoyment of the visible world, is one of the great goods we enjoy. Blindness would be a great loss, and a brief gustatory pleasure would not compensate for it. These sorts of comparisons are so trivial and obvious that we do not stop to think about them. We can produce such examples endlessly. Reflection on them is of little or no practical value, but it serves to remind us how confident we are not only about what is good, but about when one good is superior to another. Many other judgments would be far more difficult to make, and fortunately we rarely have to face them: which, for example, would we give up if we could have only one: the pleasures of sound or those of sight? It would be pointless to dwell on such difficult choices until we are forced to do so, and often the answers will vary from one person to another depending on the peculiarities of the particular course of life he has chosen so far.

Ages ago, before we human beings became language users, the kind of development that was good for each of us was, in many ways, utterly different from what it then became when language transformed our cognitive, affective, and social lives. Being nonlinguistic was not then the grave defect (if it was a defect)—the severe diminution in well-being—that it is now. There can be and have been smaller transformations in the components of human flourishing than this. Our way of conceptualizing the human mind can change, and that in turn can change the mind. For example, we talk now about the powers of the imagination in new ways: we want our children to develop these powers and to enjoy activities that give free rein to this mental faculty. That picture of healthy human development is not and has not been possessed by all individuals and all cultures. And those who think of the imagination as a faculty to be cultivated will of course try to cultivate it—their theory about what a healthy mind is will alter their minds and those of their children. Inventions, discoveries, and technology are also engines of change in our conception of what it is to flourish. Before we thought with numbers, our mathematical capacities lay dormant. Before there were chess pieces, no one could develop the combinatory, strategic, and geometric skills of a chess player. It is not far-fetched to think of each of these changes as not merely changes but as improvements. Perhaps they have been costless, or their costs have been minimal, and as a result human life has, on balance, been enriched. But the more important point is that some of the faculties and powers of the human mind may exist at certain times but not others; or at any rate the wherewithal for developing them may be available at certain times but not others. Our psychological potential, like our physical potential, is subject to alteration, and when that happens, the components of flourishing alter as well.

36. More Examples of What Is Good

Developmentalism is an attempt to answer two types of questions. First, what is it for something to be good for someone? Second, which things are good in this way? To the first question developmentalism replies: when it is good for S that P, that is because the occurrence of P is productive or part of flourishing. In response to the second, it specifies what flourishing consists in for this species or that. For a human being it consists in the maturation and exercise of certain cognitive, social, affective, and physical skills. But can we give a more concrete answer to the second question than that? Do we *need* one?

To see what is at issue, consider once again Ross's view that pleasure, knowledge, virtue, and the proper apportionment of pleasure to the virtuous are good.[10] That is his answer to a question—what kinds of things

10. Ross, *The Right and the Good*, pp. 134–141.

are good "sans phrase"?—that we have dismissed (sections 17, 21), but even so, we should note an enviable feature of his theory: he tells his readers in concrete detail what he believes they should want and pursue. In many cases we can recognize whether someone knows something. If it is knowledge that we want, we should study the sciences, read reliable authors of nonfiction, open our eyes to the world, and so on. Similarly, we can recognize what pleasure is and have a good idea about how to get it. And we can recite a long list of virtues, although there may be some qualities whose credentials as virtues are in doubt. In any case, no one should complain that Ross has not been specific enough about what is good.

The conative theory can be construed as an answer to only the first of our two questions. To that first question, it replies: when it is good for S that P, that is because P involves the fulfillment of a rational, properly informed, and reflective desire or plan that S has. But even though it proposes no answer to the second question, it would be unreasonable to hold that against the theory, for we know very well what we have to do to arrive at answers to that question. To know what is good for S, we need only find out what S wants or plans. That of course will not always be easy, but at least in a large number of cases, observation of a person's behavior or careful self-reflection will give us an answer. Since it is not every desire whose satisfaction is good, according to the conative theory, but only those that are rational and so on, we need to do a bit more work beyond observation or introspection to know what is good for someone. Even so, one of the attractions of the conative approach (section 30) is that it can easily be made determinate, and therefore can be easily applied to our everyday concerns. With it in hand, we have a concrete method for answering our second question.

It is reasonable to ask how well developmentalism does on that score. The answer is that we are filled with concrete, developmental ideas about what is good or bad for people—developmental in that what lies behind these ideas is the assumption that it is good for us to put into action the psychological and physical skills we began to acquire as children. What kind of jobs do we think of as bad jobs—bad, that is, for the person who does them? They are mindless, repetitive, emotionally stifling, socially isolating, physically debilitating tasks, devoid of anything that can be enjoyed. But with a moment's thought we can also give a long list of jobs that have at least something to offer to a worker in the very doing of them—if that worker is temperamentally suited to and qualified to perform them and she therefore enjoys her work. The powers of thought and feeling whose origin can be traced back to childhood education can be put into play by an extremely large number of social positions, and they are often sought partly for this reason and not only for the good they do for others. It is good for a doctor (and not only her patients) that she be successful in healing; good for a poet (and not only her readers) to write good poetry; good for an actress (and not only her audience) to inhabit convincing roles; good for a cook (and not only the restaurant-going public) to make delicious meals. We can think of countless cases of this sort, and all of them depend on our confidence that the exemplary performance of complex tasks that make use of our cognitive, affective, and social powers is good for the person who achieves that goal.

But it is not only well-defined social roles that have this duality of giving room to one's own good as well as that of others. For example, being a loving person, when this is not mere sentiment but is suffused with social intelligence, is an activity that brings into play a complex set of affective and cognitive powers that are directed at the well-being of others, but whose very exercise constitutes a good for the person who possesses them. When, for example, we occupy the role of a friend and perform that role well, we enjoy giving the people we like the help, comfort, and amusement they need. Of course, we think directly about their good and do not use them as mere instruments for our own self-improvement or material advantage. But we *like* doing things for them—not to do so would constitute a grave defect as a friend. And one reason we find this so enjoyable is that being a good friend is in some respects like having a good job: it offers abundant opportunities to be a comforter, a helper, a companion; and when we do these things, we put into play the sophisticated psychological skills that gradually took shape as we emerged from childhood. For similar reasons, someone can set his heart on becoming a parent: it is for his own good that he wants to raise a family, not as a way to have helpers in his old age, but because he thinks he will be a good father and he wants to develop and exercise the caring skills called forth by the love of children. Another example: a single person may want to find someone to marry in part because he thinks that the complex affective and interactive skills needed by a good marriage partner are ones that he will enjoy acquiring and exercising.

Athletic activity is immensely enjoyable because of the complex physical and psychological skills it requires. It is a form of physical flourishing, but it often involves acute mental and emotional skills as well—quick decisions, perseverance, control over anger, and so on. But uncompetitive physical activity can also be enjoyed as a form of physical flourishing. Swimming well is an exercise in physical grace and vigor. A walker can find pleasure in the very act of walking—that too is a complex, learned activity, as we are reminded when we are recovering from an injury or disability. Someone too old to walk any longer has suffered not only the loss of a means of transportation, but the enjoyment of the use of his legs.

There are many other ways, besides putting our bodies in motion, to take pleasure in actualizing our physical powers. We flourish as observers of objects and users of our eyes when we become conscious of the world as a thing to be looked at and studied. We enjoy looking more carefully at nature or at beautifully crafted artifacts. We appreciate tastes, sounds, smells; we classify, study, and mix them. All these learned activities are ways in which we exercise control over and enjoy the use of our sensory modalities. To lose any of them—to become blind, or deaf, or unable to taste and smell—is not merely to lose instrumental means. The ability to take in and meet the world by means of the senses is one of the powers that a healthy baby should have not only because she will need them to achieve her ends, but because the development and exercise of these powers are among the components of a flourishing human life.

These platitudes are not ones that a conative theory or hedonism can properly explain. Consider someone who is born with irreversible blindness and who never develops a desire or a plan to see. The conative theory will count this as a misfortune if that person develops plans the successful execution of which would be facilitated by sight. But that theory cannot say: it would be noninstrumentally good for him to have the use of his eyes. It must take that same stand toward someone who is born with an incapacity for affective or linguistic responses to other people. Its only access to the notion of good or bad fortune is through the medium of desires and plans; it has no way to express the ideas that are so easily expressed when we make use of the notion of a flourishing human life, fully equipped with all the powers and faculties that a human being can have. Strict hedonism is similarly handicapped by its need to account for the badness of blindness solely by appealing to the intensity of visual pleasures: it holds that it is that pleasure alone that explains why it is good for someone to be able to see. But we do not value the enjoyment of our eyes because of the intensity of the feeling we get from seeing. (In fact, this is normally a rather calm pleasure.) What is good for us is the activity we enjoy—looking at objects—and not just the feeling we get from that activity.

The developmental theory gives a longer and more complex answer to the question "What sorts of things are good for human beings?" than Ross gives to his question, "What sorts of things are good?" He names four, and he thinks there are no others. Developmentalism, by contrast, begins with a root idea and sketches in broad strokes what well-being is: it is flourishing, and in the case of human beings, that consists in the exercise of cognitive, social, affective, and physical skills. That is a mere sketch; if it could not be filled in, it would be useless. There is no mechanical or systematic procedure for filling it in; we simply proceed inductively with examples that can be multiplied indefinitely. Nor is the list we produce meant for all time. Vocations, sports, social roles come into existence and can go out of existence, and even while they abide, the human skills they put into play can vary from one generation to another.

Our survey of concrete human goods has been, by implication, also a way of saying what sorts of things are bad for people. What is non-instrumentally harmful to a human being? We have already given some examples: blindness, and any other loss of a sense; the loss of limbs, or anything else that would diminish our physical enjoyments; extended solitary confinement; the loss of language; the blunting of all affective response; cognitive deterioration; and so on. Some of these harms can be self-imposed: one can, for example, want to blind oneself, and one can willingly refrain from preventing the onset of blindness. What someone wants and seeks, with perfect information and careful reflection, will nonetheless be bad for him, if it impedes the flourishing of his faculties. (More will be said about "un-flourishing" in sections 38–39, 41–43.)

37. Appealing to Nature

Is developmentalism an attempt to base ethics on nature? So it may seem. It says: look to the flourishing of plants and animals. It also says: look to the powers we have at birth—the powers, in other words, that nature has given to us. That might be interpreted to mean that according to developmentalism, what is good for us is whatever is natural for us, and whatever we are born with must be used, because nature does nothing in vain.

If developmentalism had to rely on such crude ideas as these, it would be unacceptable. But it does not need them, or anything resembling them. Facts about plants, animals, and natural powers do play a role in the thinking that lies behind developmentalism. But it is important to see that there is nothing controversial or exceptionable in the use it makes of those facts.

Here is how they are used. Begin with some concrete and commonly accepted examples of what it is good for people to do. When, for example, we enjoy eating good food with good friends, and spending the evening dancing, that is good for us. When someone loves writing, does so with flair, skill, and imagination, and enjoys a successful career as a writer, that is good for him. Now, *why* are these activities good for those who engage in them? What is it about them that justifies calling them good? The conative theory is one attempt to answer that question, and it has failed; the fulfillment of desires and plans is not even part of the account of what makes these things good. Hedonism is another failed theory, though it contains a partial truth. What both theories try to do, but do poorly, is to find some common feature that good things have that explains their goodness.

Developmentalism is an attempt to do a better job of this. It takes such examples as these as genuine cases of people doing what is good for themselves and proposes an explanation of their goodness. Admittedly, the diners, the dancers, and the writer are all doing what they want. They are all enjoying themselves. But when we examine those common features, we find that they do not work in other cases. Developmentalism proposes an alternative: when we enjoy food, when we interact with friends, when we dance, when we love language, we are enjoying the use of skills that originate in our inherent powers and emerge more fully through a process of training.

In a way, there is an appeal to nature here, but its role must be properly understood. Developmentalism does not begin with an a priori commitment to the idea that whatever nature gives us must be good for us. Rather, it finds it plausible that these enjoyments—of food, friends, dancing, writing—are good; and, like any other theory of well-being, it looks for unifying elements among these examples. Nature comes into the picture at this stage: our sense of taste, our sociability, our physical capacities, our language skills were the origins that led, eventually, to such sophisticated activities as dinner with friends, dancing, and writing. We say that nature gave us something good in all these cases, but in saying that, we are standing in judgment of nature, not bowing down to it as the arbiter or determinant of what is good. We are free to arrive at the conclusion that some natural powers are bad for the person who has them.[11] In fact, we might even say that about many or all of them. If we did arrive at that conclusion, the education of children would have to become a process of destroying their psychological propensities and replacing them with something entirely different. (Could such a project ever succeed?) But, as it happens, there is no reason to suppose that nature has gone so badly astray. What it has given us we can, at least for the most part, make some good use of.

When developmentalism appeals to the notion of flourishing and reminds us that plants, animals, and humans all can be said to flourish, it is not proposing the foolish idea that we humans should learn a lesson about how to live by looking to the way other living things do it.[12] It does not claim that we should make use of our natural capacities because, after all, that is what lions and roses do. Its idea, rather, is that it would be foolish to *begin* with the assumption that whereas it is good for

11. If, for example, one finds that one's sexual organs impede one's affective and social powers, one would be justified in altering them. In doing so, one transforms part of one's body (and impedes the powers one could exercise through their use) in order to enjoy the exercise of affective and social powers that one correctly judges to be central components of well-being.

12. Philippa Foot argues that a free-riding wolf is defective (*Natural Goodness*, p. 16), but it would be an illegitimate appeal to animal behavior as a model for human behavior to infer (as she does not) that a free-riding human being is *therefore* similarly defective. A further question is whether one should say quite simply, as she does, that a social animal that fails to help others and, in doing so, benefits itself really is defective. It is tempting, rather, to relativize: to say, that is, that such an animal is defective when judged by one standard (the good of other animals), but not by another (its own good). Since there is no basis for saying that an animal should benefit others even at some cost to itself, absolute judgments about whether free riding is a defect are baseless. This is not so in the human case: here we correctly assume that some degree of sacrifice for the good of others is reasonable and that noncooperation is therefore a defect. Note, further, that the standard by which we normally evaluate domestic animals is *human* good: a good dog is one that serves its owner's needs. Therefore, it is not necessarily good for a dog to be a good dog. Nothing can be inferred from this about whether it is good to be a good person. For a general discussion of the difficulties of basing ethics on biology, see Philip Kitcher, "Biology and Ethics." The concept of free riding is given precision in discussions of collective action. For a general overview, see Russell Hardin, "The Free Rider Problem."

all other living things to flourish, it is not good for *us* to flourish. After all, flourishing consists in the growth and development of the capacities of a living thing: why should that be good for plants and animals, but not for us? The claim that flourishing is bad for us would have to be supported by arguments to the effect that, when we consider what our natural capacities are, we find that the development of many or all of them would undermine our chances to obtain what is good for us to have. What theory of good, what common ideas about what is good, would allow such arguments to succeed? Only a complicated religious story would do: God once gave all human beings good natural capacities, but we sinned; as part of our punishment we have been given some natural capacities that are bad for us to develop; to prepare ourselves for the life to come, we had better do what we can to impede those natural propensities; and so on. (Note how important it is for this account to appeal to an afterlife: impeding the growth of our powers makes sense, even according to this religious outlook, only as a means to some further goal.) If we do not accept this story, or some metaphysical equivalent to it, we have no reason to resist the idea that flourishing is good for human beings. That already plausible thesis about our species is made all the more plausible because it is an instance of a more general truth: it is good for *any* living thing to flourish. And, having accepted that general idea, we are committed to saying that the specific activities or processes that constitute flourishing are good for us.

The idea behind developmentalism is not the absurd thesis that we should set aside any thoughts we have about human good and substitute for them a theory of good derived from animal behavior. Rather, it rests on the plausible assumption that a theory is strengthened when it is made more general and systematic. If a theory of goodness can fit its account of human well-being into a larger framework that applies to the entire natural world, that gives it an advantage over any theory that holds that "G is good for S" is one kind of relationship for human beings and a different kind for all other creatures.

38. Sensory Un-flourishing

A theory about what is good is not, all by itself, a theory about what is bad. It can easily seem otherwise, because we might suppose, unreflectively, that what is bad for someone is simply the absence of what is good for him. If that were so, there would be no further work to do in constructing a theory of badness beyond working out a theory of goodness; we would simply add one more sentence, saying: "And when these states of affairs, which are good for S, do not obtain, that is bad for S." Thinking about hedonism should be enough to show that this cannot be right. Hedonism holds that what is bad for someone is not the absence of pleasure but the presence of pain. A state of affairs that brings no pleasure is not good, but neither is it bad.

Even so, it might be thought that all the important work has been done once one has said what is good and what it is for something to be good. Should it not be immediately apparent, to anyone who has worked through these issues, which things are bad? Good and bad are contraries; so too, according to ordinary ways of thinking, are pleasure and pain. If one supposes that pleasure is good, it should not take much thinking to arrive at the conclusion that pain is bad. Similarly, if one holds that the only good is the fulfillment of one's wishes and plans, then not much further thought is needed to arrive at the idea that the only thing that is bad is having a wish or plan that is not fulfilled.

What should developmentalism say about what is bad for human beings? It might be thought that, for it, what is bad must consist in the absence of what is good, not the presence of something opposite to what is good. There is no English word that would normally be counted as an opposite to "flourishing." Furthermore, what is bad for a plant are the many ways in which it can fail to do the things in which flourishing consists—to grow, or to produce the foliage that belongs to healthy specimens of its species, and so on. That might lead us to suppose—mistakenly, as we will see—that developmentalism must say the same about what is bad for *any* living thing. What is bad for a human being, then, would be the nonoccurrence of any state of affairs that is good for all human beings. If, for example, it is good for a child to enjoy his exploration of the world, then it is bad for a child if he does not explore the world, or does not enjoy doing so. In fact, that does not sound unreasonable. It would be implausible to say that if a child does not explore the world it is neither good nor bad for him. He ought to be exploring the world because that is good for him, and it is bad for him if he does not. Similarly, if one is a swimmer who loves to swim regularly, then any injury that makes one unable to swim, or any loss of access to places where one can swim, is bad—not merely not good.

But to move entirely in this direction would be a serious mistake. Of course, developmentalism should say that *among* the things that are bad for us are those that in some way interfere with states of affairs that are good for us. But it must not stop there. Like hedonism, it should work with three categories: good, bad, and indifferent. Again, like hedonism, it should put certain pains—we will soon say which—in the bad category. But there are many other bad things besides certain pains and impediments to getting what is good.

Consider the sensory aspect of human life, and think of all the ways in which we can suffer from unpleasant disorders besides physical pain. We can feel so cold that we shiver uncontrollably. We can feel overheated, parched, hungry, thirsty, dizzy, nauseated, exhausted. We may be subjected to foul tastes and smells, horrible sounds, and blinding lights. On any reasonable account of what is bad for a human being (and much that is said here would apply to other animals as well), these are all bad for us. Of course, many of them interfere with our ability to go about our normal business, and so they are bad in part because they deprive us of what is good. But that is not the only reason that can be given for being averse to them. These are, in themselves, ways of feeling bad. They should be counted as components of un-flourishing, as bad developments or disturbances in a human life. Hedonism is partly right: there is a sensory component to human well-being, and there is a way of faring poorly that is not just the absence of doing well.

When we list, as we just did, the many kinds of unpleasant sensations that we can experience, we are guided to a large extent by various features of the human body. We can be made to experience what is distressing and unpleasant through our eyes, ears, throats, tongues, stomachs, flesh, and so on. When we feel bad in these various ways, the powers of these various organs are being used to ill effect. What we feel is not pleasure—something positive—but, rather, various forms of distress or unpleasantness—something negative. We are not merely in neutral territory as sensory beings. In that sense, the sensory system we have been given by nature is disordered and not functioning as it should, from the point of view of our well-being; rather, it is made to go in the opposite direction. These disturbances could therefore be called forms of un-flourishing. We might say that our auditory system is un-flourishing when, by means of it, we take in noises that we cannot abide; or, rather, that we are un-flourishing, as auditory beings, when this happens. We are in this respect sinking into negative territory: un-flourishing.

The sensory experiences under discussion—physical pain, nausea, bone-chilling cold—would not be bad for us to feel were they not things we dislike. (The physical conditions that cause these feelings—a burn, a virus, a low temperature—would continue to have bad consequences even if we did not dislike the feelings; but we are not discussing the instrumental badness of what accompanies these feelings.) In that sense, it is partly because we dislike them that they are bad for us. It would be a mistake, however, to suppose that their badness is to be explained solely by our reacting to them with dislike, and not even partially by the quality of the sensation to which we react with aversion. The quality of that experience—what nausea, for example, feels like—is what we react to when we try to avoid feeling it, and we justify our negative reaction on the basis of that sensation. There is no reason to say that the explanation for the badness of what we experience has nothing to do with the quality of our experience, and to make it consist solely in the reactive sentiment of disliking that experience.[13]

The things we dislike differ enormously, and our disliking them is sometimes a reaction we try to correct because it has no justification. A child may dislike helping his sister, but his dislike is not something we cater to. We can reasonably say not only that he should help his sister, whether he likes doing so or not, but also that it is bad for him to dislike helping her—that his relationship with her would be better for him if he were to overcome his distaste. Similarly, someone may dislike the way a drink tastes upon first trying it. That may be an unfortunate reaction, and it might be worth his while to learn to relish the drink. It would have been better for him had he not immediately reacted negatively to the drink. But when we think about pain, nausea, dizziness, exhaustion, and so on, our attitude is that these things are to be disliked because of the way they feel. Admittedly, if we could somehow train ourselves not to dislike them, they would no longer be bad for us. But the fact that their badness rests on a subjective condition does not by itself constitute a reason to remove that condition. It is not bad for us to dislike them. Our dislike is a justified reaction to the way they feel. So there is no rea-

13. Contrast my view with Christine Korsgaard's discussion on this topic: "The painfulness of pain consists in the fact that these are sensations which we are inclined to fight" (*The Sources of Normativity*, p. 147) and "Pain is nearly always bad . . . because the creatures who suffer from it object to it" (ibid., p. 154). The distinction I am drawing—between the reason pain is bad and a necessary condition of its being bad—is one instance of a general distinction (between disfavoring and disabling) that Jonathan Dancy emphasizes in *Ethics without Principles* (pp. 41–45).

son to stop disliking them. In many cases, needless to say, it would be impossible to stop disliking them. But that truth should not be confused with another: there is no reason to stop.

It should also be kept in mind, throughout this discussion, that we are setting aside the instrumental benefits of reacting aversively to pain and other negative stimuli. It would be dangerous to stop disliking the pain induced by a fire: we would not pull our arm back from the flame, and we would lose its use. But when one's arm is being painfully burned, that is bad not only because it is disabling, but also because of the way it feels. When someone is tortured by having his arms and legs broken and then is killed, something very bad happens to him before his death, and that badness cannot be explained simply in terms of the loss of his capacities. It would be good for him if somehow he could bring himself not to dislike the pain. Assuming that he cannot, what he is made to experience is bad for him.

What is it about pain, dizziness, nausea, and other such sensations that justifies us in classifying them as things that are bad for us? One way to answer this question is to say: the way they feel. That is what I have been insisting upon. But we can give a fuller answer by fitting that reply into a larger framework. What is good or bad for a living thing always has something to do with its closeness to or distance from living the kind of life available to a flourishing member of its species. Animals that have perceptual systems do well if the organs and mental processes that are part of those systems operate well, and those animals fare well, as sensory beings, to the extent that they have certain kinds of experiences and not others. Just as the deterioration of the eyes constitutes one kind of disorder for an animal—an organic disorder—so too is a disease that causes pain whenever the animal tries to use its eyes, or makes it vomit whenever it eats. Similarly, normal human beings react aversively to certain sensory stimuli, and their aversion is caused by the quality of the experience they have. There is no reason to set aside those experiences when we consider how well or badly their lives are going. The kind of sensory experience human beings have is one aspect of their lives that is appropriate to evaluate when we ask ourselves what is good or bad for them. And if an experience is one that they have good reason to dislike, because of the way it feels, and the way it feels gives them no reason to like it, then having that sensation is reasonably considered a kind of disorder, a sensory pathology, an untoward state of affairs in their lives, and therefore something that is bad for them.

Not every occurrence of the sensations we have discussed here—nausea, pain, dizziness, and so on—is bad, even to some extent. Some children love to make themselves dizzy. Pain is sometimes so mild and brief that it is not minded at all. Other pains might be welcomed as an ingredient of a complex experience that is no less joyful than it is painful. Like the bitterness of a bittersweet food, their presence is not regretted at all. Other pains are not welcomed, but neither are they avoided, and reasonably so. Some women, for example, choose to give birth without taking medication that would reduce the intense pains of labor because they welcome the full and natural experience of their bodies. What we experience when we are in pain is permeated with the emotions we are feeling at the same time, and when those emotions are joyous and the pains willingly encountered, they can lose the badness they would otherwise have and become not bad at all, despite their intensity. Not all pain is bad pain—pain that is bad for us.

Nonetheless, in a great many cases, the sensations we feel when things go awry in our bodies—chills, exhaustion, nausea, dizziness, pain—are pathologies of the sensory system. When they occur, we, as sensory animals, are not merely in a neutral state; we are not merely missing something good—the flourishing of our faculties—but are in a state of un-flourishing.[14]

39. Affective Flourishing and Un-flourishing

Our picture of how a human being should develop is, in part, a picture of the growth of emotional response. To be completely devoid of affect— to live a life that contains no joy, no love, no laughter—would be extremely bad. One would be missing experiences that any human life should have. A disease or injury that robbed a child of the ability to have emotional interactions with his social world would be a great evil. But of course that does not mean that whenever we feel an emotion of any kind, that is good. There are negative emotions: anger, sorrow, fear, despondency, shame, guilt, disgust, frustration, exasperation, anxiety. What is meant by calling them negative? Like the sensations discussed in the previous section (of pain, cold, heat, dizziness), they have a certain feel to them, and that feeling is experienced as a kind of tension or

---

14. I have rejected in this section my earlier thesis (advanced in "Desire and the Human Good") that pain is not intrinsically bad.

turbulence: they are burdensome, upsetting, stressful. By contrast, positive emotions—joy, laughter, love, wonder, admiration, pride—are accompanied by a sense of buoyancy, expansion, and delight. Emotions are like sensations in that they admit of positive and negative valence. Their sensation-like aspect is precisely what gives them that valence. It is not a tautology to say, "A positive emotion is good." To call it positive is to remark on what it feels like; to call it good is to evaluate it.

A simple theory of what is good or bad in the emotional life of a human being would say: whenever someone feels a positive emotion, that is good for him, because of the way it feels; whenever one feels a negative emotion, that is bad, because of the way it feels. After all, *sensations* can be good or bad because of the way they feel; emotions are experienced as well, and the way they are experienced seems to be a proper grounding for classifying them as good or bad.

The idea that all positive emotions are good and all negative emotions bad may sound too simple to be true, but we should be careful to reject it for the right reasons if we reject it at all. What counterexamples can be proposed to defeat it? Consider sorrow. It is a matter of common sense to think that when someone you love dies, you *should* feel sorrow—at any rate, some degree of sorrow, for some period of time. But even if we accept that piece of common sense, that would not by itself justify rejecting the simple thesis. That thesis holds that whenever one feels a negative emotion, that is bad *to some extent* for the person who feels it. So a defender of the simple thesis can say, in response to our counterexample, that although it is good *on balance* to react with sorrow to the death of a loved one, it is nonetheless bad to some degree to react in this way. That, he might say, is because more harm than good will be done if no sorrow is felt. His idea might be that when one suppresses all sorrow and does not permit oneself to respond in this normal way, one's mental life eventually becomes disordered, and one's ability to cope with one's social world is severely diminished. The sorrow is still there in another form, not consciously felt but nonetheless causing trouble. Better, then, to undergo a catharsis: feel the sorrow, bad though that is, because that is a small price to pay when one considers the psychological costs of not feeling it.

The psychological theory that lies behind this defense of the simple thesis may or may not be true; we need not try to assess it here. What we should do instead is ask why we should believe that it is even to some extent bad for us to feel sorrow. The defender of the simple thesis will reply: because it is a negative emotion. That is a remark about the way the emotion presents itself to us, the deflationary way it feels, the bodily sensations that give sorrow its peculiar color and texture. Looking at that experience, the defender of the simple theory says: feeling that way is bad for one. This is precisely the kind of argument we endorsed in the preceding section when we discussed pain and other sensations. We agreed that when these sensations are disliked, they are bad—not solely because we dislike them, but because of the way they feel. Since that thesis about sensations was accepted earlier, it might be thought that a similar thesis about our emotional lives should also be accepted. But there are important dissimilarities between the two cases.

Recall, to begin with, that we left room for the existence of pains and other sensations that are not bad. Pains can be welcomed, or tolerated, as ingredients in a complex experience. Something similar is true for emotions. The sorrow one feels, no less than physical pain, can be tolerated or even welcomed. One can want sorrow to come, as one takes in one's loss; one can be relieved and glad when it does come—not because one thinks of it as a price one must pay to avoid even greater future harms, but because it would be a debility to be incapable of feeling sorrow or other emotions that express one's rational assessment of one's situation. Someone whom one has loved is now gone forever; someone it was good to be with will never be present again. If one makes that judgment, it is healthy to experience the feeling, negative though it is, that normally accompanies it. Affectlessness would be an affliction for a human being; better to react to situations with the feelings that are appropriate to them. When that happens, one is functioning well, not badly, and the sorrowful feelings one experiences are not a debit in one's wellbeing, not even a small one. It is the absence of the person one loved that is the loss, not one's sorrow.

These remarks apply equally to other negative emotions. It is not necessarily bad, even to a small degree, to feel angry, guilty, ashamed, frustrated, anxious, or afraid. Fears that are planned—those provided by scary movies, for example—can enhance one's pleasure precisely because of their negativity. It is reasonable to want to be the sort of person who becomes angry when there is good reason to do so; to feel afraid in truly dangerous situations; to feel guilty or ashamed when one goes astray and needs to change. Of course, all these feelings are indeed bad whenever they are uncalled-for or excessive. If someone is angry but in fact nothing that merits his anger has happened, then there is nothing to be said in favor of his anger, and everything to be said against it: the very way anger feels makes it bad to feel, unless it is accompanied by other psychological factors that deprive it of the badness it would otherwise have.

So negative emotions are not necessarily bad to feel, even to some degree.[15] What of positive emotions: are they always good to feel, to some degree, simply by virtue of the way they feel? Consider again (section 8) someone whose sense of humor goes badly awry because of an injury, and who laughs uncontrollably and incessantly—with a genuine feeling of amusement—at what no one else finds funny. Or think of someone who feels a rush of passionate love for every human being he encounters. Such cases are similar to one we considered earlier: the dysfunctional child in a constant high administered by drugs (section 32). It is implausible to say that these conditions are good even to some degree, since we would do everything in our power to avoid them. It would not be better to gush constantly with some intense and inappropriate emotion than to be affectless. Being addicted to a single emotional high can be compared to a diet of nothing but rich chocolate, day in and day out. The taste of chocolate may remain, but whatever small pleasure it gives becomes sickening. Similarly, the positive feeling that is a component of obsessive laughter or love may abide, but that feeling no longer has any significance in one's life since it never varies and never forms a bond with another person. Positive emotions are good only when they are felt in a certain context. Their positivity—the buoyant, inflationary sense they bring—diminishes in value to nothingness when they no longer have their normal setting.

We should therefore reject the simple theory under consideration,

---

15. More precisely, the fact that an emotion is negative does not by itself make it bad for someone ever to feel it. This leaves open the possibility that there are certain negative emotions that are always bad to feel, not simply because they are negative, but because they possess other features as well. It might be said, for example, that it is bad to feel contempt for oneself; self-loathing is not something that one should, for one's own sake, feel at certain times and on certain occasions; rather, it should be entirely excluded from one's emotional repertoire. Similarly, it might be thought that such garden-variety emotions as envy, spite, and schadenfreude are always to be avoided because they poison one's relations with others. However we are to assess such claims, the case against antisocial emotions should not rest entirely on the point that the way they feel puts them into the category of negative emotions.

which holds that to some extent positive emotions are always good and negative emotions always bad, regardless of the context in which they are felt. It will not help matters, however, if we modify this universal generalization and turn it into a statement about what holds true for the most part. We have no reason to say, for example, that for the most part it is bad to feel angry, or sad, or guilty. If one has those feelings when they are appropriate, and with an appropriate intensity, why should it be supposed that it is bad to experience them? The status of negative sensations—dizziness, nausea, chills, and so on—is quite different. These are *always* bad, unless one manages to stop disliking them.

The simple theory should be replaced by the thesis that the negative emotions can be felt too often and the positive emotions too infrequently. To see what this idea amounts to, consider someone who is angry all the time; each day brings him a fresh reason to be angry, and he responds appropriately. Something in his life has gone wrong—and not only because there are unfortunate events to which his anger is a response, but also because too often he is experiencing (however justifiably) the emotion of anger. The negativity of that emotion does not by itself make it true that whenever one feels it, something bad is happening. Nonetheless, if anger fills someone's life, that is bad for him, and part of the explanation for this is that it is bad to have that feeling too often. It would certainly be better, for the sake of his emotional life, if he could change his environment so that the number of situations he encounters that call for justifiable anger are fewer. One reason for making such a change lies in the harmful physical effects of constant anger, but that cannot be the whole story. Anger is a negative emotion; it is not a pleasant feeling to experience. That by itself does not make it bad to feel on each and every occasion it is felt. But when the frequency of anger reaches a certain threshold, those bouts of anger, each appropriate to its occasion, are, taken as a group, bad. There is no saying exactly where that threshold lies. Certainly, constant anger is bad. But it is also bad to be angry almost all the time, or more often than not. More than occasional anger is bad, because of the way anger feels (section 44).

The same holds true for all the other negative emotions. To live in constant fear, or with constant sorrow, guilt, shame, envy, jealousy, or hatred, is bad. So too is a life devoid of positive emotions. It is bad to have little or no laughter, joy, affection, or tenderness in one's life, or never to experience a sense of happiness and well-being. These positive feelings may have beneficial consequences—one's body might be more resistant to some diseases if one has a generally positive outlook—but that is not the only reason to welcome them. Just as physical pain is bad because of the way it feels, so the warm affection we feel for others, or the robust sense of well-being that we can attain when all goes well, is in itself good for us to experience.

40. Hobbes on Tranquillity and Restlessness

If one thinks that human well-being consists solely in the quality of one's conscious experience, one may be led to a pessimistic conclusion because it can look as though the human mind cannot help being dissatisfied. We are propelled toward interaction with the world by some form of conation—goals, plans, acts of will, desires—but it seems to be built into the very nature of these forces that they are forms of dissatisfaction. To want is to be moved toward what one does not have; it involves the thought that one should not be where one currently is in time. It necessarily disrupts one's tranquillity, for if one were utterly at peace, one would not seek any change in one's situation. So Hobbes says: "*Continual success* in obtaining the things which a man from time to time desireth, that is to say, continual prospering, is that men call FELICITY; I mean the felicity of this life. For there is no such thing as perpetual tranquillity of mind, while we live here; because life itself is but motion, and can never be without desire, nor without fear, no more than without sense."[16] And later: "The felicity of this life, consisteth not in the repose of a mind satisfied. For there is no such *finis ultimus*, utmost aim, nor *summum bonum*, greatest good, as is spoken of in the books of the old moral philosophers. Nor can a man any more live, whose desires are at an end, than he, whose senses and imagination are at a stand. Felicity is a continual progress of the desire, from one object to another; the attaining of the former being still but the way to the latter."[17] This is what leads Hobbes, several lines later in this same chapter, to "put for a general inclination of all mankind a restless desire of power after power, that ceaseth only in death." (Compare this to the Duke in Shakespeare's

16. Hobbes, *Leviathan*, pt. 1, chap. 6 (emphasis in original).
17. Ibid., chap. 11.

Measure for Measure: "Happy thou art not [when alive]; / For what thou hast not, still thou striv'st to get, / And what thou hast, forget'st.")[18]

Surprisingly, Hobbes does not observe, in these remarks, that when we are conscious of the progress we are making toward the achievement of our goals, that gives us a certain amount of felt satisfaction. Nor does he make the more subtle point that we might even prolong our progress toward the completion of our goals because we are getting so much enjoyment from the use of our powers. (Think of a writer who keeps adding new chapters, putting off the day when he will no longer be working on his book.) He identifies the felicity of which we are capable with success, or an ongoing series of successes, not with awareness of progress toward success or the enjoyment of our skills. Nonetheless, the point that we can be pleased that we are moving toward our goals or exercising our talents does nothing to undermine his thesis that tranquillity is unavailable to us because of the nature of desire. Desire involves an awareness that a state of affairs that should obtain does not and thus disrupts our peace of mind.

What Hobbes is talking about is *unalloyed* tranquillity: complete contentedness with our condition as it presently is, and complete assurance that it will continue without end. We are not in that state of mind when we lack what we want; nor are we in it even when we get what we want, because new desires and goals immediately take the place of old ones. Restlessness and discontent are part of our nature. Hobbes can concede that we are capable of achieving some favorable mixture of tranquillity and distress. If we have adequate resources, we might have a high degree of confidence that our current desires will be fulfilled, but the very fact that they are not yet fulfilled, or that when they are fresh anxieties will arise, shows that our tranquillity is at best partial.

Hobbes's psychological observations, however acceptable they are as pictures of the human mind, are of no *normative* significance unless it is *better* for someone to experience unalloyed tranquillity than to have the kind of conscious experience that involves some degree of anxious concern. He does not argue for that thesis but merely assumes it, presum-

18. *Measure for Measure,* 3.1.21–23. Similarly, Raymond Geuss writes: "The complete satisfaction of desire is radically unstable, and even, to put it paradoxically, inherently unsatisfactory as a general human goal because any satisfaction of a given desire will give rise to a new desire" ("Happiness and Politics," p. 107).

ably because he thinks his readers will readily accept it. Perhaps that is because he takes it to be obvious to everyone that *all* negative forms of consciousness—all pain, discomfort, anxiety, fear, sorrow, and anger—are bad to some degree, and that it would be better for us to live a life entirely free of these experiences. But we have already seen why that general thesis should be rejected. Having rejected it, do we have any reason to suppose that a life of total tranquillity would be a good life for a human being?

In fact, we have good reason to reject that idea. Certain forms and degrees of adversity—circumstances that challenge us, give us obstacles to overcome, and thus pose impediments to the satisfaction of our desires—are universally recognized as desirable. We want some of our desires not to be too easily satisfied. A game that is too easy to play is no fun. A task that presents no difficulty is unchallenging. We are not disturbed by impediments to the satisfaction of our desires in these situations; we welcome them. Without them, we would lose all interest. Our anxiety over the possibility that we may fail is not a negative but a positive feature of these situations; it is a precondition of excitement. In fact, just as pleasure can be taken in fear, or pain, or dizziness, we can take pleasure in our anxiety, and not merely in the overcoming of obstacles. Periods of utter tranquillity, in which we are totally unmindful of anything that opposes us and enjoy that form of consciousness, may sometimes give us precisely the kind of relaxation that we need. But there is no reason to suppose that human life would be at its best if it contained nothing but that kind of pleasure, and that all other forms of consciousness are defective because they fall short of it. Hobbes invokes the ideal of a peak experience, a perfect form of consciousness, by comparison with which all other kinds must be judged partial failures because they are mere mixtures of good and bad features. In fact, he points out that we have no idea what our lives would be like if we had the kind of "felicity" by comparison with which all other forms of consciousness are defective. It would not be the "felicity of this life," he says, but of some other. Its pleasures are, he adds, "joys, that now are as incomprehensible, as the word of Schoolmen *beatifical vision* is unintelligible."[19]

Although certain forms of negative consciousness—grief and anger, for example—are ones that we reasonably would like to eliminate en-

19. Hobbes, *Leviathan*, pt. 1, chap. 6 (emphasis in original).

tirely or reduce to a minimum, that cannot be said about the condition we are in when we want something to be the case that is not yet the case. If we would like to be relieved of that kind of negativity in our affective life, we are, as Hobbes recognizes, hoping for the termination of the conditions of human life.

41. Flourishing and Un-flourishing as a Social Being

The components of well-being, we said earlier (section 35), are the various ways in which we enjoy our physical, sensory, affective, social, and cognitive powers. Notice that some of the points made in our discussion of *affective* flourishing and un-flourishing have consequences about the kind of *social* life it is best for us to have. To be filled with anger, hatred, and jealousy throughout one's life is no one's conception of a good life. The way we experience these emotions—their burdensomeness—gives us good reason to look for a way of living in which we do not feel them too often. One solution to that problem would be to live in total isolation from other human beings. But that would be like choosing blindness as a remedy for a painful eye disease: the pain will be gone, but so too will all enjoyment of the visual world. Having no social relations at all with other human beings will eliminate the problem of negative social emotions, but there is a better solution for those who can achieve it: to have affectionate and nonconflictual relationships with other people—relationships in which one feels warmly toward others and that seldom, if ever, give one reason to be angry or jealous. The degrees of emotional warmth and closeness of personal relationships vary enormously, ranging from the familiarity of a second self to the tepidness of civic cordiality. It is impossible to achieve intimacy with a great many. The best one can hope for is to share the deepest mutual affection—love—with a few, and to have some liking for or felt connection with everyone else who is not a mere stranger in one's social world. These sorts of relationships with others cannot be sustained for long unless one has achieved a certain kind of self-mastery and social intelligence. One must not merely experience certain warm feelings and sympathies, but learn how to express them and to become effective in one's efforts to treat others well (section 35).

Many of us would experience a strong sense of isolation, a feeling of loneliness, if we lived entirely apart from others. But our desire to avoid that feeling is not the only reason there is for choosing a way of living that brings us into relationships with others. While living in isolation, our feeling of loneliness might diminish over time, or even disappear entirely. Perhaps some people would not experience even a brief sense of isolation. Even so, the absence of affectionate relationships would be a diminution in well-being; those who are socially isolated are in one respect worse-off than others, just as the deafness of those who cannot hear is a loss for them. There may be compensating gains in the lives of isolated people (just as there sometimes are for those who do not hear), and they need not experience loneliness or a sense of loss. But they lack something that would be good for them to have.

Is it good to be loved, and not only to love? Good to be the recipient of affection somewhat less intense than love? Those who are dead can be loved, but they no longer flourish, and therefore it is not good for them that they continue to be loved. (That is no reason to stop loving them: section 67.) So we should change our question and ask instead: is it good for someone to *feel* the love or affection of others? More fully, is it good to perceive regularly and with pleasure the expressions and signs of love and affection?

This is something nearly everyone in fact wants, but consider someone who has rid himself of this desire. He genuinely does not care whether others love him or care for him. It is reasonable to doubt that it is psychologically possible for someone to maintain this attitude of indifference and at the same time feel some affection for others. If that is impossible, then such a person has indeed lost (if he ever possessed) the good that consists in loving others. But that would not show that the sense of being loved is itself an element of well-being, and that when one does feel loved one is, because of that very fact, better-off.

Such a person is indifferent to receiving human warmth, and so we should say the same thing about him that we would say about someone who is indifferent to the pleasures of physical warmth or to any other sensual pleasure. If one is unable to taste food with pleasure, or reacts to all food with indifference, that is a loss. If one does not enjoy the warmth of the sun or a fire, that is a loss. But it is no less a loss to be indifferent to receiving the affection of others. That is one way of being a chilly person, a person who does not participate in the pleasures of human interaction. (The other way is to have and express no affection for others.) The goodness of both giving and receiving affection is the reason we prize reciprocity in friendships. In these relationships each individual benefits in two mutually reinforcing ways, by demonstrating and enjoying the receipt of affection.

What if someone senses what he takes to be love or affection, but is mistaken in his perception? That is, he is not loved—he only thinks he is. He is not really living in a welcoming world, but he has the same kind of conscious experience as someone who does live in such a social environment. We should think of him as someone who possesses a simulacrum of a good, not the real thing. What is good for him is to perceive with pleasure that he is loved, and this he does not perceive, though he thinks he does. It is not merely a certain kind of consciousness that is good for us, but the operation of various powers. Someone who is only dreaming that he is swimming is not getting the good that comes when one really does swim with pleasure: he is not actually performing a graceful and exuberant feat of physical organization. Similarly, our lives as social beings flourish only if we really are loved and perceive this with pleasure. Being loved is not by itself good, for someone who is loved may not be conscious of being loved—he may even be dead. Nor is it good merely to be in a pleasant state of mind that is unconnected to reality (recall the example, used in section 32, of a constant high). Not every pleasure is good. The good of receiving love must be understood as what one has when one perceives with pleasure that one is loved.[20]

---

20. I offer some further reflections. No one is made worse-off merely by virtue of the fact that others denigrate him behind his back or think poorly of him. (Of course, such talk and such thoughts can have further consequences that do in fact make him worse-off.) We do not bring about something bad for a villain merely by thinking to ourselves, or saying to each other, that he is a bad person. (Otherwise, we could punish known criminals without having to apprehend them.) Being despised by the world at large is not by itself a harm. But if someone is the victim of *unfair* evaluations—if he is falsely thought to be a bad person and does not receive the esteem he deserves—then someone who perceives the unfairness of those evaluations has good reason to oppose them, because of the general harm undeserved blame can cause. If, for example, an admirable head of state is unfairly called a tyrant, the general acceptance of that accusation can interfere with the good he does. There is even good reason to oppose slanderous statements made about those who are no longer living. The general acceptance of the charge that Abraham Lincoln was a tyrant, for example, would have significant consequences for contemporary political life. Although those who are no longer alive can be treated unjustly in this way, it is not they who are harmed by such treatment, but others. Fictional characters can also be unfairly treated by literary critics, and it can be worthwhile to oppose such treatment because our ideas about the representation of imaginary individuals can have consequences for the way we treat real people. Furthermore, since we can reasonably admire and even love historical figures (section 67) and fictional characters, and such emotions are components of affective well-being, defending them against unfair criticism can serve our own well-being (although that is not what we aim at when we come to their defense).

42. Cognitive Flourishing and Un-flourishing

The absence or deterioration of basic mental competencies—to use language, to deliberate, to order one's experience into a meaningful narrative, to recognize people and remember events—is a loss. Psychiatric disorders are exactly that: disorders—bad for the person who suffers through them. That does not mean that the mere possession and use of basic mental skills is noninstrumentally good. But taking pleasure in their use certainly is. Someone who delights in using language, solving mental puzzles or practical problems, telling stories, or making things is, to some extent, doing well precisely because he enjoys the exercise of his cognitive powers. It is not simply his being pleased by something or other that is good. Nor is it the mere use of his mind. But when the process of using one's mind for this or that purpose, or for no purpose at all, is enjoyed, that is good.

Ross, we have noted several times (sections 16, 17, 22), holds that knowledge is good—good, as he insists, "sans phrase." To support that thesis, he asks his readers to envisage two states of the universe that are similar in all respects, except that in the first "the persons . . . had a far greater understanding of the nature and laws of the universe than those in the other." "Can anyone doubt," he asks, "that the first would be a better state of the universe?"[21] His claim is that it is better *that* the first universe exist, regardless of which facts its knowers know; but he does not say that it is better *for* anyone that he has knowledge. He should be given credit for not saying that, for the thesis that knowing P, regardless of the content of P, is noninstrumentally good for the knower is utterly implausible. Many of the propositions we know to be true (that such-and-such is someone's telephone number, for example) would be of interest to us, and would be worth calling to mind, only if we could make use of them; and if we could, that of course would show only that our knowledge of them is instrumentally valuable. If we do think of knowledge as intrinsically worth having, what we are likely to have in mind is the thrilling *process* of acquiring a body of knowledge about a subject that fascinates us—not the mere *state* of possessing that knowledge. It would not be absurd for someone to say that coming to understand a branch of mathematics is good in itself because of its intrinsic beauty.

21. Ross, *The Right and the Good*, p. 139, and see also p. 145.

But even that claim, though hardly absurd, is open to question: if a student learns the subject, but is utterly bored by it, has he done something that is good for him? When we change the example and consider instead a student who *loves* learning a subject, it becomes far more plausible to say that this is a good thing for him to do.

It is striking that Ross takes it to be utterly obvious that the first state of the universe is better than the second. In effect, he holds that it is unarguably true that one should acquire knowledge of a proposition, regardless of its content; and he takes this to be self-evident without affirming that it is good *for* anyone to acquire that bit of knowledge. But surely one can reasonably doubt that one should acquire a piece of knowledge when it is not good *for* anyone—oneself or anyone else— that one do so.

Ross, it should be remembered (section 23), appeals to "a widely accepted classification of the elements in the life of the soul" to lend further support to his conception of what is good: cognition, feeling, and conation. Knowledge, he thinks, is good because it is the ideal state of cognition. But why should we agree that it is a better state for the mind to be in than all others? Chess players, crossword enthusiasts, readers of novels, poets: they are not seeking knowledge of facts, but when they enjoy these activities, their minds are in good condition—no worse condition, at any rate, than that of knowers of facts. A theory of well-being should be catholic: the cognizing mind flourishes not merely when it enjoys learning what is so and why it is so, but also when it is pleasurably engaged in all kinds of complex problem-solving and language-using activities. It is only when pleasurable cognition impedes further development that it loses its status as something that is good (section 44).

Inquisitiveness about the world is one of the necessary elements in any infant's kit of cognitive and affective tools. Properly nourished, it leads to all manner of intellectual play and the enjoyment of learning; a child or adult who has lost the curiosity he once had is not flourishing as a cognitive creature. The argument is not that we have certain powers and inclinations when we are young, and therefore their development must be good for us. Rather, we notice, as we systematize our thoughts about what is good, that they fall into a pattern, and the notion of an inherent power waiting to be developed plays an organizing role in that process of systematization (section 37). An adult's enjoyment of complex cognitive skills and the wonder he feels at the world he comes to understand can be seen as the flowering of a child's curiosity, and the narrative of human well-being in this way follows the same developmental pattern found throughout nature.[22]

43. Sexual Flourishing and Un-flourishing

Our physical, sensory, affective, social, and cognitive powers seldom operate in isolation from each other. Very few things we do employ only one of them. A good example of the way in which they can be brought together is provided by the enjoyment of our sexual powers. Human sexuality at its best is as much in the head as in the body; it is an intricate cognitive, social, affective, sensory, and physical interaction with the world. An injury or disease that prevented a child from developing sexually would be precisely that—an injury or disease, and not a mere physical alteration that left him no worse- or better-off.

It does not follow that every sexual pleasure is good for the person who feels it. To see why this is so, we should begin by recalling one of the conclusions we arrived at when we discussed hedonism (section 33). When a state of affairs is good for someone, it must bring pleasure, but its pleasure does not on its own explain why it is good. If someone is pleased, we must know something about the cause or object of that pleasure before we can determine whether it should, for his sake, be given a place in his life.

Someone who thinks that all sexual pleasure is good may accept this. His idea will be: the very fact that someone's pleasure is *sexual* is enough

22. Compare this account to T. M. Scanlon's discussion of the intrinsic value of scientific knowledge (*What We Owe to Each Other*, pp. 90–94). He too assigns an important role to curiosity about the natural world, and he sees "the highly developed capacities of many individuals" (ibid., p. 94) as among the "rational responses to our justified curiosity" (ibid., p. 93). "A person who responds to nature in this way is right to do so, and someone who fails to have this response is missing something" (ibid.). Elsewhere he says: "One cannot respond to every value or pursue every end that is worthwhile, and a central part of life for a rational creature lies in selecting those things that it will pursue. It thus makes a difference whether an aim has been adopted" (ibid., p. 119). Someone who is uncurious about nature is missing something valuable; the same is true, Scanlon would add, of someone who is indifferent to friendship (ibid., pp. 88–90, 123–124). But every life fails to respond to certain values, and so someone lacking an interest in nature or friendship is not necessarily defective—provided what he pursues is worthwhile (and no less valuable than are science and friendship). How is that judgment to be grounded? How should we construct a list of things that are valuable, and what entitles something to be on the list? The developmental approach to well-being is an attempt to answer those questions.

to show that it should, for his sake, be given a place in his life. But why should the mere categorization of a pleasure as sexual be sufficient to secure this conclusion? To see what is at issue, consider someone whose sole sexual pleasure is rape, and who spends much of his time planning and carrying out sexual assaults. Is it good for him to succeed because when he does so he feels pleasure? Of course, what he does is odious because of the great harm it does to the victim; that is not at issue. Our question is whether we are forced to the conclusion that what he does is beyond criticism, from the point of view of what is better or worse for him, simply because the pleasure he gets is *sexual* pleasure.

We should wish that this person had had a better course of sexual development, and we should hope that we can change him, so that he enjoys sex but in a different way. If one suspected that one's teenage son was developing the sexual psychology of a rapist, one would be very worried indeed about his future well-being, and one would try to change his direction so that he could engage in a better form of sexual activity. Why so? Because there are so many better kinds of sexual pleasure for him to feel. Rape is a pleasure infused with feelings of hostility, anger, or rage—all burdensome feelings. It is devoid of the sexual pleasure that consists in giving sexual pleasure. So it lacks the positive affective and social aspects that other forms of sexual experience have. If possible, it should be replaced by a sexual orientation that allows someone to combine, in a single experience, receiving sexual pleasure from and giving sexual pleasure to someone for whom he has some liking—if possible, someone he loves. We should call the rapist's pleasure a bad pleasure, meaning by this that it is worse by far than the many kinds of sexual pleasure that are good for him to have.

In certain situations—for example, when someone is in prison—the pleasure of rape might be the only kind of interpersonal sexual pleasure available. Rape would combine the pleasures of domination and of sexual release; and in a prison no better kind of sexual life may be available. But accepting that point is entirely compatible with those made in the preceding paragraph. We would not wish that kind of sexual life upon anyone; it is one of the aspects of prison life that makes it horrid. That rape is, in certain situations, better for the rapist than something else does not show that it is, in general, good to some degree for someone to be a rapist. In the setting of a prison, the extinction of all sexual desire might be a better outcome for someone than its persistence if that opened space for other activities (studying in the prison library, for example). That is certainly not the kind of judgment we should make about sexual pleasure in general. The extinction of sexual desire, in favorable circumstances—that is, when there are attractive and likeable people to whom one can give and from whom one can receive sexual pleasure—would be a great loss.

It is not only in prison that one would reasonably wish for the extinction of sexual desire. When it is never sated, but always felt as a burdensome and alien force that distracts one's attention and displaces one's affective and cognitive life, it is something one can reasonably wish to be without. Fortunately, eros is not always like that.

Hedonism (section 32) must hold that the intensity and duration of pleasure is all that matters in sexual life; and since sexual pleasures can be extremely intense, hedonism goes badly astray here. Assume that the pleasures of the rapist are no less intense than any other kind of sexual pleasure. Then the hedonist ought to say that, for one's own good, one should put rape on the menu of sexual encounters that one has. Such a rapist would have no hostility toward his victims: he would rape as a matter of principle, and not out of anger or frustration. Of course, a utilitarian hedonist would take into account the great harm done to those who are raped. But he would have to say that it would be to everyone's advantage to engage in rape to some degree—if one could get away with it.

Similarly, a conative theory would have to say that if someone prefers to lead the life of a rapist, and this preference is rational, properly informed, and reflective, then it is good for someone to lead that life. But we have seen that, like hedonism, this theory does not subject desires and plans to a full enough battery of evaluations; it too easily counts a goal or desire as good for someone to achieve, because it says too little about how a human life should go for the good of the person who is living it. The only failing it can find in rape derives from the grave harm the rapist willingly does to another. A more satisfactory conception of well-being can be achieved only by adopting a more substantial stand than this on what counts as healthy sexuality.

44. Too Much and Too Little

We think that a good life has a certain shape, and that thought lies behind certain quantitative judgments we make about what is good or bad for people. A certain amount of something or other will do no harm; but there is such a thing as too much of it, because at a certain point it begins to do harm. For example, it does a child no harm to watch an inane TV program for a half hour each week. But it does harm a child to watch inane TV programs all day and every day, no matter how much he enjoys doing so. A child's cognitive powers should grow and flourish. If his mind is filled with idiotic entertainment, that displaces the kind of thinking he should be doing for his own good. So it is not the case that the enjoyment of any cognitive process whatsoever is good, just as it is not the case that it is good to enjoy every kind of sexual pleasure. There is a pattern of development that should take place, and when desires are satisfied or pleasures felt in a way that impedes this development, that is a loss.

We noticed this phenomenon in our discussion of affective un-flourishing (section 39). It is not bad for someone to feel anger when anger is the appropriate response, even though the feel of anger makes it a negative emotion. So too for many of the other negative emotions: stress, frustration, fear, and sorrow. It would be a bad mistake to lead one's life in a way that involves the smallest possible exposure to situations that cause one to feel these emotions. But a life *filled* with stress, frustration, fear, and sorrow is not a good life, and the possibility that a way of life might have this affective texture certainly counts as a reason for avoiding it if one is considering one's own good. Why should that be the case? Why is a large amount of negative affect bad, but a small amount not bad? Why aren't both small and large amounts bad to feel, though to different degrees? The answer is the same as the one we gave in the preceding paragraph: a good life has a certain shape. More precisely, it should be filled with joy, affection, laughter, and a sense of well-being. In small quantities, the negative emotions do not displace those positive feelings. But when they constantly accompany one's activities, they drive out the positive affects, and one's life is disfigured by its negativity.

We also saw that it is good for someone to perceive, regularly and with pleasure, that he is loved (section 39). But there is such a thing as having too great a need for that kind of warmth. If someone constantly demands expressions and signs of affection from every individual in his social world, he exhibits a level of neediness that is not only a nuisance to others but too high for his own good. An insatiable craving for affection would be an affliction because it would displace the kinds of reciprocal interactions and joint activities that make a relationship desirable. Similarly, a life filled with constant and uncontrollable laughter, or intense love felt for everyone one encounters, would drive out all else and disturb the complex contours that a good life should have (section 39).

Here is one further example, this one drawn from sexual life. A certain amount of masturbation harms no one. But if someone masturbates all day and every day—if that is his sole activity (aside from sleeping and eating)—that is bad. (Not wrong, but bad for the masturbator.) Why so? Because it bends his life out of shape: it leaves too little room for other things that are good for someone to do—all the cognitive, affective, social, and physical pleasures that life, as we normally picture it, should have. We are not bonobos or chimps. When we ask what it is for a human life to go well, we reply by bringing forward a rough sketch of what the possibilities are for a human being, and this sketch is based on our picture of the human mind and body. When a life contains too little that fulfills these possibilities, we judge it to be thin, narrow, constricted—too distant from the flourishing life a human being can have when all goes well. Hedonism and the conative theory of well-being, as we have seen, have no conception of the shape that a human life should have, and that is what makes them so implausible.

No element of a good life should be maximized. What is good for someone should take its proper place in his life, falling somewhere in the range of neither too much nor too little. It should not displace all else. Plato was right, as we noted earlier (section 4): good is produced when excess is avoided through the imposition of measure and balance.[23]

45. Comparing Lives and Stages of Life

When we know what the components of well-being are, we can compare one stage of a person's life with another, and in some cases we can say that he is worse-off, or better-off, than he once was. We do this sort of thing all the time. For example, if someone loses many of his cognitive, physical, and social capacities—as sometimes happens in old age—he is

---

23. Plato *Philebus* Stephanus pp. 64d–e. Needless to say, certain excesses may benefit others: a medical researcher whose devotion to his laboratory experiments leaves no time for significant social interaction or anything else that is worthwhile may nonetheless be doing socially useful work. But it would be unreasonably pessimistic to assume that any project of great social utility must disfigure the life of the person who undertakes it.

worse-off than he was before. But here is something remarkable: that comparative judgment about old age commits us to saying that a newborn baby does not yet have as good a life as he will come to have later if he develops properly and lives in favorable circumstances. His cognitive skills are rudimentary, his use of his body is not yet under his control, his affections are underdeveloped, he cannot yet fully enjoy the love he receives, his sex life is not yet what it can later be. What is remarkable about this is that we do not think of a healthy and normal baby as doing poorly, even though he falls far short of having the kind of life he will have later. The reduced capacities of an old person draw our attention because we cannot resist comparing them with the fuller powers he once had; we assess his well-being by comparing it with the standard established during his earlier years. But we do not use that same standard of comparison for a baby. Instead, he is doing well if he functions in the way that a normal baby should—even though that level is far below what it is likely to be someday.

Adulthood is the period of life during which we normally come to the height of many of our cognitive, affective, and social powers. But it would be foolish to say that someone's adulthood is always a better period of time for him than his childhood, or even that this holds true for the most part. Consider a child who loves to learn and to play, who basks in the love of his family and is liked by all his friends and teachers. When that child becomes an adult, he may enjoy nothing that approaches the blissful circumstances of his youth: he may have a job he hates, he may despise and be despised by the members of his community, and so on. The fact that some of his mental and physical skills operate at a more advanced level than they did when he was a child will do him no good if he does not enjoy their use. Do more lives follow this pattern of deterioration than not? That is not a question that has *philosophical* interest, or one that philosophers can help answer. What a theory of well-being can do is find the dimensions along which lives should be compared when we ask whether one person is better-off than another, or whether someone's well-being has increased or declined.

We can easily construct examples in which we compare the lives of two different people. Suppose S loves his mentally demanding and emotionally satisfying eight-hour-a-day job, is surrounded by people he loves and by whom he is loved, and enjoys playing tennis regularly. T equally loves his equally challenging and equally satisfying eight-hour-a-day job. But he is deeply lonely and physically inactive. S has every good thing that T has, and more; so S is better-off than T. If one were offered the choice of living the kind of life S has or the kind of life T has, one should, for one's own good, choose the former.

In other cases, S may be slightly better-off than T in one dimension, but so much worse-off in all other dimensions that we would not hesitate to say that, all things considered, T is better-off than S. In still other cases, we would judge two very different sorts of lives to be roughly equal in goodness, because the advantages one of them has along certain dimensions are balanced by its disadvantages along others.

If some of the dimensions along which we make such comparisons—the various ways in which we can flourish—differed greatly in importance, that would complicate matters. But there is no reason to suppose that cognitive, affective, social, and physical powers do differ in this way; they all have roughly equal weight as elements of well-being. Of course, the consequences of losing certain faculties ramify throughout the whole range of one's life, and others have far fewer consequences. Brain damage, for example, is a more serious matter than the loss of a toe. But we need not pursue these issues here. Circumstances are often favorable enough to allow us to develop normally along all the several dimensions of well-being.

46. Adding Goods: Rawls's Principle of Inclusiveness

All theories of well-being should accept a simple principle of addition for goods: a larger bundle of goods is better than one that is missing one or more elements of that bundle. The larger bundle has precisely what the smaller one has, and more besides; and so one would be worse-off were one to choose the smaller bundle.[24] This is the principle we relied

---

24. There are of course disadvantages in taking on too much—for example, in devoting oneself to so many pursuits that one enjoys each less or fails to develop one's skills as fully as one could if one had fewer interests. In such cases, a smaller number of projects can easily be better than a larger number. But when that is so, the diminution in the number of activities pursued is compensated for by something good—the greater enjoyment of the development of one's powers; and so, even though one is developing fewer powers, the "bundle of goods" one has is in fact not smaller but larger. The principle I have in mind holds that when one bundle of goods (A) contains everything good that the other (B) contains (for example: as many powers developed, with as much enjoyment, for as long a period of time), and in addition more that is good, then one is better off to have A than B.

upon in the previous section when we compared stages of a single life and compared the lives of different individuals. When the principle is made more concrete by being expressed in the terms used by developmentalism, it holds that if two lives differ in that the first flourishes in all the ways that the second does, but in additional ways as well, then the first is better than the second. Nothing would be gained by saying that if someone fails to abide by this principle when he makes choices about how to live his life, he is *irrational*. But if he flouts this principle and his choices are effective, he will certainly be *worse-off*.

Strict hedonism does not reject the principle that a larger bundle of goods is better than a smaller one; rather, it says that one bundle is larger than another not by containing additional kinds of goods, but by containing pleasures of greater intensity and duration (or more pleasures of equal intensity and duration). Similarly, the conative theory accepts the principle of addition. A nice formulation of it, adapted to its conception of the good, is offered by John Rawls (who calls it the "principle of inclusiveness"): "One long-term plan is better than another . . . if it allows for the encouragement and satisfaction of all the aims and interests of the other plan and for the encouragement and satisfaction of some further aim or interest in addition."[25] Rawls speaks of long-term plans here because he is thinking not of someone who is deliberating about how to accomplish goals he already has, but of someone who is deliberating about future goals that he might have if he decides to cultivate an interest in them. We are, in other words, to imagine someone whose future is to a large extent shapeless: he might enter into any number of careers, cultivate any number of interests, and so on. How is he to make this decision? Rawls's reply is: more is better. More specifically, whenever one finds that two plans of life differ in that the first has and accomplishes all the purposes of the second, and more, one is to choose the first. In fact, he holds that to do otherwise would be irrational.

Notice how different this method of making long-range plans is from the one that we normally use. When someone has his whole future ahead of him and asks what purposes he should cultivate for his own good, we think he should answer this question by considering the various dimensions of well-being: which of the various options before him will allow him to flourish as a mentally active, emotionally and socially

25. Rawls, *A Theory of Justice*, p. 363.

engaged person? We work with a concrete menu of goods, adjusted to the peculiar temperament and talents of each individual; and if one career will cultivate all that another career would, and more besides, we think the first is better. Suppose, for example, that following plan A would lead one to become both a successful chess player and a successful tennis player, whereas plan B would offer only the first of these goods. Even if one currently does not aspire to become either a chess or a tennis player, one knows that plan A should be chosen over plan B if one chooses one or the other. Why so? The developmentalist answer is that plan A leads to flourishing along two dimensions, mental and physical, whereas plan B leads to only one of those. But Rawls explains why plan A is better in an entirely different way: it is better because by choosing the life of a chess and tennis player, one will have a larger number of purposes that are accomplished. The desirability of life A has nothing to do with chess or tennis and the way in which these activities would enhance one's powers. Rather, it is more desirable because it leads to the cultivation of one extra interest and the achievement of that goal. For Rawls, the content of the goal has no bearing on the issue. That is precisely where the weakness of the principle of inclusiveness lies. We do not cultivate new interests for the sort of reason proposed by that principle. We do not acquire an additional purpose simply in order to have one more purpose that can be accomplished.

Rawls does think that an objection can be raised against the principle of inclusiveness, but it is not the one just brought forward. Rather, it is this: "A person may say that since he does not have the more inclusive interests, he is not missing anything in not deciding to encourage and to satisfy them."[26] To this Rawls's reply should simply be that the person who adopts the less inclusive plan certainly *is* missing something: since what is good for a human being is the satisfaction of rational desires, a plan that offers less satisfaction offers less of what is good. It is irrelevant that someone who follows plan B will not mind the fact that he plays no tennis because he has no desire to do so.

Instead of responding in this way, Rawls makes two remarks in defense of the principle of inclusiveness. The first relies on an assumption that he builds into the principle: it tells us to choose the more inclusive plan, provided that in doing so one does not stand a smaller chance of

26. Ibid.

accomplishing the goals one will acquire. With that assumption in place, Rawls points out that a less inclusive plan takes on the risk that a smaller proportion of one's purposes will be accomplished. To return to our examples: if plan A offers both a 50 percent chance of success as a chess player and a 50 percent chance of success as a tennis player, whereas plan B offers nothing but a 50 percent chance of success as a chess player, then the first alternative makes it more likely that in the future one will be doing *something* one wants to do. Plan B runs the greater risk that one's life will be empty; with plan A, by contrast, failure as a chess player still leaves a chance of some happiness, since one might nonetheless be a successful tennis player.

But that reply takes advantage of the unrealistic hypothesis that more inclusive plans do not, by virtue of their greater ambitiousness, diminish one's chances of succeeding with each of their components. In the real world, one's chances of becoming a success as a chess player *are* likely to diminish if one pursues not only that task but in addition that of becoming a successful tennis player.

Rawls's second remark about the principle of inclusiveness is that people will tend to choose the more inclusive plan because doing so will give them more pleasure. In saying this, he is not trying to show that we *should* choose the more inclusive plan, but only that we probably *will*. Why so? He replies: human beings "prefer the more comprehensive long-term plan because its execution presumably involves a more complex combination of abilities."[27] And then he invokes what he calls the "Aristotelian Principle," which holds that "human beings enjoy the exercise of their realized capacities (their innate or trained abilities), and that this enjoyment increases the more the capacity is realized, or the greater its complexity."[28]

Rawls's expectation is that under conditions of freedom, when human beings are given the chance to make long-term plans not only about how to accomplish their current purposes but also about which goals to cultivate in the future, they will choose more inclusive plans because the greater complexity of such plans provides more enjoyment. People's taste for greater complexity will lead them to develop their capacities. He thus arrives at the conclusion that under favorable conditions, hu-

---

27. Ibid., p. 364.
28. Ibid.

man beings will find it good to realize their capacities—to flourish—when they follow their preferences. And when that happens, it will in fact be good for them to realize their capacities. Note the contrast between his approach to well-being and the developmental account. For Rawls, the exercise of "innate or trained abilities" is good because it is rationally wanted. But developmentalism reverses the order of explanation: it holds that we should develop desires to realize our capacities because it is good for us to do so. Rawls is eager to show that a just society equipped with adequate resources is a community in which individuals will develop their powers and join together in the common pursuit of excellence.[29] With that idea he pays a compliment of sorts to the view that well-being consists in flourishing. In a way, he agrees: although he holds that well-being is the satisfaction of rational desire, he expects that flourishing is what rational individuals will freely choose.

But the principle of inclusiveness, as Rawls formulates it, is not one we use or should use to guide our decision making. We abide, rather, by the principle that the more elements of well-being we have, the better-off we are. If we had to choose between an option that allows a child to develop all his powers and another that allows for the development of only some of them, we would not have any doubt that the former option is the one that is better for the child. That is because more good is better than less. Satisfying more desires is not always better, and experiencing more pleasures is not always better—unless the objects of those desires and pleasures make them good for someone to have.

47. Art, Science, and Culture

Is it good for someone to develop a love of literature, film, music, painting, philosophy, history, science—or, at any rate, of good specimens of these kinds?

The question needs to be refined before it can be addressed. Consider any of the items on this list—the enjoyment of reading good fiction, for example. (For remarks about history, see section 67.) We want to ask: is it good for someone to develop a love of that kind of activity and to spend his time pleasurably engaged in it? But that question is still not sufficiently precise. We need to say something about what the other op-

---

29. Ibid., pp. 456–464.

tions are. What alternatives would be bypassed, what opportunities foreclosed, by someone's developing that interest? If we want to ask whether developing a love of literature is good for someone, we should be prepared to say what that activity is being compared with. What is it better than?

We might mean to ask: is it better for someone to develop that interest than *not* to? More precisely, we are to consider someone who currently has no interest in literature, and we then imagine his life taking one of two different directions. In one direction, he continues to have precisely the same interests, desires and plans that he currently has. In the other, he has those same interests, desires, and plans; but in addition, without giving anything up, he also develops a love of literature and enjoys reading good fiction.

When the question is formulated in this way, it is all too easy to decide how to answer it: yes, when doing so is costless, it is better to develop a love of reading good fiction than not to. To defend that answer, we merely have to say how such an activity, pursued with pleasure, promotes, in some way, one of the components of well-being. The enjoyment of literature, we can reasonably say, is an exercise of one's cognitive and affective powers. It activates and enlarges one's powers of imagination, social understanding, and appreciation for the riches of language. It builds on the pleasure we take, as children, in storytelling, and it admits of endless variation and development. As one becomes a more experienced ethical agent and learns more from one's social interactions, one can bring to and take from one's reading a deeper understanding of human beings.

The truth of these platitudes is sufficient to show that *something* worth having is added to one's life if one becomes a reader of imaginative prose, poetry, and so on. And since, by hypothesis, nothing is lost, the value of developing an interest in this activity is obvious. We need merely appeal to the simple principle of addition for goods, discussed in the previous section: a larger bundle of goods is better than one that is missing one or more elements of that bundle.

But it would be implausible to suggest that *only* in these circumstances would it be good for someone to develop a love of literature— that is, only when that activity can be included in someone's life at no cost. The degree of goodness of literary pleasures is not so minute that no trade-off would be worth accepting in order to gain that good. Consider, for example, someone who enjoys playing checkers all day and every day. We offer him two options: he can remain, for the rest of his life, a full-time checker player with no time for reading; or he can play checkers somewhat less often, and with the additional time he has he can learn to enjoy good fiction, and he will continue to do so for the rest of his life. It would be implausible to claim that he should remain as he is. Checkers exercises one's combinatorial, deliberative, and spatial skills, but in very limited ways. It does not offer unending new opportunities for innovation, growth, imagination, creativity, insight, or understanding. It develops, to a small degree, certain aspects of the mind, but literature develops, to a high degree, certain other parts. It is inexhaustible in what it offers our emotions, imagination, and understanding. The fact that different mental skills and pleasures are being compared when we measure checkers and literature against each other does not mean that there are no respects in which one of them can be judged to be better for us than the other. The loss in well-being that would occur, were someone to play checkers somewhat less, would be well worth accepting to make room for the pleasures of reading good fiction.

Simple games like checkers, of course, have real value. Because they are for most people mildly interesting but not extremely demanding, they can provide a good way to relax; and for children of the right age, they provide good exercise for the mind. But someone who is capable of developing a love of literature should, for his own good, give up at least a little bit of his checker-playing time to do so. Someone who is incapable of developing a love of literature and whose only mental pleasure is checkers is handicapped by a cognitive or linguistic disability. It would have been better for him had his powers been greater.[30]

---

30. Does it follow that it would be wise for us to increase our powers if we could do so? If, for example, genetic engineering could make us, or future generations, better athletes, should we embrace such alterations? It would be pointless to make *everyone* a better competitive runner or tennis player; but it *would* be worthwhile to remedy the defects of those who are currently handicapped as runners or to improve the skills of those who cannot participate in sports. When our experience of life shows us that those who are defective in one area of human excellence do not thereby gain in some other area, we have good reason to remedy those defects when we can. But it does not follow that improving the set of skills of *all* human beings would be good for us. This allows for the possibility that in certain spheres we are *all* defective, and that the elimination of that defect would be beneficial. For example, people are generally quite bad at making intuitive probabilistic judgments. If we could genetically engineer future generations in a way that eliminates this widespread deficiency, human beings would make fewer costly mistakes. But there is no reason to increase someone's powers, unless doing so removes a deficiency; and something can be identified as a deficiency only by means of a theory of well-being.

A conative conception of well-being lacks the resources for acknowl-edging this point. It can make the sociological observation (if it has em-pirical support) that most people who develop an interest in literature are glad that they accepted a small loss in some other good activity in or-der to do so. It can also claim that most people who are given opportuni-ties to learn to take pleasure in literature, film, music, painting, and so on, will choose to make use of those opportunities. But it refuses to as-sert that there is any reason they *should* do so. It is therefore forced to the conclusion that if, at some future time, no one takes any interest in these activities, and everyone instead fills his days with a steady regime of checker playing, no diminution of human life would have occurred, be-cause those generations of simpler people would be no worse off than we are. But if that conclusion is to be accepted, what reason can there be for schools and parents to encourage children to develop a love of mu-sic, film, art, and so on—except for whatever small instrumental value they have? To accept the conative theory is not to be a philistine, but it is to accept indifference to artistic and intellectual achievements as an atti-tude that is beyond rational criticism. It is to say of such achievements: some people just happen to like these things.

It should be kept in mind that developmentalism is not a doctrine about how social and political institutions should be designed. It is a theory about what it is for something to be good for someone and about which things are good. Political consequences can be drawn from it only if it is combined with a theory about which undertakings are appropriate for a political community. Developmentalism must not be seen as a ver-sion of what Rawls calls "perfectionism"—a term he uses for any politi-cal theory that "direct[s] society to arrange institutions" in a way that promotes "the achievement of human excellence in art, science, and cul-ture."[31] Leaving political theory to one side, developmentalism exploits the idea that what is good for any being is its flourishing. It applies this

31. Rawls, *A Theory of Justice*, pp. 285–286. Rawls conceives of what he calls "perfection-ism" not only as a political theory, but also as a maximizing doctrine (ibid., p. 22). So defined, perfectionism is committed to saying that the good of human beings who cannot be perfected in the relevant way—who can achieve little or nothing in the way of "art, science, and cul-ture"—must receive little or no attention, and that such "defective" human beings must be used for the maximization of "the realization of human excellence" (ibid.). Our goal must be to make the universe contain as much excellence as possible, and those who cannot be excellent are valuable only as means to this end. Rawls associates the doctrine with the theories of Aris-totle and Nietzsche (ibid.), and he notes that perfectionism might be used to defend slave labor as a necessary condition for "the achievements of the Greeks in philosophy, science, and art" (ibid., p. 286). But since the developmentalism I present here is not combined with the princi-

to the human case by observing that the flourishing of human beings has cognitive, affective, social, and physical dimensions. The application of that general idea must be sensitive to time and place. As we noted (section 22), when human beings became language users, one of the components of their cognitive well-being changed, and it became a drawback for an individual to be incapable of speech. Something similar can be said about an individual who lives in a community in which the institutions of "art, science, and culture" play a pervasive role. If someone lacks the resources to participate in those institutions, that is a loss for him. But what should be done by political institutions to address that loss is a further question. It is tempting to say that political institutions should, as a matter of justice, try to remedy that loss—but to assess that idea, one must move beyond the theory of what is good and ask whether civic institutions should address themselves to all the components of the well-being of their members. Rawls holds that only certain kinds of goods—the ones that are of concern to the parties in the original position—must be promoted as a matter of justice. That thesis is compatible with a developmental conception of the good. If, however, *all* the dimensions of human well-being are the appropriate concern of the political community, then it is not implausible to suppose, as many people over many centuries have supposed, that public educational institutions should encourage an interest in "art, science, and culture."

48. Self-Sacrifice

We can find a further indication that developmentalism is merely a matter of common sense if we bring to mind ordinary assumptions about what it is for someone to make a willing self-sacrifice. To do so is to give up some good one wants or needs for oneself to fulfill a duty or to bene-

---

ple that good should be maximized, it is not committed to any form of neglectful treatment or indifference to human beings whose capacities for normal development are limited or impeded. On the contrary, there may be much that can and should be done for those whose cognitive, affective, social, or physical functioning is impeded. (Since they are needier than others, the case for addressing their needs may be unusually strong.) A developmental approach to well-being is not committed to saying that there are certain human beings who, because their capacities for good development are impeded, are less worthy of love or care than those who are more fortunate. Unlike the perfectionism to which Rawls is rightly opposed, it does not rank human beings according to their capacity for cultural achievement and does not single out those whose powers are greater as more worthy of love, respect, or institutional support.

fit someone else. As the term is most often used, it has both a subjective and an objective element. Someone who does what in fact harms himself and benefits others is not necessarily engaged in an act of self-sacrifice—his motive might be to benefit himself at the expense of others. But when someone thinks of himself as acting for the good of others and willingly accepts a loss of well-being as a necessary condition of success, then the subjective element of self-sacrifice is in place. We would not comfortably describe him as engaged in an act of self-sacrifice, however, if we thought that in fact he is not disadvantaged by what he does. Notice how different this is from a mere willingness to compromise. To compromise is to give up, as a result of negotiation, something that one is recognized as wanting, and it does not matter whether what one wants is good for one to have. Self-sacrifice, by contrast, always involves a loss, and not merely the renunciation of what is desired.

Examples of self-sacrifice are easy to construct if we think in terms of the various dimensions of well-being that we have identified. Here is one. Suppose a parent, to earn enough money to give his child an expensive education, gives up a job that makes full use of his talents and in its place accepts a post that is intellectually and emotionally deadening and physically dangerous, but provides a large and steady income. Developmentalism and common sense count this as an act of self-sacrifice—no coincidence, since developmentalism is rooted in widely accepted assumptions about what is good. (Hedonism too would count this is a great loss, but it radically departs from common ideas.)

Proponents of a conative conception of well-being will have a difficult time if they want to explain why such an act should be counted as a self-sacrifice. The problem is that the parent is following a master plan: he works to make money, and he makes money to achieve his highest aim (the education of his child), an aim that propels him forward for a long period of time and organizes his whole life. Not only is the achievement of that goal something that he wants and aims at—it is what he *most* wants, it is his *highest* goal. So, since the root idea of the conative theory is that what is good for someone is constructed out of his conation (when it is rational, and so on), that theory will be hard-pressed to explain why it need not say that the parent's act is, on balance, not a self-sacrifice. If his plan succeeds, his highest goal has been achieved. Admittedly, he would have liked to achieve that highest aim without giving up other things that he wanted. But we cannot always get everything we want, and at least he achieved his highest purpose. It seems that the co-native theory is stuck with the conclusion that self-sacrifice is impossi-ble. Since it always involves a planned loss of things that are given up in order to achieve what one seeks even more, it always involves—despite its being called "self-sacrifice"—a net gain.

An ungrateful child might tell his parents, after they have made many sacrifices for him, that he owes them nothing in return, because, after all, they chose to live as they did. They wanted to do their duty, and they got exactly what they wanted. In saying this, the child is drawing upon the widely accepted idea that what is good for someone consists in get-ting what one wants. The conative theory of well-being, no less than developmentalism, is a matter of common sense. Even so, we can recog-nize, by focusing on how repugnant a child is who thinks along these lines, that the piece of common sense that the conative theory repro-duces must be rejected.[32]

Not every self-sacrifice, of course, is as severe as the one used several paragraphs above. And sometimes we do in fact gain something as a re-sult of our sacrifices, even though the good that we gain is not one we aim at and does not motivate our sacrifice. A father who loves to play the violin during his spare hours may decide to give that instrument to his child, accepting a lower degree of well-being for himself out of his love for his child. Perhaps he will gain something even better in return: the greater love his child will have for him and a more intimate relationship between them. But he need not have given up his violin for this reason—he may, on the contrary, have expected his child to leave home soon and to live at a great distance. Intimate relationships typically involve some willingness to accept some degree of sacrifice for the sake of the other person, and the character of an intimate relationship can change radi-cally when individuals sense that the other person is not willing to incur any losses in well-being. Each is then willing to act for the good of the other, but not if any sacrifice is involved. It is good for people to enter into and sustain *some* relationships in which each individual is confident

32. For further discussion, see Mark Overvold, "Self-Interest and the Concept of Self-Sacrifice"; and Stephen Darwall, *Welfare and Rational Care,* pp. 3, 24–27, 52–53. To solve the problem, Darwall proposes that what is good for S is what someone who cares for S would ra-tionally want for S, rather than what S wants (ibid., pp. 4, 7, 45–48, 53). But that reverses the usual and correct order of explanation: because something is good, it is what someone who cares for S would want, not the other way around.

that sacrifices would be made on his behalf. Such relationships provide the sort of attachment and commitment that enhance our well-being as affective beings. In such friendships, each stands ready to be worse-off in some respect; but in a different respect they are, because of that willingness, better-off—though this is not the calculation that stands behind their being prepared to make a sacrifice.

It is not only intimate friendship that requires a willingness to accept a loss of well-being along some dimension. Some of the qualities normally counted as virtues—justice, honesty, courage—make that same demand, as we will see (section 52).

49. The Vanity of Fame

We have classified many types of states of affairs as good for human beings, and many others as bad. What should go into the neutral category, the category of things that are neither good nor bad? A great deal—more than anyone can say. It is neither good nor bad for me, or for anyone else, that a circle contains 360 degrees, or that "Chicago" is the name of a city, or that the planet Neptune exists. Only a small number of types of things are good for human beings, and a small number bad: these are the components of flourishing and un-flourishing that we have discussed. But neutral things are unlimited. It looks like a category all of whose members are of no practical significance. (Of course, some neutral items have great instrumental value, and are of great interest to us for that reason.)

But within that unlimited category, there are a small number of items that deserve special attention because under certain conditions people develop a desire for them, despite the fact they are not in themselves good. Consider, for example, the desire for fame—the desire, that is, that an extremely large group of people know some facts about oneself: perhaps just one's name, but, if possible, other facts as well—namely, facts about what one is famous for. Julius Caesar's fame continues to grow, as each new generation learns something about him, if only his name. Is he better off as the number of people who have heard of him increases? Of course not. And yet, it is possible that Caesar wanted to be famous. He may have wanted there to be a large number of people in every generation who know at least something about his life. Perhaps he wanted this to happen because he thought that fame is good, or perhaps he wanted this to happen without giving any thought to what is good. In any case, if he thought that fame is good, he was wrong. That is what developmentalism claims: it puts the state of affairs of being famous in the category of things that are neither good nor bad. Acquiring a certain amount of fame during one's lifetime might, in certain circumstances, be a useful means to a good end. But it lacks noninstrumental goodness.

The conative conception of well-being cannot agree. It is committed to saying that if someone wants to be famous both during his lifetime and afterward, or aims at these goals, then it is good for him to be famous during his lifetime (whether he is aware of being famous or not), and good for him to be famous after he has died. When his fame grows after his death, that causes a change in an earlier state of affairs: it increases the level of well-being he had when he was alive. (If one does not exist at a certain time, one cannot become better-off at that time. So if posthumous fame is good for someone, one's earlier well-being is altered by what happens later.)[33]

Nothing recommends the idea that fame is good for those who want it, and it is another strike against the conative theory that it must accept this idea. But it might be objected that we have too quickly dismissed the desire for fame. Perhaps what some people want is not being famous, but the pleasant awareness that they are famous. Their well-being does not increase after they die, even if their fame grows; but, according to this suggestion, the enjoyment of fame—not fame by itself, or the acquisition of fame by someone who wants it—is good.

But there is no way to make this suggestion work if some of the points made earlier were accepted. We rejected the thesis that every sort of pleasure, no matter what its cause or object, is worth having (section 32). There are pleasures that are not good for someone to have, even if he wants to have them. So we cannot say that the enjoyment of fame, simply because it is the enjoyment of something, is good. If the enjoyment of fame is good, there must be something about someone's being *famous*, and not merely about his finding pleasure in it, that helps explain why that is so. What could that be? The fact that being famous is what he wants? No, because of the point just made: there are pleasures that are not good for someone to have, even if he wants to have them. If

33. That is, if events that occur after one's death could affect one's well-being, they would do so by adding to or detracting from the well-being one had while alive, not be adding to or detracting from posthumous well-being. A distinction is being made here between the time at which an event is good for someone and the time at which it occurs.

there were something about being famous that explained why the acquisition of fame should be counted as an advantage or improvement in one's life, provided that it is enjoyed, then we could be assured that the enjoyment of fame is good. But nothing about fame is capable of doing this job.

Consider once again a child in the course of his normal development. At a certain point in his life, he will acquire the concept of fame, and he will at that point be capable of forming a desire for it and enjoying its acquisition. Should those who care for his well-being try to inculcate that aspiration in him, on the grounds that it will be noninstrumentally good for him to become famous? If he does acquire this new ambition and must make room for its fulfillment by taking time and energy away from other goals, what should be sacrificed? Which of his cognitive, affective, social, and physical powers should develop less fully, in order that he become extremely well known and enjoy that fame? Suppose he can become extremely well known, and can enjoy his fame, by becoming the victim of a heinous crime—one that leaves him incapable of any further development. Would those who care for his well-being be tempted to commit that crime for his sake? The hypothesis that the enjoyment of fame is good has nothing to recommend it.

And yet some people have a burning desire for fame and will move heaven and earth to acquire it. That desire has none of the defects that conative theories typically acknowledge to be defects: people are not irrational merely because they want to be famous. Renown is not something they want only because they lack certain pieces of information. Their desire is not something they will necessarily renounce if only they give more thought to it. There is no way to criticize the desire for fame, except to say that its object is not something it is good to have. But it should not be at all surprising that human beings sometimes have desires whose objects fall into this category. Nature has not installed in us some wonderful mechanism that guarantees that what propels us forward and focuses our minds on certain courses of action will bring us to something it is good for us to have. Somehow or other, we have to take steps to learn about what is good for us, and even to care about what is good for us; that is not a topic about which we inevitably come to have tacit knowledge merely by virtue of having desires. Yearnings, hankerings, cravings, hungers will propel us forward toward objects of all sorts—good, bad, and indifferent. We might hanker after what others around us want, simply because we do not want to be without whatever

it is that they have (section 27). So the fact that some people hanker after fame should not lead us to suppose that it is good for them to have it
or to enjoy its possession.

The desire for fame must not be confused with other desires. Its object
is simply that one be known by many others. It should be distinguished
from the desire to be admired, appreciated, or respected for one's skills
or accomplishments. A singer who is gratified by the warm applause of
her audience need not have a general desire to be famous, or even the
more specific desire to be famous as a fine musician. When she is
pleased by the enthusiastic response of her audience and shows her audience that she appreciates their response, she is participating in a relationship that has some of the characteristics of a friendship. Earlier (section 39), we reached the conclusion that if someone is indifferent to the
affection of others, she is missing one of the pleasures of human interaction; her social powers are not flowering to the fullest. In the same way, a
performer who is indifferent to the appreciation and admiration of her
audience cuts herself off from one kind of valuable human interaction,
and she is made worse-off by that very fact. (She is also likely to perform
less well, but that is a different matter.) On the other hand, indifference
to *impersonal* evaluations of one's work is not by itself a loss (though it
may have good or bad consequences).

The desire to become famous for some accomplishment—athletic superiority, virtuosity as a musician, the signing of a peace treaty—is not
merely a desire to be famous. It is a complex double goal: to achieve
something worthwhile, and to be widely known for having done so.
Merely becoming widely known for an achievement cannot be good if it
is agreed that nothing is good in the absence of pleasure.[34] Is it good to
be pleased by the fact that one is famous for some accomplishment? We
have seen that it is not good to have the pleasant awareness that one is

34. Nagel imagines a case in which, after an author's death, "the belief becomes current that
all of the literary works on which his fame rests were really written by his brother, who died in
Mexico at the age of 28" ("Death," p. 4), and he proposes that we count this as bad for the author. But if that judgment rests solely on the assumption that a conative approach to well-being
is correct (he wanted to be known for his accomplishment, and the frustration of that desire is
bad for him), it cannot be sustained. There is good reason for us to care about the proper attribution of authorship to important literary works: someone is speaking to us in them, and we
enhance our appreciation of them if we know who that individual is. (See section 47 on the
good of literary works.) We need not assume that in order to justify this concern about proper
attribution, we must conceive of ourselves as benefiting the author by thinking well of his
works.

famous. Having arrived at this conclusion, it would be implausible to suppose that nonetheless someone's being pleased by the fact that he is famous for having done something impressive or worthwhile should be counted as something that is good for him.

50. The Vanity of Wealth

Unlike fame, material wealth (not bare adequacy of resources for survival, but a large number of financial assets) is of great instrumental value, and developmentalism can explain why. A conative theory of well-being would say that whenever people need large sums to satisfy their rational desires, it is good for them to have those sums. That is not acceptable, because when rational aims are bad for someone to achieve, it is bad for him to have the resources for doing so. Developmentalism affirms the great value of wealth by using an entirely different approach: it points out that good schools, hospitals, athletic facilities, parks, theaters, museums—the public institutions that cater to all forms of flourishing—require a vibrant economy. Furthermore, our lives go best when we have interesting jobs—jobs that do not deaden us, physically, intellectually, and emotionally—and that kind of work is available to large numbers only when the economy is well advanced. So, if we are to flourish, economic institutions must also flourish.

Is it good for an individual to be rich—to have a much higher net worth than most other members of his community? No one really thinks so. A young child might be extremely rich and have no awareness of that fact. But is it good for someone to take pleasure in the fact that he is wealthy? That is a pleasure that one can give oneself simply by thinking, as one gazes upon one's possessions or glances at one's financial records, that one has so much more than others. Many people aspire to have that pleasure. They of course also want to do the things that money will enable them to do, but the attraction of wealth is not limited to its utility. Even when people have so much that they cannot possibly use it all, they still take pleasure in having that much, and often they want more and more.

But if there is nothing good about the pleasant awareness that one is *famous*, then the same is true for the pleasant awareness that one is *rich*. The same argument applies: enjoying wealth is not shown to be good simply because it is an enjoyment, and there is nothing about wealth that would explain why its acquisition in large quantities is by itself an improvement in one's life. The same thought experiment about childhood development can be repeated: which cognitive, affective, social, and physical powers should develop less fully in order that a child come to love having riches far beyond what others have and far beyond what can be used to good effect? No one would make that trade-off on behalf of his child.

In this case, too, the conative conception of well-being is at a disadvantage. It lacks the resources for criticizing a person or a society for being materialistic—for being in love with possessions and money for their own sake and leaving too little room for what is genuinely good. Because it does not evaluate goals by looking at their content, it must say that if one's goal is to have more wealth than everyone else, it is good for one to progress toward it and attain it. It is free to add that if one can develop additional goals, and achieve them as well as the goal of superior wealth, one should do so (section 46). But we should ask someone who wants to enjoy material supremacy to reexamine that aspiration, not merely to have other aspirations as well.

51. Making Others Worse-Off

It would be a burden to live one's life with the sense that nothing one does has the slightest effect on anyone's well-being, one's own or that of others. Many avoid this oppressive feeling by assuming that at least some of the things they do are good for someone—for themselves or for others. But it is remarkable that human beings can take pleasure in having a *negative* effect on others. As we noted in section 27, we can pursue, over long periods and with great relish, the goal of making our enemies suffer. Brief flashes of anger give us a sense of what this is like. Anger can harden into enduring hatred, which can organize all that one does. Here is another item—the suffering of one's enemies—that can be added, along with fame and riches, to our list of goals that are often pursued but not good to achieve, however much progress toward them and success in attaining them may be enjoyed. Someone else's being worse-off does not make one better-off. An awareness that a person one hates is suffering can be enjoyed; in fact, it is possible to enjoy seeing any human being or creature suffer—even those toward whom one has no particular feeling. But enjoyment is good only when it takes certain objects (sections 32, 49). There is nothing about S's being worse-off that can make it plausible that T's enjoying it is good for T.

It is of course widely recognized that in certain conditions people are willing to accept enormous losses in order to inflict injuries on others. Those who look at blood feuds from the outside perceive their madness. But why not take them to be complex mixtures of good and bad? A feuding tribe that devastates its enemies gets precisely what it wants and can dance in the streets: that, it might be said, is the good part, for them. The losses they incur must be acknowledged, but might it not be difficult to say whether, on balance, there is more good for them than bad? But that is an absurd question. The common conviction of outsiders that the humiliation and suffering inflicted on a clan's enemies is not, by itself, a good thing for the clan, however much its members may enjoy it, is correct. This is not a case in which good and bad come in roughly equal measure, because when S observes T's suffering with pleasure, that is not good for S.

Aiming at the destruction of another can bring in its train much that is good for the person who has this aim. Destroying an aggressor can have enormous instrumental value. Furthermore, the very steps that are taken to prepare oneself for battle can be good for the person who takes them. A social role can be a good one to occupy, because of the way in which it exercises the powers of the person who fills it, and yet it may be a role that essentially involves harming, or threatening to harm, others. Nearly all societies have soldiers, or warriors, or police officers, or knights, or positions that are similar to these, in that they require the perfection of one's ability to fight with and harm others. In many cases, the physical skill needed for the successful performance of these roles is only one component of the job. They also call for skills of perception, thought, and emotion: self-control, alertness, ingenuity, persistence, the ability to size up opponents, and so on. Some of these skills are comparable to those of a great athlete, and these too count as positions that call forth and exercise the development of one's powers. But harming someone else—bringing it about that someone else is worse-off—is not itself good for the person who inflicts the harm, even when it is enjoyed. It may take nothing more than a push to send one's enemy off a cliff and to his death.

A society in which the role of warrior is the only one that allows for the development of the powers of its members faces a serious problem.

Its military success is unlikely to endure forever. A community will not flourish (that is, many of its members will not flourish) over a long period unless it makes available to them a wide variety of social roles that do not have as their object the vanquishing of foes. It will have to find or create the resources needed for the development of inner powers that do not have as their raison d'être the suffering or death of others.

It is false that whenever someone wants and seeks what is bad for others, or fame, or economic supremacy over others, that is bad for him. The preparation he makes for success, or the consequences of success, may in fact be extremely good. A desire to achieve great fame in the art world might lead someone to develop and enjoy intricate visual and mental skills. A burning desire to become wealthy may lead someone to perfect the complex social, affective, and cognitive skills needed by an entrepreneur. The enjoyment of making progress toward and achieving these aims—fame, riches, destruction—is not good, but what progress and success bring may be.

An objector may ask: why not think of human beings as possessing destructive powers that they must, for their own good, develop and enjoy, just as they must take pleasure in exercising their cognitive, affective, social, sensory, and physical powers? The idea that underlies this question is that, contrary to the arguments of the preceding paragraphs, it is good for us enjoy doing what is harmful to others because in doing so our aggressive powers flourish.

The reply is that although we can describe human beings as having destructive powers—they certainly can, in most circumstances, develop the ability to harm others—it does not follow that it is noninstrumentally good to develop, exercise, and enjoy them. It should be kept in mind (section 37) that developmentalism does not start from the abstract assumption that it is good for human beings to exercise their powers. It arrives at that generalization by starting from concrete cases. When we consider the sorts of activities it is good for us to engage in, we find that the best explanation for their goodness consists in the way they involve the enjoyable use of our bodies, senses, emotions, and intellect. We are not led to the conclusion that, for our own good, we might do best to extirpate these powers or to use them only when it is instrumentally valuable to do so. On the contrary, we find that our well-being consists precisely in the full flowering of these powers, just as the good of any living thing consists in its flourishing.

So when it is suggested that human beings are best understood as having destructive powers, and that these are no less important to express than the others we have been discussing, we should reply that when we work out the implications of this suggestion, we see no merit in it. Recall the point that one can push another person to his death with almost no effort. If that is counted as the activation of our destructive powers, there is no plausibility in the idea that such an activity is noninstrumentally good. Admittedly, human beings sometimes take pleasure in seeing other human beings and other creatures suffer; that is part of what might be meant when it is said that we have a destructive or aggressive nature. But that part of what is natural to us—if it is natural—should, unlike other parts, be extirpated because it does us no good. That it does us no good is the conclusion of a philosophical argument, the outcome of an inquiry into well-being. As we noted earlier, what nature gives us is not necessarily good. Like social practices, nature too is a fit object for philosophical examination and evaluation.

52. Virtues and Flourishing

Plato asked: is it good to be just? That is, if someone is just, is that good *for him?* He thought it a matter of the greatest importance to show that it is.

Ross assumes that Plato was asking an unimportant question. He holds that the moral virtues are good "sans phrase"—not good *for* anyone. He says: "We are directly aware that conscientious action . . . has a value of its own. . . . Our reason informs us of this as surely as it informs us of anything, and to distrust reason here is in principle to distrust its power of ever knowing reality."[35] He thinks that to see that hedonism is false, we need only conduct this thought experiment: imagine two states of the universe in which there are equal amounts of pleasure, but in one of which all individuals are thoroughly vicious, and in the other highly virtuous.[36] Obviously, the universe that contains good people is better. It is good that good people and their morally good actions exist, and in this sense virtue is good "sans phrase."

But it is hard to believe that one should cultivate or nourish a personal

35. Ross, *The Right and the Good,* p. 82.
36. Ibid., p. 134.

quality about which it can be truly said: having that quality does no good for anyone—neither for the person who has it, nor for any others. Justice, honesty, and kindness are poor things if they fall into this category. In any case, there is no reason to treat the question "What is good for human beings?" with disdain—as though it could have no practical importance or philosophical interest. And when we do ask that question and consider some of the answers proposed by our philosophical predecessors, we inevitably face the question Plato raised: are justice, honesty, and other qualities that are normally taken to be virtues good for anyone? Are they good only for those who receive just and honest treatment? Or also for those who treat others in these ways? These questions cannot be answered by Ross's method of imagining contrasting states of the universe.

In certain conditions, an honest person will suffer greatly because of his honesty. He will reveal information that others use to deprive him of material resources that have served him well. As he consults his financial records about the way in which his family farm was acquired, his honesty may force him to make disclosures that lead to the loss of the farm. Imaginary examples are easy to invent; real cases are scarce, because that degree of honesty is uncommon.

But this only shows that when one has and exercises a quality that is normally counted a virtue, one may suffer very bad *consequences*. It leaves unanswered the question whether there is anything good about being honest—good for the person who is honest. Plato wants to show that justice is the greatest good one can have, but we are not asking whether the virtues are so much better than everything else that it is worth having them, even if one thereby loses everything else. There is a much simpler question that should be asked: is being a good person good *at all* for the person who is good? Or is being a good person a total loss from the standpoint of one's own well-being?

Suppose someone does not know how to be honest, fair, kind, or trusting in *any* of his relationships. That will have devastating consequences: his social ineptitude will show, and he will have great difficulty entering into cooperative or affectionate relationships with others. No parent would want his child to be so lacking in virtue; that would be bad for his child. A parent supervising the education of several children will try to teach them how to be honest, fair, kind, and trusting in their interactions with each other. If one of those children is incapable of acquiring these attitudes, he is cut off from the rest of the family, and being cut off in this way is by itself a deficit. A social bond that exists among the others does not extend to him. They voluntarily make certain sacrifices for each other by playing fairly and not taking advantage of occasional positions of superiority. Though some of the children, through stealth and strength, might have been able to acquire certain advantages—larger portions of pie, more toys—had they not been fair to their siblings, each, by virtue of his fairness and honesty, enjoys a benefit that the virtue-less child does not have. Each good child enjoys the sense that he is welcomed as a member of a cooperative group, and each welcomes the others in that same way. Each shares a sense of community with the others. A child who belongs to such a family would lose that sense of belonging if he transformed himself into a defector from cooperative schemes—even if his defection went undetected. The defecting child would no longer have an emotional bond with the others, though he might have more ice cream.

What about relationships with those who are not family members? Each member of family F might be honest and fair in his treatment of the other members of F, but dishonest and unfair in his treatment of all others. That might bring certain gains, and it would be a reasonable strategy if the members of all other families are following the same strategy. But a society in which all families treat outsiders in this way will function poorly. Its political leaders will be corrupt and will use their power to enrich the members of their own families, even if this impoverishes the other citizens. That attitude will prevail throughout the whole economic and social structure. Some families may do extremely well (as measured by material resources), but if so, they do so at the expense of many others. Or there may be a rough equilibrium, with no family doing much worse or better than the others. In any case, there is something that would be good for all of them to have that none has: there is no shared sense of justice, no feeling of allegiance to the community, no perception that one's interests will receive consideration from those who are not related by blood. Since no one expects to be treated fairly or with kindness or honesty, relationships of trust outside the family are fragile at best. That by itself is a loss. In such a society, no one cares about and therefore no one enjoys working with outsiders. Whatever alliances are formed are vulnerable to defection and therefore filled with suspicion. Though in each small social world constituted by the family the relationships are warm, the general social world, which everyone must inhabit, is chilling.

That is not a picture of an ideal political community. It would be far better for all if each felt at home in many different subcommunities and in the general political community, not only in his family. It would also be better for each person to share with all other members of society a common conception of justice and a felt assurance that all citizens are committed to treating each other with justice, honesty, and consideration. When such a society has been established, there may nonetheless be a few citizens who feel no sense of connection with others in this way. Assume that they want to be fair only to members of their small circle and are indifferent to all others. Their inability or refusal to feel a sense of membership in any other group is their loss. Other members of society enjoy a shared sense of justice, but those who defect emotionally—who cut off their affective ties to all but a few—lack this. They stand a chance of gaining material advantages that others will not seek. But they had better succeed in gaining those advantages—otherwise their social disconnectedness will be a net loss. And they must really be advantages—not just things they want.

A just person who is deprived of a needed material resource by the political community, and who thinks that in losing this advantage he is being treated justly, has an affective reaction to his loss that compares favorably with the reaction others have if they have no sense of justice, or if their sense of justice differs from that of the community. They regard this way of being treated as a double loss: not only must they part with something that is instrumentally valuable; in addition, they cannot help feeling resentful toward the system that has done this to them and toward those individuals who make that system work. If their sense of grievance persists, that will poison their affective lives, and one component of well-being will be unavailable to them. By contrast, a just person who loses a needed resource, because, as he realizes, it is fairly taken from him and he had no legitimate claim to it, will be glad that justice is being done. He may regret the loss of a material resource, but his situation is better than it might have been, precisely because he has a sense of justice that brings him into harmony with his community. A widely shared sense of justice is a collective asset, not only because it smoothes the path to other goods, but because it constitutes a desirable affective condition.

A just person who sees that he is being treated unjustly, and is losing certain material goods as a result, might mind the unjust treatment and not the loss of goods. Suppose a child receives a smaller piece of pie and recognizes that this is because his mother is treating him unfairly. He may not care about pie, but his sense of justice will be offended. His affective life would be better if he could bring himself to be the sort of person who does not mind being treated unjustly. Similarly, someone who is suffering a great deal of pain would be better-off if he did not mind it. And someone who is angry all the time would be better-off if he were incapable of anger. But it does not follow that we should try to make ourselves insensitive to all pain, or incapable of anger, or devoid of a sense of justice. It would be better to be *susceptible* to burdensome affects and sensations, but to feel these things seldom, if ever. The ideal condition, as regards justice, would be to have a sense of justice that is shared by all others, to treat all others justly, and never to be treated unjustly. Someone who meets this description will feel entirely at home in every corner of his community.

We have been focusing on some of the ways in which being a just person can partly constitute the flourishing of one's affective life, but we should not overlook the point that the theory and practice of justice can be a welcome component of one's life as a thoughtful person. What justice is and what it calls for are topics that require considerable thought, and the acquisition of insight and understanding in this area is as demanding an intellectual accomplishment as any. The life of a fair-minded judge who has studied the law and enjoys seeing justice done is the kind of life one can reasonably want to live if it suits one's temperament and interests. If someone has these skills and predilections, it is good to be just—good *for him* that he is just. But we should not think of the office of a professional judge, working in a political system that relies heavily on legal expertise, as the only kind of social role in which the cognitive skills of a just person are put into play. Every parent of two or more children needs to develop the skills of a fair-minded arbitrator. For that matter, family life—even that of a childless couple—inevitably calls upon each of its members to make some contribution to the fair resolution of conflicts. Similarly, friends must share a sense of fairness. In addition to these small and intimate circles, there are countless jobs in which a sense of justice must be put into play. If many of the institutions of a society leave room in their daily operation for individual and collective deliberation about what justice requires, then every member of society will need to develop the skills and attitudes of a just person and can enjoy using them.

None of this proves what Plato sought to prove: that being a just person is so great a good that it is worth having even if it brings with it the loss of all other goods. Our conclusions are more modest: justice in one's relation to the whole of one's social world is one component of a flourishing life; if someone is entirely unjust—unjust to everyone—that by itself detracts from his well-being.

53. The Good of Autonomy

If I allow my health to deteriorate, that is bad for me. If, in addition, I deliberately make you unhealthy, I am giving you precisely what I give myself. One might mistakenly infer from this that there is only one bad thing that happens to you, a diminution of only one good, when I undermine your health. But that is not so. When I take it upon myself to do what undermines your health, I am the one who is making decisions about what happens to you. You therefore suffer in more than one way. Someone other than you is making decisions about what happens to you—someone not of your choosing. That is not a problem I create for myself when I allow my health to deteriorate. In doing so, I exercise control over what happens to me.

Since our well-being consists in the exercise of our powers, and among these powers are those that are involved in reasoned choice, it is bad for us when matters that we can decide about, on our own, and take pleasure in controlling are taken out of our control.

Having less control over certain matters can bring compensating gains and at the same time can allow us to turn our decision-making powers toward matters of greater significance. Suppose our environment could be so controlled that ill health becomes almost an impossibility: the water we drink not only tastes good but is healthy; our food is not only nutritious, delicious, and various, but cannot cause disease or weight gain; airborne diseases are eliminated; and so on. We are better-off—we are all healthy—though we have fewer choices to make. We cannot decide to overeat, or to drink polluted water, or to become sick. But though our rational faculties are not faced with choices in these areas, that loss is not a diminution in well-being; and even if it were, it would be outweighed by a compensating gain (health). There would remain many areas of our lives over which we could continue to exercise rational control, and our powers of practical choice in these areas could be exercised as fully as they were before.

One of the great goods that a child must be trained to acquire and enjoy is the ability to make up his own mind about areas of his life that are important to him—what job he will have, whom he will marry, with whom he will associate, where he will live, and so on. If major choice points do not exist, if every important aspect of his life is planned for him, his cognitive powers are not challenged, and he is not called upon to exercise his imagination. No room is left, in his decision making, for creativity, individuality, and exploration. That does not mean that children or adults should be given the option of eating unhealthy food, drinking bad water, and smelling foul air. These ills can be made unavailable to us without diminishing our powers.

If I take it upon myself to control everything in your environment, so that you no longer have effective control over *anything* that you do, then I do you great harm by turning you into a passive creature who has no decision-making powers or skills. My manipulations might have some good effects: if, for example, I use my great power over you to protect your physical health and make your environment tranquil, that is good for you, but it is a small benefit in comparison with the harm done to you when you are left with no decision-making authority.

Powerful elites—political, economic, professional—can easily misunderstand or ignore the good of the public. That is one kind of reason in favor of democracy, but it is not the only one. Even when elites are responsible and trustworthy, the public loses something of great value if it is turned into a politically powerless and purely passive recipient of their attention and benefits. Developmentalism is not a political theory—it is only a theory about what is good—but it can play a role in explaining why some of the central values of liberal democracy—self-governance, liberty, autonomy—are indeed valuable. Flourishing is what is good for any living thing, and among the powers of a human being that flourish, when circumstances are fortunate, are the cognitive skills used in critical and autonomous deliberation. It is not because people often dislike being controlled by others that authoritarian governance is at best a stopgap measure; in fact, in certain conditions people will grow accustomed to passivity and will fear its loss. If a political theory must be based, at least to some extent, on a theory about what is good for people, then developmentalism will provide a better basis for political theory than any conative conception of well-being.[37]

The notion of "autonomous deliberation" used in the preceding paragraph is the familiar idea we invoke when we talk about a person having an independent mind and in this sense governing himself. An autonomous person, so conceived, does not merely make decisions; he makes *his own* decisions, he judges *for himself*. That is entirely compatible with his seeking the advice of others—provided that the advice is not followed slavishly but is critically scrutinized and evaluated according to his own standards. If someone begins each day by consulting an authority figure about how the rest of the day is to be spent, and he merely does whatever he is told to do because he assumes that, whatever the content of that advice he is receiving, it must be good advice, his actions cannot reasonably be regarded as an expression of any independence of mind. He has, in effect, decided to mimic the mind of another; in fact, it could be said that he has no mind of his own. Admittedly, the decision to hand over the conduct of his life to another person may have been voluntary and wholehearted. He chose to arrange his life in this way, but nonetheless, his way of life is inimical to the development and expression of autonomy. He may be entirely content with his lot, but that does not show that he is really ruled by himself and not by another. Consider a political analogue: when a public official voluntarily hands over his office to another, it is the latter who now rules and not the former, even though he initiated that transfer of power. Just so, when one hands over, however voluntarily, the concrete details of one's choices to another, it is the other person who rules.[38]

---

37. Among the many recent attempts to place a conception of freedom or liberty at the center of political theory, those to which I am most sympathetic are Raz's (*The Morality of Freedom* and *Ethics in the Public Domain*) and Fleischacker's (*A Third Concept of Liberty*). Neither proposes a developmental conception of well-being. But Fleischacker's advocacy of social conditions that develop a citizen's ability to exercise his own judgment (pp. 3–20, 32–87, 243–278) can easily be accommodated by such a conception. Raz, by linking well-being with the pursuit of valuable goals (*The Morality of Freedom*, p. 298) and affirming the value of autonomy (ibid., p. 390), makes autonomy a component of a well-lived life—something whose protection he takes to be the primary business of political morality (*Ethics in the Public Domain*, p. v). My discussion departs from Dworkin's (*The Theory and Practice of Autonomy*, pp. 3–47), in that he characterizes individuals as autonomous even if they renounce or fail to achieve what he calls "substantive independence" (ibid., p. 23). Needless to say, my thinking on this subject follows the lead of Mill in the third chapter of *On Liberty*.

38. No doubt several different conceptions of autonomy are in circulation, and it would be fruitless to insist that the word should be attached to only one of them; what matters is to ob-

It would be a mistake to suppose that whenever someone devotes himself to the well-being of others, he becomes unable to exercise the independence of mind I am calling "autonomy." To be responsive to the needs of others is not to be ruled by others. (Think of a doctor who takes control in an emergency.) A person who judges for himself what he is to do is not thereby confined to thinking only about what is in his own interest to do. Nonetheless, there are ways of being responsive to others that do involve a surrender of one's autonomy, as the example used in the preceding paragraph shows. But it is not only when one slavishly follows orders or slavishly accepts advice that one delivers one's mind to another and surrenders one's agency. If one person's love of another takes the form of a mindless willingness to do whatever his beloved wants, autonomy has been surrendered. If one is uncritically complaisant in one's relation to others, one is constantly subject to their will and develops no standards for deciding whether one should try to please them. One is not truly acting, but being pushed and pulled by the sweet lures of agreeable relations. Similarly, if one is overwhelmed by the power of another personality and mimics him in every aspect of his life—his tastes, appearance, preferences—one's mind has, in effect, been invaded by another's. It is not difficult to understand what Oscar Wilde is talking about when he says, paradoxically: "Most people are other people. Their thoughts are someone else's opinions, their lives a mimicry, their passions a quotation."[39] Nothing is amiss when one person's opinions agree with another's, or when one person is persuaded by another. But Wilde is referring to something more pernicious: the highly

---

serve distinctions among different kinds of autonomy. Autonomy as independence of mind is one kind of good, but that is not to say that no other psychological state that might be labeled a form of autonomy is good. There is also a kind of autonomy that consists in the exercise of a will that is unconstrained by external or internal coercive forces; that condition is compatible with slavish but willing subordination to the advice, example, or commands of others. It is no doubt noninstrumentally bad for someone (to some extent) if his will regularly labors under such constraint, even if what he is compelled to do is instrumentally good for him (to some extent). That he *unwillingly* does such-and-such is bad; but that he unwillingly does *such-and-such* may be good (as a means).

39. Wilde, *De Profundis,* p. 76. This well-known epigram occurs in the midst of a discussion of Christ. It is preceded by Wilde's approval of Emerson's statement, in a lecture entitled "The Preacher," that "nothing is more rare in any man than an act of his own." Wilde believes that the widespread absence of independent thinking and action can be remedied by an alteration of social conditions, and that the sort of individualism he favored is "latent and potential in mankind generally" ("The Soul of Man under Socialism," p. 132).

imitative nature of human beings and the threat this poses to the development of a mind and will that are capable of departing from others when doing so is justified. The pattern of mental development that is most desirable for a child is one in which he learns how to control his imitative propensities, to develop a mind of his own, and to enjoy its exercise. When a child at some stage of development rebels against authority, that urge can be put to good use.

As I noted above, a democratic state is in serious trouble if large numbers of citizens are too pliable and slavish to serve as an effective check on the power of elites. For then the various goods (security from danger, clean water, roads, and so on) that governments might provide citizens when they are well administered can all too easily be denied them. So it is both good in itself and instrumentally valuable for people to develop and exercise the mental powers that constitute autonomous agency. That good, of course, is not something that anyone can reasonably expect to be unlimited in extent. In groups governed by majority rule, the minority is barred from getting its way, and so there is a limitation in the expression of their autonomy. But when no group in a polity dominates any other, and educational institutions are in place that foster the development and expression of autonomy in all citizens, no one can reasonably complain—certainly not on the grounds that his own way of thinking about collective projects is not always accepted by others and therefore cannot issue in action.

Autonomy, so conceived, is something that is more fully exercised in certain kinds of work than others. When all the tasks one must perform are prescribed by one's employer and leave no room for deciding how to go about performing a task well, they do not allow for the expression of autonomy. Among the many inequities of most economies is the great disparity that exists between different kinds of remunerative labor, some of them leaving no room for independent thinking and others requiring it as a matter of course. So long as the work world offers so few opportunities to achieve this good, most citizens must look to periods of leisure for their only concrete opportunities to exercise genuine control over their lives and to escape "the totalitarian claims of the world of work."[40]

40. Josef Pieper, *Leisure: The Basis of Culture*, p. 39.

The struggle for mere survival or the mere essentials of food, clothing, and shelter is no less a bar to the development and enjoyment of an independent mind than is political domination.

Important as it is, autonomy is only one good among many, and its value must not be exaggerated. It is certainly not a precondition for the existence of all other human goods; nor is there is any basis for holding that it is preeminent among goods and outweighs all others. Someone who makes up his own mind about the kind of work he will do and the person he will marry might make extremely poor choices and suffer greatly as a result. A marriage arranged by a couple's parents might be a very good match—a much better relationship for the married couple, in fact, than the one they would have gladly chosen on their own. Similarly, a job to which one is assigned by the state may be one that develops one's mind and is thoroughly enjoyed; it too might do one more good than the job into which one might have drifted on one's own.[41] Something valuable is lost when independence of mind is not developed or exercised; but certainly not everything. We should not pretend that nothing good ever happens to those who live in nonliberal societies. Nonetheless, liberal institutions—that is, social arrangements that give individuals control over the major aspects of their lives—are founded on the reasonable hope that people can be educated not only to think for themselves but also to think well (about their own good), and that they will often make better choices about these matters, when those choices express an independent mind, than would others (parents, government officials, religious authorities) who decide on their behalf.

---

41. Consider someone whose marriage or profession has been arranged for him and not initially selected by him; and suppose that all goes well: he enjoys the full exercise of his capacities and is successful by every other measure. It might nonetheless be suggested that he would have been even better-off had he himself chosen that marriage partner or that line of work. For in that case, he would have not only all the goods that we have already posited that his life includes, but, in addition, the good of having a partner or profession of his own choosing. The suggestion is not that he would *enjoy* his life all the more had he made his own decision; it is rather that there is a kind of autonomy his life lacks if it is selected for him; and it is intrinsically good for someone to possess that kind of autonomy. I do not find this a compelling thought experiment: as I see it, a way of life initiated by someone else's choice is not for that very reason worse for the person living it than the same way of life that is self-selected.

54. What Is Good and Why

In his last book, Bernard Williams wrote: "There is a danger that if trust-worthiness (or anything else) is regarded as having an intrinsic value, it will be supposed that there is nothing else to be said about its valuable-ness—it is good because it is good, and that is all there is to be said about it. . . . What we want . . . is some insight into these values, . . . an insight that does not reduce them to the merely instrumental."[42]

If developmentalism has any merit as a philosophical theory about what is good, it lies in the general strategy it proposes for accommodating Williams's point. And surely Williams does have a good point. It is unilluminating to be told that knowledge is good, virtue is good, pleasure is good, and so on. It would be no more illuminating to be told that knowledge, virtue, and pleasure are good *for* us. Any theoretician who makes such a claim will be asked, why? One way of responding to that question will be to look for the ways in which these values lead to other values—but that will only push the question back one step, because we will be asked why what is produced by them is worth having. (And it would be particularly silly to claim that pleasure is good for its consequences.) A different way of responding might simply be to dig in one's heels: these items are good in themselves, as you can see simply by carefully reflecting on them. That is Ross's approach, and hedonists may also adopt it. Isn't it obvious, the hedonist will ask, that pleasure is good?—and it is indeed hard to find anything useful to say in response to that question.

Developmentalism proposes that we can achieve some insight into what is good for us by tracing the development—and that means healthy development—of a human being over the course of a lifetime. As we have seen in our discussion of the virtues and the value of autonomy, it seeks to understand why valued features of our lives are valuable by seeing how they fit into the life of a properly developing child. It does not simply assert that justice, honesty, and autonomy are somehow valuable. It asks a more specific question: are they good *for* us? And then it uses a rough picture of the powers of a human being—cognitive, affective, sensory, and so on—as a template in which whatever is good for us can be situated. To say that justice and self-governance are good for us, and to

---

42. Williams, *Truth and Truthfulness*, p. 90.

explain why, is to take a step toward a more concrete specification of what a flourishing life is—more concrete than is provided by the bare assertion that it consists in the use of our cognitive, affective, and social powers. Illumination about well-being is to be obtained by a process of making the general and abstract more detailed and precise. But this is not a process that comes to an end at some fixed and easily recognizable point. Every account of what is good for a human being must be a sketch that is specific enough for certain purposes but not for others; further elaboration and further inquiry are always possible. That is true not only because the story we tell about our powers is always subject to revision or expansion, but also because we can always find new insights about what is good for us by deftly giving greater detail and density to the rough picture of human well-being that we all take for granted.

We have come to the end of our discussion of the two intimately connected subjects of this work: what is good and why. We can best understand what is good by seeing what is good *for* someone. And seeing what is good for someone is not a matter merely of possessing a list of disparate items that have nothing in common beyond their having been joined together on that list. What is good for any living being? We should reply: whatever is a component of or a contributor to its flourishing. Can we say not only what is good for someone, but why? That is, do we merely have to accept or reject, without explanation, an assertion that it is noninstrumentally good for S that P? Our way of responding to the question "What is good?" also provides an answer to this second question. Why is it good for someone to have friends? To be just? To have an independent mind? To learn how to swim? To have a sexual partner? To relish food? To love music? To reply to these questions, we tell a story about the healthy development of the various powers of a human being. Our story has explanatory force because it allows us to see how the items about which we are being asked have a place within a convincing and attractive picture of human life as it should be lived when all goes well. To the question "Why is flourishing good?" we can reply by giving a more concrete specification of what the flourishing of this or that species consists in: flourishing is not good as a means to some further end, but because *this* (and here we fill in the details) is what it involves. The goodness of each separate component of flourishing is better understood when it is seen as part of a larger whole, and the goodness of the whole is better understood when it is seen not merely as an unspecified abstraction but as a complex whole that is constituted by *these* concrete parts.

"Questions of ultimate ends are not amenable to direct proof. Whatever can be proved to be good must be so by being shown to be a means to something admitted to be good without proof. The medical art is proved to be good by its conducing to health; but how is it possible to prove that health is good? The art of music is good, for the reason, among others, that it produces pleasure; but what proof is it possible to give that pleasure is good?" Thus Mill, in the first chapter of *Utilitarianism*.[43] Hume argued for a similar point—that "ultimate ends . . . can never . . . be accounted for by reason"—and he inferred, "Something must be desirable on its own account, and because of its immediate accord or agreement with human sentiment and affection."[44] Mill and Hume argue for their conclusions by way of example, but they spend too little time on their examples. They simply assert that there is no way to show that health is good, or that all pleasure is good, or that all pain is bad. But the health of an organism is its flourishing, and we can explain why flourishing is good by considering the components of which it is the whole. Pleasure is *not* good nor pain bad in all cases; we see that this is so, and why it is so, by recognizing how pleasure and pain can be, or can fail to be, integrated with other components of a well-lived life (sections 33, 38, 49–51). "Human sentiment and affection" do not "account for" ultimate ends, as the failure of the conative approach to well-being shows. Philosophical reflection "accounts for" ultimate ends not by inferring truths about what is good from premises devoid of empirical content, but by systematizing commonsense notions of what is involved in a flourishing life for this or that species.[45]

43. Mill, *Utilitarianism,* pp. 207–208.
44. Hume, *An Enquiry Concerning the Principles of Morals,* app. 1, his emphasis.
45. Common sense, as I noted earlier, is a good place to start when one has nothing better. Although it is not the only or necessarily the best standard for testing a philosophical theory, it should be abandoned only when we find reason to do so.

FOUR

The Sovereignty of Good

55. The Importance of What Is Good for Us

Although the two principal questions posed by this work have now been addressed, there remains a third, which was raised in Chapter 1 but left unanswered: what role should good and bad (that is, what is good or bad *for* some living being) play in our thoughts and actions? Utilitarianism places these values at the center of all good practical reasoning by holding that the quantity of good and harm we do is the only consideration that should figure in our deliberations. We rejected, almost from the start (sections 4, 12), the principle that good should be maximized. Even so, good and bad may play an essential role whenever we reason well to a practical conclusion. That is a possibility we should now explore.

Certainly *one* reasonable test to apply to a proposed course of action is to ask: will it do anyone some good, or impede some harm? In extreme circumstances, an alternative under consideration might fail that test and nonetheless be one's best choice. Every other option might do great harm; it would then speak in favor of one's action that it is harmless, even though it does no good.

What we would like to know, however, is whether we need to look outside the realm of what is good or bad and to acknowledge an entirely different sort of consideration, having nothing to do with what is good or bad for anyone, that speaks in favor or against what we propose to do. To speak metaphorically: we would like to know whether there are multiple and independent routes for arriving at practical conclusions, some of them passing through what is good or bad but others bypassing good and bad entirely.[1]

---

1. One way to use the word "deontological" would be to apply it to any theory of practical

John Rawls, it should be recalled (section 5), holds that when an action is morally wrong, it does not matter that it does some good, or even that it does more good than any alternative. He conceives of rightness as an alternative route to practical conclusions: it bypasses goodness, construed as the satisfaction of rational desire.[2] It does not matter that

reasoning that holds that, at least in some cases, the proper path to a practical conclusion completely bypasses any consideration of what is good or bad for someone. That would be close to the way C. D. Broad proposes to use the term: "Some people judge that there are certain types of action which ought to be done (or avoided) in all or in certain types of situation, regardless of the goodness or badness of the probable consequences. This is what I call the 'deontological' application of 'ought'" (*Five Types of Ethical Theory*, p. 162). Correspondingly, Broad suggests, one uses "ought" in a "teleological" way when, on the basis of some consideration of good or harm, one arrives at the conclusion that one ought to do something. A teleological theory, then, would be one that impugns deontological uses of "ought" and sanctions only teleological uses. Broad's distinction occurs in his discussion of Henry Sidgwick, who distinguishes two broad approaches to the study of ethics, one of which is "prominent in modern ethical thought" and investigates "the true Moral laws," and the other of which inquires into the "'True Good' of man" (*The Methods of Ethics*, p. 3). John Rawls uses the terms "deontological" and "teleological" differently. For him, "deontological" is defined negatively: a theory is deontological simply by being an ethical theory that is not teleological (*A Theory of Justice*, p. 26); and a theory is teleological when "the good is defined independently from the right, and then the right is defined as that which maximizes the good" (ibid., pp. 21–22). All theories that deny that good should be maximized are to be called deontological, according to this usage, and so the "theory" proposed in this study (if "theory" is the proper term for it) would be deontological. Because this way of speaking lumps together radically diverse approaches to practical reasoning, I find Broad's way of using "deontological" more fruitful—if that term has some useful role to play in the classification of ethical theories. The approach I am proposing would, in that case, be called teleological rather than deontological. But for reasons made clear in Chapter 1, my approach is not teleological in Scanlon's sense of the term (*What We Owe to Each Other*, pp. 79–87).

2. Two principles of moral rightness—namely, the principles of justice that are to govern the basic structure of society—are adopted by the parties in the original position in light of such "social primary goods" as "rights, liberties, and opportunities, and income and wealth" (Rawls, *A Theory of Justice*, p. 54). The theory that underlies these forms of rightness cannot be understood apart from a theory of goodness. Nonetheless, "the welfare of society as a whole cannot override" what is wrong because unjust (ibid., p. 3). Rawls does not claim that *all* principles of rightness are selected on the basis of "social primary goods," or that these goods provide even a roughly accurate measure of well-being. Must every principle of rightness be chosen in the original position by a process of reasoning that adverts to something that is good for someone—even though such a good need not be one of the "social primary goods"? Why might a principle of rightness not be chosen in the light of some consideration having nothing to do with anyone's well-being? It is difficult to know how Rawls would have wished to answer these questions, and what basis there is in his framework for responding in one way or another. He affirms that "the two main concepts of ethics are those of the right and the good" (ibid., p. 21), but this by itself does not imply that for every principle of rightness there is a good that it secures. And yet, if rightness is not at least for the most part the securing of something good, what is it about goodness that accounts for its being one of the two main concepts of ethics?

a morally wrongful action satisfies rational desires, even when it greatly satisfies the rational desires of a great many. Since it violates a principle that would be accepted in the original position, its wrongfulness nullifies its goodness.

Rawls is right that the satisfaction of a rational desire, or even the rational desires of many people, should sometimes bear no weight in an individual's or a group's deliberations. But since goodness does not consist in the satisfaction of rational desires, he has not shown that we sometimes properly bypass goodness in our practical reasoning. What we must investigate is whether goodness and badness, *properly understood*, provide only one source of practical justification.

Earlier (section 8) we observed that the merit of many widely accepted social norms consists in the way in which they protect what is good or impede what is harmful; and we are most inclined to acknowledge exceptions to these rules when we think of cases in which violating them does no harm. The theory of well-being proposed in Chapter 3 gives us no reason to doubt that thesis. We assumed that university rules against plagiarism, for example, promote the good of students; and the developmental conception of well-being supports that claim, since we count the enjoyment of our cognitive powers as one component of a flourishing life (section 42). The norm that prohibits adultery serves, at least in many cases, a useful purpose because of the way in which sexual infidelity often undoes the good that comes with affective and sexual intimacy (sections 41, 43). Looking for exceptionless prohibitions, we cited those that forbid us from inflicting serious physical harm merely for the fun of it (section 8). Since that sort of pleasure is not good for anyone to feel (section 33), and the harms are so grievous (section 38), it is understandable that these principles should be exceptionless. When we ask whether a proposed course of action should be rejected because it violates a widely accepted social norm, or is a legitimate exception, we are not bypassing considerations of good and bad—not if the rule is a good one. What entitles a rule to our consideration is the good accomplished by its observance.

But perhaps our survey of moral rules in Chapter 1 overlooked some that have nothing to do with what is good or bad for people. Should we not keep our promises, for example, whether doing so is good or bad? Must we not refrain from interfering with people against their will, even if intervention would promote their good? Ought we not honor and respect the dead, even though this does them no good? Perhaps the realm of moral rightness is a source of reasons that bypass goodness altogether, even when we think about goodness along developmental lines. Those possibilities must be examined more carefully. What we will find is that here, too, justification adverts to good or bad. In fact, we can fully understand the reasons for keeping promises (when in fact they should be kept), or not intervening paternalistically (when we should leave someone alone), or honoring those who have died (when they are to be honored), without taking into account the moral rightness of doing so (sections 57, 61, and 67). We will find that the utilitarian's inattention to moral wrongness is justified (sections 7, 65).

To hold, as I believe we should, that all justification proceeds by way of good and bad—that no realm of practical reasons floats free of what is good or bad for someone and competes with them—is not to downplay the importance of answering the question "To whom should one do good?" Utilitarianism goes astray by supposing that this question is of no independent importance because it is always to be answered by looking to the greatest quantity of good. As W. D. Ross emphasizes in his critique of utilitarianism, "the highly personal character of duty" must not be overlooked. "If the only duty is to produce the maximum of good, the question who is to have the good . . . should make no difference."[3] But if one has promised to deliver some good to S, that gives one a reason for delivering that good *to S*. The justification for keeping a promise adverts to something good that it accomplishes (section 57), but who it is that one benefits with that promised good can hardly be a matter of indifference. Similarly, if S is T's father, then S must pay extraordinary attention to T's good, and he must not leave aside the question of who benefits from his actions. Once we choose or are justifiably assigned various social roles, we must take them into account in our deliberations (sections 12, 57). If we try to abstract from those concrete assignments and ask ourselves, "Whose good should I be promoting?" there is no possible answer to our question (sections 11–15).

By contrast, there is an immediately appealing way to answer the question "Whom should one try to *harm*?" The answer is: no one and no thing. That does not mean that one should reject any course of action that does some harm to someone. The harm we cause must sometimes

3. Ross, *The Right and the Good*, p. 22.

be accepted as a regrettable though necessary cost, but it should never be accepted unless some sufficiently great good compensates for it. Why should we not allow someone to destroy a forest, or any other living things, for the sheer pleasure of doing so (section 2)? Simply because he does harm, and no good compensates for that damage.

Justice, as it is sometimes conceived, requires that those who have treated others badly should, for that reason alone, be treated badly in turn. No one's good need be served by punishment, according to this theory; rather, we are required to punish merely because the scales of fortune and misfortune have become unbalanced and need to be set right. Legal punishment, it might be said, is the state's attempt to bring suffering to those who deserve it. But the idea that we should devote ourselves to making certain people worse-off for no reason except that they deserve such misery is unappealing (section 58).

Some accept a closely related principle, one that applies not to our actions but to our mental life; they think that we should want bad people to suffer in proportion to their badness, and we should be glad when their unhappiness is proportional to the gravity of their vices. According to Ross, it is good that this should happen; this is one of the four good things, to be set beside pleasure, knowledge, and virtue.[4] But we should reject this conception of justice (section 59). We should instead accept a way of thinking about this virtue that does not bring it into conflict with the project of doing what is good for people (section 60). Principles for allocating goods—on the basis of need, or merit, or equality—are among the factors that should be taken into consideration when we decide to whom we should be doing good. So conceived, considerations of justice do not bypass the whole realm of reasons that advert to what is good for people, but they operate within that realm, directing us to benefit these people rather than those, or these people as much as those.

There is another way in which the importance of what is good for someone might be downgraded. Good poetry, it might be said, is valuable; so too is good science, good philosophy, good painting, and so on. But *why* are these things valuable? One way of answering that question is to say: because, upon consideration, we find that we are justified in valuing them. Such an answer studiously avoids making any claim about what is good *for* anyone. In effect, it denies that good poetry need be

4. Ibid., p. 138.

good for anyone in order to be good as poetry. Clearly that is not the way we *always* think about the evaluation of something as good of a kind. Rather, when we call something a good thing of a kind, we often support the assignment of that high grade by referring to the way in which the item in question benefits someone or other. I noted at the outset: "Food is good by being good *for* the person who eats it. Plans are good when their results are likely to be good *for* those affected by them. A good friend is good *for* the person to whom he is a friend" (section 1). Similarly, we should look for a way of explaining why good poetry should be read that rests on the idea that writing, listening to, and reading good poetry is good for those who engage in these activities (section 69). Whenever we defend the claim that something is valuable, we should do so by locating that valuable item in the framework of well-being.

The hypothesis we should put to the test is that all the elements of good practical reasoning are, in some way, good-related or bad-related: they must say which sorts of goods and harms are in view, whose good and harm are in view, how much good and how much harm are in view, why that good or harm should be done to that person and not another, and so on. There must be a premise that says how the act under consideration plays a role in advancing or protecting someone's well-being. There must also be a premise that explains why *this* agent should act for the good of *that* beneficiary or *those* beneficiaries. If there are countervailing considerations, these must point to some harm that the act under consideration would do, or some individuals whose good this agent should not be neglecting. In these several different ways, good and bad lie at the center of practical justification. Once we know everything we can know about facts that are related to goodness—what is good (including what is best), what is bad (and worst), to whom one should do good, the strength of competing considerations based on good and bad, and the proportionality of burdens and benefits—there is nothing further one needs to learn in order to decide how to act. If that is so, good is indeed "sovereign," to use Iris Murdoch's phrase: it is the "master value" of practical life and the focal point of practical thought.[5]

---

5. The title of the present chapter is taken from Iris Murdoch, *The Sovereignty of Good*, which seeks to restore goodness to the position that Plato assigns it in his *Republic*.

56. Good's Insufficiency

Suppose you are told that if you do V, the result will be good for S. You are told what V is: some simple act that will cost you a little time and will deplete your resources slightly. (V might be writing a check for one dollar.) But you are not told anything about your beneficiary, S, or the way in which what you do is good. You are completely confident in your interlocutor: some good will indeed happen to some living being. But you are not told whether that living being is a plant, or an animal, or a human being.

Is the information you have been given sufficient to permit you to draw the conclusion that you should do V? No. For one thing, S might be a plant. Plants should not be wantonly destroyed, but there is no reason to make a special effort simply for the sake of their good. We should benefit them only if that in turn helps someone else who should be helped; they fall below the threshold of merited direct concern. Gardeners love tending to their gardens, and it is good for *them* that they do so (it gives their sensory systems a treat); it is for the good of human beings (and perhaps animals as well) that we tend to the plant world.[6] That is because the only kind of good a plant can have is inferior by far to the kinds of goods that human beings can enjoy. When a human being grows to the full height and weight that proper nourishment allows and is free of physical disease, he attains the kind of good that a plant too is capable of. But if that were the only kind of good human beings could have, our lives would be far less rich than they can be when things go well enough. That is all that plants can achieve—and it is not enough to make it worthwhile to take action merely to make them better off. There

6. Some members of the plant world (stately oaks, for example) are *grand*—that is, they satisfy one of our aesthetic standards—and their wanton destruction is for that reason especially objectionable. The contribution they can make to the flourishing of our senses gives us a special basis for protecting them. We should not merely refrain from destroying them for no good reason (a forbearance we should extend to anything or anyone that can flourish); we do well (for our sake) to protect and cultivate them. But there is no reason to extend our care to something merely on the grounds that it is a living thing, or that it is a living being for which some things are good and others bad. (Recall the possibility mentioned in section 2: some living things may be too simple to count as flourishing or failing to flourish, and so there may be no such thing as what is good or bad for them.) In any case, many living things (harmful viruses, for example) must be destroyed, and these should fall below the threshold of our concern if we are to have some chance of going on with our lives.

are much better things for us to do. The more humanlike a living thing is—the more it has cognitive and affective powers and lives in a social world—the richer the life of which it is capable, because the kinds of goods it can possess are of a higher order. But the fact that plants can be harmed should count for something in our practical reasoning: that is why we need to justify any harm we do them by showing that we are not being needlessly or wantonly destructive.

That establishes an important point: the mere fact that an act would do some good is never, by itself, enough to support a conclusion about what should be done.[7] That thesis can be supported in several other ways.

Suppose you are now given more information: you are told that S is a human being. Even so, you should ask for other facts before you decide whether to infer that you should do V. For suppose that a different act, W, which costs you no more than V, would be better for S than V would be. Then, if you do one or the other, it is W, not V, that you should do. You should ask your informant to see to it that your investment brings about what is best for S, not merely what is good for S.

But you still do not have as much information as you need, for you know nothing about S except that he or she is a human being. You have no idea whether you have any significant personal relationship to S. (You might: S might even be you.) You do not know how well-off S is. Should you be helping someone whose needs are greater? Should you be helping S at all—if S is not yourself or someone else whose well-being is already of some concern to you? If S is a complete stranger, helping him or her will leave fewer resources for doing what is good for the people to whom you have already made commitments and who are objects of your concern. You should therefore not help S in the absence of further information.

7. This point reveals that something has gone amiss if intrinsic value or goodness is defined as "to be promoted," and what is noninstrumentally good for a creature is regarded as one species of intrinsic value. This is one of the defining features of what Scanlon calls a "teleological" conception of intrinsic value (a conception he opposes). See *What We Owe to Each Other,* pp. 79–87. It is a further question whether ethical theory or practical reasoning has any use for a conception of intrinsic value when this is construed as a genus of goodness of which the things that are good for some individual form only one species. Certainly, each of us needs to know whose good it is that we should be promoting, and also what is good for these individuals. But if what is good for someone plays the central role I assign to it, and the kinds of things I claim are good for human beings really are so, there is no wider realm of intrinsic value or goodness of which what is good for individuals forms only one part. See below, section 69.

The hypothetical situation we have been discussing is of course artificial, but it is a useful way to make a philosophical point: to draw a practical conclusion, one needs more than a general conception of what is good; one must also know something about who the potential beneficiaries of one's actions are, and about how one is situated in relation to them. To make this point is not to say (quite correctly) that in addition to one's general knowledge about the sorts of things that are good, one also needs to know which particular actions will bring it about that something good is done. Rather, it is to generalize on the point Ross makes against utilitarianism when he discusses promises.[8] When we have made a promise to someone, and what we have promised to do is something that is good, then we have given ourselves a partial answer to the question "Whose good should I attend to?" A promisor, having made a promise, cannot view himself as being in the business of maximizing the good—treating all potential beneficiaries on a par and merely deciding how to squeeze as much good as possible out of his resources. Rather, he must allocate his resources in a way that helps someone in particular—the beneficiary of the promise (who may in fact be himself), because he owes it to the promisee (not himself) to do so. But Ross's point about promises is just one example of the way in which our social relations help us answer the question "Whose good should I promote?"

The practice of promising gives us the option of picking out some person or group as the object of our special concern for a length of time of our choosing, and of delivering a good of our choosing to that person or group. It is one small example of the ways in which social communities provide structure to our lives by carving out various practices by which we do good for ourselves and for others (section 13). Many of these practices are long-term and good-specific. Teachers, farmers, builders, warriors, parents—the list is extremely long, is always undergoing transformation, and is always open to question. These are social roles for which we need training, and when we learn them, we enter into relationships with others through which we do what is good for them. They are like the practice of promise keeping, in that they give us some help in answering the question "Whose good should I promote?" If S is a doctor and T is her patient, then S should help T in a certain respect. The fact that T is ill does not give everyone in the world some reason to

8. Ross, *The Right and the Good*, pp. 22, 37–39.

help her get better or to want her to get better (sections 14–15). But if
S is specially trained to provide a certain good to others and has a relationship with T, that makes it appropriate that S should provide that
good to T. From these facts, it can be inferred that S should do so. Truths
about flourishing and un-flourishing do not by themselves allow us to
draw conclusions about what to do, but when they are combined with
truths about the roles we inhabit, and about the specific tasks of doing
good that we choose or are assigned to us, then conclusions can be
drawn about what we should do. (At times the role we inhabit is foisted
upon us merely by our proximity to another human being and the im-
mediacy of his need: a person is in danger, and only a few are close
enough to help.)

That does not mean that we should unthinkingly accept whatever social division of labor we find in place. Some of the jobs people perform
may do no good at all, or they may do a great deal of harm as well as
good. We can ask whether there should be professional politicians, or
warriors, or prostitutes, or university professors, or friends, or promise-
makers, or executioners, or gangs, or whether adult children are the
ones who should care for their ailing parents. But the social division of
labor into which we are born and trained gives us a starting point for our
reflections: this is the way we do good now, and if we think there is
something wrong with these social roles, then at least we know what it is
that has to be changed. The project of doing good gets off the ground by
making changes in or working with the ways of doing good with which
we are familiar. In the absence of some division of labor in our good-doing practices, practical reasoning would not be able to take us toward
any conclusions about what to do.

The general theory of what is good will certainly contribute, to some
degree, to a critique of current social practices and roles, but it cannot
do that job entirely on its own. (It says, for example, how children
should develop, but not whether the family is the best environment for
children.) When we set about doing some good, we must think not only
about what is good in general, but also about the sorts of goods we want
to specialize in giving, which people we want to provide those goods to,
whom we want as friends, whether we want children, and so on. These
typically play a far larger role in structuring our good-doing activities
than do the promises we make, but the same general point applies to
both: practical conclusions must draw upon two kinds of premises, one

of them based on a general picture of what a flourishing human life is, and the other appealing to the particularities of the social world in which we are embedded.

57. Promises

If one has made a promise, one should, for that very reason, keep it—or so it is thought. According to some philosophers—Ross, as we noted (section 56), is a prominent example—this is one of several principles to which we should give some weight in our moral reasoning. I will pay special attention to promise keeping because it might be thought of as something we should do, even when doing so does no good. If so, that would refute the hypothesis proposed in section 55.

Ross does not in fact claim that promises should be kept even when doing so does no good. What he insists upon is this: when we have made a promise to do V, but some alternative to doing V would bring about more good, it is not true that in all cases we should choose that alternative.[9] That is because the promises we have made should always bear a certain amount of weight in our deliberations. Even though (according to Ross) we have a prima facie duty to do as much good as we can, the duty to keep a promise can, in certain cases, have greater stringency.[10] When these two duties come into conflict, sometimes one and sometimes the other will take precedence; which it is will vary according to circumstances.

Notice that this leaves open the possibility that the only promises we should keep are those that do some good. Ross simply leaves that issue aside, since it has no bearing on his principal goal, which is to replace utilitarianism with a theory that contains many more duties than the duty to do as much good as one can.[11]

But it might be thought that what Ross had in mind—or at any rate, what he should have had in mind—was that we have a duty to keep promises for no reason other than the fact that they are promises. Ac-

9. Ibid.
10. Ibid., pp. 19–20.
11. At one point he assumes that keeping a promise will always do a certain quantity of good—though, often enough, not as much good as the promisor might be able to do were the promise broken (ibid., pp. 34–35). If my fulfilling a promise would produce 1,000 units of good, it must not be broken merely in order to produce 1,001 units by doing some alternative.

cording to this way of thinking, it is in the very nature of promises that we have reason to keep them—a reason that has nothing to do with whether keeping them does any good. It might happen to be the case that keeping a promise does some good; but if so, it is not the good that keeping a promise does that justifies keeping it. It is justified, when it is justified, because it is an act of promise keeping. As Ross says: "When a plain man fulfils a promise because he thinks he ought to do so, . . . he thinks . . . much more of the past than of the future. What makes him think it right to act in a certain way is the fact that he has promised to do so—that and, usually, nothing more."[12]

It is obvious that not all promises should be kept. Suppose S is a professional killer and has promised T, his boss, to kill U, a juror who will not be bribed. All things considered, what should S do? Obviously, he should not keep his promise. In fact, nothing speaks in favor of his killing U. It is not the case that, on the one hand, the fact that he made a promise to kill U goes some way toward showing that he should do so; whereas, on the other hand, the fact that keeping his promise will involve killing U goes some way toward showing that he should not. That he promised to kill U does not even begin to justify his making an effort to do so.[13] If Ross assumes that every promise carries some weight, he is mistaken.[14]

12. Ibid., p. 17; compare with p. 37.

13. We should separate the question whether S has some reason to kill U from the question whether S is answerable *in some way* to T, the person to whom he made the promise. He might, for example, owe it to T to explain why he is reversing himself and will not honor his promise; but even if he does owe T that much, it does not follow that he also has some reason to kill U because of his promise. It is a further question whether S should, all things considered, give T the explanation to which he is entitled. Suppose his doing so will harm some and help none (not even T); in that case, I suggest, he need give T no explanation. Even if T has some claim on S, not all claims need be redeemed. For the view that promises always must receive great weight, see Margaret Gilbert, *On Social Facts,* p. 379: "If someone acknowledges that he has taken it upon himself to do something, it is hardly intelligible for him to deny that he has sufficient reason to do that thing. Indeed, it appears that he must accept that he has a strong sufficient reason to do that thing, one that can only be overridden in exceptional circumstances, if it can be *overridden* at all" (her emphasis). She explains in a footnote that breaking a promise might in some cases be excusable, even if it is never rationally justifiable.

14. It might be suggested that although promises to undertake what is morally wrong are void *ab initio,* all others are to be honored. But that leaves it unclear what should be put into the category of morally wrongful acts, and why this category should bear so much weight. Suppose that, in a period of self-loathing, I promise my enemy never again to lift a finger for my own good: such a self-limitation would not normally be counted as morally wrong, and yet it is hard to see why any significant weight—indeed, any weight at all—should be attached to this commitment.

But it might be thought that when it *is* the case that a promise should be kept, the reason it should be kept—the only reason—is that a promise has been made. That, of course, is not what a utilitarian would say. A utilitarian would insist, rather, that when keeping a promise does no good, it is pointless to keep it. The point of *making* a promise is—or should be—to do some good. And similarly the point of *keeping* a promise should be to do some good. When goal-directed activity is seen to have no point, it should stop, and there is no point in doing what does no good. So says the utilitarian. That is a thesis that deserves a hearing, and it is entirely distinct from the principle that lies at the heart of utilitarianism, one that we earlier rejected (section 4): that good should be maximized.

It does not normally happen that one person sets himself the goal of asking another person to make a promise, but is indifferent to what the content of the promise is. (It might happen in the following way: S bets T that T cannot induce U to make a promise, because S thinks U has a policy of never making promises.) Promises are usually made because someone has a goal other than making a promise, and the promise is used as a device to bring about that goal. For example, a wife wants her husband to stop smoking, and she induces him to promise that he will quit. Her goal is to do some good for her husband by getting him to stop smoking, and she thinks that since he will honor a commitment he makes to her, he is more likely to quit if he promises her to do so.

Suppose he does promise, but it is then discovered that all the evidence for the harmfulness of tobacco was fabricated, and cigarettes are shown to be highly beneficial. It would do no good for the husband to keep his promise, as he and his wife now recognize. All things considered, what should he do? There are several possible answers.

First, it might be said that a promise is a promise, and he must abide by his commitment, regardless of what he or his wife would like. Obviously, that will not do.

Second, it could be said if he wishes to continue smoking, he must first ask his wife to release him from his promise. She should do so; but if she does not, he must refrain from smoking. That will not do either. By hypothesis, she now realizes (as he does) that it would be best for him to continue to smoke. There is no longer any reason for her to want her husband to stop smoking, as they both realize. So there is no reason that he must first be released from his promise before he may justifiably smoke. He is no longer obligated by his promise; if he mistakenly asks to be released, and she compounds his error by declining, he is not re-quired, by virtue of his promise, to stop smoking. The force of the prom-ise has been nullified by its pointlessness. (There are, of course, cases in which the proper course of action *is* to ask to be released from a prom-ise—for example, when the burdens of keeping it are much higher than promisor or promisee could reasonably have foreseen.)

Third, it might be said that although there is some reason to keep the promise, there is a stronger reason not to do so. But our rejection of the second reply shows why we should not accept this one either. Hus-band and wife used his promise to her as a means to achieve a certain goal; as it turns out, what they thought was helpful is actually harmful. There is now no point or value in keeping the promise simply for the sake of keeping a promise. So, this is not a case in which there is some-thing to be said for keeping the promise, and something else to be said against it. If an act does no good whatsoever—is in fact harmful and is recognized as such—then the fact that it was promised has no force as a justification. The fact that it is pointless is precisely what deprives it of that force.[15]

None of this implies that promises have no justificatory force. When the husband promised his wife to give up smoking, a new reason for do-ing so was added to a reason that already existed. It was already the case that he should not smoke. Then, when he promised not to, there was all the more reason not to. Now he has assured her that he will refrain from smoking, on the assumption that this practice is harmful, and it would be disloyal to her, as well as harmful to himself, were he to continue to smoke.

---

15. A promise can also lose its point when the good it was meant to achieve has already been accomplished before the promise is honored. Suppose you have two broken alarm clocks and I promise to fix one of them by the end of the day. Before I have a chance to do so, however, another friend of yours happens along and fixes one of the two clocks. When I arrive in the eve-ning to honor my promise, you tell me that one of the clocks is now in good working order. I might of course nonetheless offer to fix the other, so that you have a spare. But I do not have to fix it, or ask to be released from my promise, because as soon as you tell me that you now have a functioning clock, it is mutually understood that what I promised to do no longer has the same value for you. The force of the promise has lapsed, and since we both see this (and see that the other sees it), I am no longer obliged by it. It would be absurd to suppose that since you still have a broken clock, I still owe it to you, until I am released from my debt, to fix your clock. (If, because of an emergency, you had to leave your apartment just before I arrived, my discovery, after I let myself in, that one of the clocks now works is a sufficient reason for me to suppose that there is no reason for me to keep my promise.)

When promises should, all things considered, be kept, why is it that they should be kept? We now see that it is a mistake to reply: simply because they are promises. Rather, we should reply: because they are *good* promises—that is, promises that do some good.[16]

We should not be misled by the example just used into thinking that whenever a promise should be kept, there already was sufficient reason, apart from the promise, to undertake the act that forms the promise's content. Suppose a father promises to spend the afternoon playing tennis with his daughter. We can assume that playing tennis is good for both. But that does not mean that it was already the case, before the promise, that father and daughter should spend the afternoon playing tennis with each other. That doing V would be good for S does not by itself support the conclusion that S should do V; many other alternatives may be equally good or better. But when S makes a promise to do V, and doing so would be good for someone, these facts join together to provide S with a reason to do V. In some cases, there is already sufficient reason to perform an act that we later promise to perform; in others, a promise joins together with a good to create a sufficient reason.

Another point should be kept in mind: A promise can be broken in a manner that does harm to the relationship between promisor and promisee. The good that is done by keeping a promise can consist precisely in the good of maintaining that relationship. Consider again the husband who has promised his wife that he will stop smoking. Suppose the new evidence about the effects of smoking is difficult to interpret; he takes it to show that smoking is not harmful, but she reads it differently and continues to urge him to stop. If he breaks his promise and remains a smoker, that perhaps will not harm his health, but it will almost certainly damage his relationship with his wife. Even though a promise is a tool to be used for bringing about a good result, there are other goods to be considered in thinking about promises we have made besides the one that serves as the point of the promise. It is not only the content of a promise that determines the good or harm done by keeping it. For this reason, one should sometimes make and keep a promise even though one reasonably believes that what is promised does no good or even does some harm to the promisee. Affection may flow more freely when we are

---

16. Cicero defends a similar idea, but he spoils it by also claiming, implausibly, that one should break a promise when doing so brings one a benefit that is greater than the loss incurred by the promisee. See *On Duties* 1.31.

willing to indulge some of the bad habits of our friends, and that can be a reasonable trade-off.

When we see no point to a promise and no significant relationship between promisor and promisee, we are baffled about whether there is any reason to keep it, or even about whether the words that were exchanged really constituted a promise. Suppose you are standing on a street corner, and a stranger approaches you and asks whether you will promise to meet him at that corner three hours later. You blurt out, "Yes," before you have had time to reflect; but by then, the stranger has disappeared, and you have no idea why he made this request. It is natural to wonder whether you have assured the stranger of anything, and whether, counting on your response, he will return. Perhaps this was a practical joke, and no promise was made. But perhaps the stranger is in fact counting on you. Do you, in that case, have some reason to meet him? How strong a reason? Strong enough to overcome competing considerations? It is impossible to say, because one has no idea what the point of the promise (if there was one) is, or even whether it has a point. But if it were the case that promises should be kept merely because they are promises, we would have to say: this promise (if that is what it was) has all the importance that any promise has simply by virtue of its being a promise.

The situation would be entirely different, of course, if the stranger had explained what his need was, or if the person who approached you was an old friend. In the absence of both these two elements—the point of a promise and a relationship between promisor and promisee—the case for doing what one says one will do, when one promises, disappears.

It should also be recognized that one person can induce another to make a promise as a way of exerting power, and not because of any interest he takes in the content of the promise. Imagine a group of nasty teenagers who take advantage of a newcomer to their circle. As the price of admission to their group, they may ask the newcomer whether he will promise to do this and that—matters that do no good, as they all realize. The content of the promises are of no interest to them; what they seek is the dominance over the newcomer that goes with his acceptance of the promises they propose to him. If, having foolishly made those promises, the newcomer reconsiders, should he be told that he must keep his word, because a promise is a promise? Or that he should ask permission to be released from the debt he owes them? Neither of the two factors that promises normally have when a case can be made for keeping them—a point and a meaningful human relationship—is present. These are not the sorts of promises from which one must ask to be released—in fact, doing so would merely perpetuate the servile relationship that the group wishes to impose on him. Since no one's good is served by keeping the promise, and it would be harmful for him to enter this group, there is no case for his keeping his word.

Promises do not all carry the same weight. In some cases, we should go to great lengths to keep our word; and if we decide not to do so, we have made a grave error. In other cases, although one is to be criticized for one's failure to keep one's word, the error one has made is minor. What makes the difference? Surely the magnitude of the good or harm that is involved. If one promises to drive a friend to the airport, and he misses his meeting because one has decided not to honor one's word, that is a serious breach; but if one promises to wear a silly hat to a party, and later decides to go hatless, that is a peccadillo. It would be absurd to invoke "the sanctity of promises" (Ross's phrase) as a reason to wear the silly hat.[17] But even when promises should be treated with utmost seriousness, that is not because the promise itself has become sanctified, but because of the great value of what was promised, or the great harm that would be caused by breaking the promise.

Sometimes the harm that would be done to a promisor if she *keeps* her promise would be so great that the damage done by its breach pales in comparison. Suppose S has promised to marry T, but she has second thoughts and now realizes that she would live a life of misery if she were to keep her word. T, we can assume, will be made worse-off by this rupture. But surely S is not required to keep her promise, merely to avoid harming T, or merely to keep her promise. Should she nonetheless attach some weight to the fact that she promised to marry T? Should we say that she is still obliged to marry T and must give serious consideration to this obligation, weighing it carefully against the considerations in favor of breaking her promise? It is hard to know whether to say that her promise carries little weight or none at all, and there seems to be no point in pursuing that question. When it is understood that the purpose

---

17. "One of the most evident facts of our moral consciousness is the sense we have of the sanctity of promises" (Ross, *The Right and the Good*, p. 37). But as G. E. M. Anscombe notes, "There are many cases of undertakings from the obligation of which a small degree of inconvenience exempts us" ("On Promising and Its Justice, and Whether It Need be Respected *in Foro Interno*," p. 15).

one should have in making a promise is, in large part, to enhance one's own well-being, and it becomes clear that keeping the promise would defeat that goal rather than foster it, the promise loses all or nearly all its force.[18]

When a promise should be kept, we can say that keeping it is the morally right thing to do, but when we are asked to explain why, the answer must always appeal to the good that is done by keeping it or the harm that would be done by breaking it. Breaking certain promises is *very* wrong, because the damage their violation does to one's relationships, or the good that one promised but failed to deliver, is very great. When one voluntarily adopts the social role of promise-maker, the importance of continuing to play that role cannot be assessed without knowing what was promised and the circumstances in which the promise was made. It is not a specialized role, like that of a farmer or engineer, that always has the same field of endeavor and always delivers the same types of goods. We assess the social usefulness of these task-specific roles by looking to the good or goods they produce. But the value of stepping into the roles of promise-maker and promise-keeper varies enormously, and it is sometimes zero or less. When a promise loses its point or never had one to begin with, and abandoning that role does no harm, breaking it is unobjectionable.

Sometimes a promise-maker and his promisee cannot share precisely

---

18. Someone who takes promises extremely seriously might say that a promise carries great weight even before it has been received by the promisee. If, for example, a letter conveys a promise to marry the person to whom it is addressed, then, it might be said, the promise-maker already owes it to the addressee to marry her, even before she reads it. In that case, it would be wrong of the letter writer to change his mind and retrieve the letter before it has been opened. That, it might be said, is a refusal to acknowledge the sacredness of promises. Most people would agree that such a position attaches far too much importance to the act of tendering a promise. But now consider the slightly less extreme position that as soon as the letter conveying a promise has been read by the promisee, it carries great weight. Why should the successful communication of the promise make so great a difference? No doubt the promisor who changes his mind and arrives on the scene just after the letter has been read owes something to the promisee—but is it now too late for him to justifiably withdraw the promise? To answer affirmatively is also to take an extreme position. Many promises, even after they have been communicated, are, in the earliest stage of their existence, like resolutions: if good reason is found for reconsidering, the fact that they have been made is not a reason to set aside the newly discovered considerations that weigh against doing what was resolved or promised. Contrast this kind of situation with the signing of a legal contract, or removing one's hand from a chess piece one has moved: in such cases, second thoughts, however well grounded, are not admissible grounds for revoking one's commitment.

the same assumptions about which goods will be promoted (or harms avoided) by means of a promise. Consider an example drawn from Petr Kropotkin's *Memoirs of a Revolutionist* and discussed by Philippa Foot.[19] An anthropologist employs a native guide who enters his service only on condition that he not be photographed—a condition imposed because of the great harm he believes such a representation would do to his soul.[20] Subsequently, an opportunity arises for the anthropologist to take such a photograph, which will have considerable value for his research, and which (he supposes) will never be detected by his guide or other members of his tribe.

It is difficult to deny that the promise should be honored, or at any rate given considerable weight—but why so if no harm will come to the native if it is broken? The good-centered or "teleological" approach to promising that I endorse cannot say that the anthropologist must keep his word because there is always a strong reason to honor promises, simply because they are promises, and regardless of their content. Rather, it must say that, were he to break his promise, he would be exposing the guide to the risk of serious injury, though not of the sort that rests on any magical properties of the photograph. There is always some chance that his act or its product (the photograph) will be detected by the native, and the distress (however unfounded) this causes will be severe. Furthermore, if the photograph is discovered by other members of the tribe, they too may be harmed; the perceived violation of a taboo can destroy the social fabric of a community. Certainly the anthropologist, being an outsider, is in a poor position to assess how much social and psychological damage the violation of his promise may cause. It would be reckless of him to put his guide and his guide's tribe at risk merely to pursue his own personal goal. Since in making the promise he undertook to serve the native, not himself, the mere fact that he can do himself some good by breaking it ought not to be a factor in his thinking. He cannot harm the native in the way the native imagines, but he nonetheless owes it to him, by virtue of his promise, to ensure that no harm (or even the risk of harm) will come to him through his photography.[21]

19. Foot, *Natural Goodness*, p. 47.

20. Kropotkin writes: "The natives, as everyone knows, consider that something is taken out of them when their likeness is taken by photography." Cited by Foot, ibid.

21. My approach to this case is compatible with the one proposed by Foot, ibid., pp. 47–51. As she says, breaking the promise would have been deeply disrespectful. But I suggest that dis-

In any case, it would be wrong to suppose that whenever we make or keep a promise, or interact with others in other ways, we should always treat them according to *their* conception of what is good for them and never our own. If someone begs you to supply him with a drug that you know will do him grave physical and psychological damage, you must decline, even if *he* does not count those consequences as harms.

It should be noticed, finally, that the teleological approach to promises will, in appropriate circumstances, countenance false promises—promises made in the absence of an intention to honor them. Suppose, for example, that a journalist can gain access to a prison only by promising the warden that he will take no photographs of prison conditions. Breaking the promise (let us suppose) harms no one, and will do great good. He ought not refrain from such a project merely on the grounds that it will require making a lying promise. Another example: a delusional friend on his deathbed asks you to promise that you will fill his corpse with gold, in order to prevent it from polluting the environment. It would be madness to keep such a promise; but that is no reason to refrain from making it if, in doing so, you will give your friend some peace of mind in his final days.[22] It is unfortunate that one cannot be open with every human being one encounters, and although we do not live in a world in which that is an option, we may nonetheless reasonably feel a pang of regret whenever we falsely make a promise. But to give every promise a significant weight in one's deliberations would be to give the mere act of promising too much weight; that mechanistic mental habit is inferior to one in which one allocates only as much value to keeping a promise as it merits. Just as a juror should reasonably regret having to find a defendant guilty (would that there were no crime), and a teacher ought to re-

---

respect in this case is constituted by putting the guide at risk. Since breaking a promise is not by itself a form of disrespect (as some of our earlier examples show), a satisfactory account of this case should go beyond the observation that the anthropologist shows his respect by keeping his word.

22. Kant's examples of lying promises are significantly different: he imagines someone who would avoid a personal difficulty (for example, a shortage of funds) by telling a false promise (that the money will be repaid on a certain date). See Kant, *Groundwork for the Metaphysics of Morals,* 4:402–403, 422). He is surely right that making a false promise for this kind of reason is objectionable: personal inconvenience is no reason for failing to repay a loan, and one's action is all the more deplorable if one knows from the start that the promise will be broken. But one can recognize this without asking how things would stand if the maxim of such an action ("when I am short of money, I will borrow money, falsely promising to repay") were to become a universal law.

gret giving a poor grade (would that all students were excellent), so we should wish that lying promises need never be told. But when a lying promise does great good and no harm, the fact that one wishes one did not have to resort to it does not constitute a reason not to make it.

58. Retribution

One way to attack the thesis that all practical reasoning should be good-centered is to argue that in certain situations we are justified in doing what is bad for someone. Good, according to this way of thinking, should sometimes move so far from the center of our thinking that its very opposite becomes our ultimate goal. That is an old idea, of course. It was a common theme of popular morality in the ancient Greek world that one should help one's friends and harm one's enemies. That can be taken to mean that we should harm our enemies simply for the sake of harming them—not because, in doing so, we help our friends. Our goal should sometimes be to diminish someone's well-being for no further reason than for its own sake. Whose well-being should one diminish? The answer, according to this harsh morality, is anyone you hate.

What is misguided about this? The obvious answer is that it is possible for one person to hate another without adequate justification. If someone is a lovely person who has never done a bit of harm, he might nonetheless be the victim of calumny and an object of contempt. He should not be hated or harmed; but the thesis under consideration is that if S does in fact hate T (whether justifiably or not), then S is justified in diminishing the well-being of T. Obviously that will not do.

Suppose, however, that T is indeed a hateful person: he has no admirable qualities and has done much harm to others. T, it might be claimed, *deserves* to become worse-off. And it might also be claimed that someone—perhaps one of the people he has harmed, perhaps a designated agent of such a victim, perhaps anyone at all—should give him what he deserves. (Keep in mind that it is possible to aim at harming someone by legal means. One may, for example, try to bankrupt someone by becoming a business competitor. We are not, at this point, discussing state-sponsored punishment.)

One can see practical problems for such a proposal. For example, how much worse-off should T be made? Who should make that decision? How should the person who makes T worse-off be selected? But there is a deeper objection. The theory under consideration says that some people should devote some of their time and resources to doing what is bad for someone. That will involve some cost, of course, for they might have used their time and resources to do some good for themselves or others. So the retributivist hypothesis under consideration is that some sacrifice in someone's well-being is a price that must be paid in order that some harm be done to someone who deserves harm.

That is an unappealing idea, and it may be wondered whether anyone really believes it. When someone thinks that he should harm his enemy because his enemy deserves to suffer, he is probably assuming that he will greatly enjoy seeing his enemy suffer, or at least knowing that he is worse-off. He wants to do harm, in other words, because he assumes that it will be good for him to do so. If that is what lies behind his desire to harm his enemy, then he does not reject the thesis that all good practical reasoning aims at some good. (Of course, he may be wrong to think that it does him some good to take revenge on his enemy: section 51.)

Our discussion, thus far, has not addressed the question of how punishment as a *legal* practice can be justified. But it is a familiar point that there are ways of doing so that affirm the good that is accomplished when a just and effective system of legal punishment is in place. A system of laws needs a coercive mechanism. Without the threat of punishment, noncompliance becomes common, and infractions undermine the good that the laws are designed to promote. The threat of punishment is idle unless a system that actually delivers punishment is in place. When a country's political and legal system operates as it should, lawbreakers whose misdeeds are fully voluntary and who are justly convicted are rightly forced to pay a significant price. They get what they deserve, and what they get is bad for them. But it would be a mistake to infer that bad things should happen to certain people for no reason other than the fact that they deserve to suffer; to make that claim would be to isolate the punitive apparatus of the state from the larger purposes for which that punitive system is designed. A full explanation of why some people are rightly made worse-off through the agency of the state must refer to the good that is accomplished by the state's whole legal system. (Protecting people from harm by incarcerating dangerous people is of course part of the full story; so too is the value of punishment as a deterrent.) If the system of law and punishment brings no benefits, if the laws are simply a pointless collection of rules, the case for making some people worse-off because they violated the laws disappears. So when it is said that some people deserve to suffer at the hands of the state, that claim cannot be sustained unless it is backed by premises that spell out the good that is done by the laws and the courts.

What would the alternative to this way of thinking look like? Suppose we entirely set aside any good that the legal and punitive system accomplishes, and look upon the courts simply as venues for the apportionment of measure for measure. The degree to which someone deserves to suffer is to be assessed and the severity of punishment is to vary accordingly, so that the balance of justice in the world is maintained. Where does such thinking take us? Suppose a criminal who has committed horrible crimes is already so miserable that death would be good for him, and he would be worse-off were he kept alive. Is that a factor to which a system of criminal justice should be sensitive? If certain criminals have tortured their victims, do they deserve to be tortured by the state—and which citizens should be selected for that job? Suppose certain criminals have skills that could be put to use for the common good: is the state to forgo the good that could come of such forced labor if that kind of work fails to make those criminals as badly off as they deserve to be? Is it a matter of no significance if offenders, having served their terms and having been made as badly off as they deserve to be, have no skills that would enable them to do something useful to themselves or others? The idea that the system of criminal justice should simply be a device for making people suffer because they deserve to suffer and need not also be a device that does some good leads to unpalatable results.

Those who favor capital punishment sometimes speak of the sense of closure and psychological peace that comes to victims or their relatives when a criminal is executed. According to that line of argument, capital punishment is justified in part because of the good it does, not simply in terms of harm. It is also sometimes said that if someone's criminal deed is terrible and the courts are just and accurate, capital punishment is not only merited but also avoids inflicting on the public treasury the burden of caring for someone who deserves no state support; it allows those resources to be used elsewhere. That, once again, is a justification that appeals to the good certain forms of punishment accomplish. It is difficult to find a plausible theory of punishment—criminal or otherwise—that sanctions doing harm to someone merely for the sake of lowering him to the level of misery that he deserves. There is a place for the notion of desert in a theory of punishment: some criminals are fully responsible for their actions and get what they deserve; those who do not deserve to be punished should not be. But we go wrong if we think of punishment in these terms *alone*. Desert must be placed in a larger context, so that we can see the good that comes of making some pay a price for their misdeeds.

59. Cosmic Justice

Ross holds that besides pleasure, virtue, and knowledge, there is a fourth good: "the apportionment of pleasure and pain to the virtuous and vicious respectively."[23] He employs his usual method for bringing his readers to recognize a good thing: we are asked to "compare two imaginary states of the universe, alike in the total amounts of virtue and vice and of pleasure and pain present in the two, but in one of which the virtuous were all happy and the vicious miserable, while in the other the virtuous were miserable and the vicious happy."[24] Ross is perhaps right to say that "very few people would hesitate to say that the first was a much better state of the universe than the second." Most of us are disturbed when those we think of as good people suffer misfortunes; and not a few are delighted when villains become miserable. Would not the universe be a better place if suffering and happiness were properly allocated—all the suffering being transferred to the bad, and all the happiness reserved for the good? If so, we should want bad things to happen to bad people, and we should be glad when they do. Each time that happens, the universe is a somewhat better place.[25]

That does not mean that we would be justified in *doing* whatever it takes to make a bad person suffer. One should not deliberately infect someone with a disease merely because he is mean and nasty. But if it so happens that a bad person contracts a disease that makes him miserable, then, according to Ross's way of thinking, a good thing has happened, and we should be pleased. Ross would not say that when a good person

23. Ross, *The Right and the Good*, p. 138.
24. Ibid.
25. These reflections play an important role in Kant's conception of the supreme good as constituted not by happiness alone but by morally deserved happiness. See *Critique of Pure Reason*, B841: "Reason does not approve happiness (however inclination may desire it) except insofar as it is united with worthiness to be happy, that is, with moral conduct" (trans. Norman Kemp Smith).

is in pain or is unhappy or is deprived of some pleasure, this is bad *for* him. As we noted (section 17), he conceives of pain, ignorance, vice, and the allocation of pain to the virtuous as bad "sans phrase," not bad *for* anyone. But we need not accept that component of his position. It accords with common sense to say that when someone contracts a disease that makes him miserable, that is bad *for* him. Not a few also hold that if someone is a bad person, he deserves to suffer; and so his infection should spread through his body, because that will be bad *for* him.

That does not sit well with the thesis that we have been exploring and that has held up well so far: we should do nothing that does no good for anyone. There is no contradiction here, but it is not easy to accept both ideas. If we should *do* only what is good for someone or other, why should we sometimes *wish for* and be *pleased by* what is bad for someone and good for no one?

The idea with which we are grappling is that sometimes what is bad for someone should happen to that person simply because it is deserved. Here is an inference to the conclusion that something should happen that bypasses any consideration of what is good for anyone. Perhaps we should *do* nothing that does no good. But should things *happen* that do no good? Should they happen because by harming someone they give him his just deserts?

This is not a question about the distribution of limited resources. It is not as though only a certain number of bad things will happen, and so each bad thing that happens to a bad person is one fewer bad thing that happens to a good person. If that were the case, then we could think along these lines: in order that a good person have less of what is bad, we want this bad person to have more of what is bad. That wish is really a wish for what is good—in other words, less bad—for someone. It is not a pure wish for what is bad for someone for no reason other than his deserving to suffer. It is a wish for what is good (for a good person), and a hope that something bad happens (to a bad person) in order to pave the way for what is good. According to this picture, it is really our desire for what is good that lies behind our ill-wishing. (Ross's thought experiment obscures this issue. His way of framing the question allows us to think that happiness should be taken from the bad in order that it be given to the good.)

The proper way to think about this issue is to consider what we should hope for, wish for, and do when resources are abundant enough so that neither good nor bad people have to suffer. Suppose a doctor is put in charge of two equally ill and suffering patients, one good and one bad, and there is plenty of medicine for both. She can relieve the suffering of both as easily as she can relieve the suffering of one, and she knows how different they are in character. Our question is about palliative care: the bad patient is not on the verge of committing a crime; like the good person, he is at the end of his days. Should she give care to both patients, or only the one who is virtuous? Both, obviously. She is not a minister of cosmic justice.

But can it be that although she should care for both, she should *hope* that somehow the medication she administers to the bad patient will be ineffective, and that he will continue to suffer? Should she be a minister of cosmic justice in her hopes, wishes, and pleasures, though not in her actions? In asking that question, we are of course asking about *our* mental lives as well. For if the doctor should wish for ill, even as she does good, that must be because all of us should wish for ill to all those who deserve to suffer.

One's mental life cannot be entirely isolated from one's effectiveness as an agent. A doctor who hopes that her patients will suffer thereby increases the chances that she will do her job poorly. All of us are in the same predicament: by dividing the world into two camps—the good, to whom we wish well; and the bad, to whom we wish ill—we are more likely to inflict harm on the latter or allow them to suffer. We are in some danger of wronging people—inflicting or allowing harm—merely on the basis of their character. And in any case, whether our ill-wishing affects our actions or not, we had better be careful that we measure our ill wishes so that they are proportionate to the deserts of the people we are standing in judgment of. That is not a task any human being is equipped to undertake. It would be difficult to know about even one person in one's social world how much that person deserves to suffer; to know this about *all* those one judges to be bad people and therefore deserving of punishment would be impossible. And why should anyone waste his time gathering that information? We should leave aside the question about who deserves to suffer and face it only when circumstances force us to take a stand—as the doctor would, if she could help only one. ("Judge not, that you be not judged. For with the judgment you pronounce you will be judged, and the measure you give will be the measure you get."[26] Thus Christian scripture. But we *should* sometimes assess character. What we should not do is wish ill to those who fall short.)

These considerations lead to the conclusion that we should be charitable in our dealings with and our thoughts about our fellow human beings. Charity is at least this much: not wishing or doing ill needlessly—that is, unless some good comes of that ill. This does not require us to wish well to all, or to make no distinctions between wonderful and hateful people. The doctor who can relieve the suffering of only one of her patients should help the one who is virtuous. Wishing and doing ill need to be justified, and they cannot be justified simply on the grounds that they are deserved. Ill will not only must be deserved, but must do someone some good. That thesis about our mental life accords well with the principle about agency that we have been examining: what does no good should not be done (unless every alternative is worse).

60. Social Justice

In the last two sections our concern has been that justice might be regarded as an enemy of what is good, for it seems that we are sometimes required to do or wish for what is bad, simply as a matter of justice. But there is yet another way in which justice might be thought of as an enemy of what is good. Whenever we do what is good for someone or for a group of people, there will inevitably be others for whom we are not doing good. Those others may complain: by leaving them out, we have acted unjustly; and, they may add, one should never do what is good if that involves injustice. According to this way of thinking, everyone's first priority should be to refrain from injustice; we are permitted to do what is good only if that requirement has been met.

Hume characterized justice as a "cautious, jealous virtue."[27] The jealous person wants others not to have an advantage that he himself lacks; he would rather that no one at all have a good if he is not one of those to have it. If justice requires that when distributions of certain goods among certain people fail to meet its standards, there must be no such

26. Matthew 7.1–2 (revised standard version).
27. David Hume, *An Enquiry Concerning the Principles of Morals*, sect. 3, pt. 1.

distribution at all so that everyone suffers, it is indeed a jealous virtue. Even if that were a correct characterization of justice, however, the thesis (of section 55) that doing good lies at the center of all good practical reasoning would not be undermined. That thesis holds that when there are considerations that speak against some undertaking, they must advert to some harm that is done by the act proposed, or some good that ought to be taken into account that the proposed act neglects. When justice is jealous, it calls our attention to someone's welfare and says: we should not go forward with our project of doing good, unless *that* person's good is taken into consideration as well.

In any case, it is obvious that doing good for some but not others is not *always* unjust. Someone who makes a promise singles out a single beneficiary; not everyone is meant to benefit from the promise. Parents are held responsible for giving special attention to their children, not other children. Universities are specially devoted to their faculty and students, doctors to their patients, states to their citizens, and so on. Yet it is true that sometimes exclusionary treatment is unjust. If parents love only one of their children, the others have reason to complain. If a business provides health benefits to its heterosexual but not its homosexual employees, that is unjust. Within social institutions, arbitrary departures from equal distributions of good are unjust; the difficulty, of course, is in deciding what is arbitrary. Acting justly is a way of organizing our answers to the question "Whose good should one aim at?" into a proper pattern. To answer that question correctly, one must consider how selecting one person or group as a beneficiary will force one to exclude other potential beneficiaries, and whether that exclusionary practice is justified.

Suppose we decide that doing what is good for *these* people is unjust, because we ought also to be doing what is good for *those* as well. Should we stop what we are doing entirely, if that is the only way to remedy the injustice that we would otherwise do? If so, justice is certainly a jealous quality, and in that sense an enemy of good. Rawls says: "Justice is the first virtue of social institutions, as truth is of systems of thought. A theory however elegant and economical must be rejected or revised if it is untrue; likewise laws and institutions no matter how efficient and well-arranged must be reformed or abolished if they are unjust."[28] Certainly

---

28. Rawls, *A Theory of Justice,* p. 3.

they should be reformed if that is feasible. But suppose one faces a stark choice: what should be done when the only way to eliminate the injustice done by an institution is to destroy it and all the good it does, or to destroy entirely the policy that creates an inequity, thereby eliminating all the good done for some by that policy? An employer, for example, gives certain benefits to some of his employees, but others are arbitrarily denied that same benefit. Should he be forced to give the benefit to no one? That would eliminate the injustice. But ending that injustice is not costless: certain individuals, perhaps many, are harmed. Should we agree with Rawls that if we cannot create a certain pattern of good, then we should not bother with good at all? That no member of a social institution should flourish, unless all within it flourish justly?

That is an extreme position.[29] Rawls does not think of justice in precisely these terms, because his conception of what is good makes it easy for him to assume that nothing of value is lost when someone is prevented by the requirements of justice from getting what is good for him. He says: "The interests requiring the violation of justice have no value. Having no merit in the first place, they cannot override its claims."[30] And he is right to this extent: it is unreasonable for an injustice to be tolerated simply to allow someone to get what he rationally wants. Nothing can be said in favor of doing what is good when good is interpreted as the satisfaction of a desire, and the desire is directed against the well-being of another person. But when good is construed as flourishing, the thesis that justice takes priority over it loses its plausibility. It is more reasonable to say that we should put up with a bad pattern in the distribution of good if the only alternative is to have no good at all.

Fortunately, these are rarely, if ever, our only alternatives. Unjust patterns of distribution can normally be reformed so that the good that was once unjustly distributed is now equitably shared rather than entirely destroyed. Certainly, the world is not so harsh an environment that we must inevitably choose between creating institutions in which human beings flourish and creating just institutions. Distributive justice cannot

29. As Rawls himself seems to acknowledge. In the paragraph that follows his insistence that we abandon well-arranged but unjust systems, just as we reject elegant but false systems of thought, he concedes: "These propositions seem to express our intuitive conviction of the primacy of justice. No doubt they are expressed too strongly" (ibid., p. 4). Perhaps then he should not be taken to mean that an unjust distribution of good must be dismantled, even if the result is the complete disappearance of the good it distributes.

30. Ibid., p. 28.

be described as jealous when it is conceived as a virtue that calls not for constricting well-being, but for dispersing what is good so that no one's well-being is arbitrarily neglected. It would be an unappealing characteristic if it did nothing but destroy unjust institutions and left nothing good in their wake. It is more charitable to think of just people as unstinting rather than jealous. The scope of their concern is not arbitrarily confined to a favored few, but encompasses all those to whom good is due.

61. Pure Antipaternalism

According to the hypothesis that good and bad lie at the center of good practical reasoning (section 55), reasons in favor of a proposed action always stem from some good in view, and countervailing reasons always advert to something bad. Against this it might be said: we must never do what is good for someone without that person's consent, or unless that person would, if properly informed, consent. Even if what you would like to do for someone is entirely good for him, and does nothing harmful to him or anyone else, you must work through that person's will or not at all. There are borders that must be respected: the borders that surround each person, protecting him from the intrusions of others, even those that are well-intentioned and beneficial. To pass through that border, to enter the little kingdom where each of us resides, you must obtain the king's permission.

What of the good a mother does for her baby or small child? Is she stepping over a boundary that must not be crossed by refraining from asking her infant to consent to the way she treats him? That of course is an absurd suggestion. But perhaps the idea of a boundary can be preserved in this way: a baby lacks the capacity to understand what is good and bad, and so in this case border crossing is permitted. Even so, it might be thought that the mother should do for her child only those good things that the child *would* consent to if he were able to.

But that suggestion is equally absurd. We have no idea what a baby would consent to. We do know something about what is good or bad for children, and when we draw upon that knowledge, that is the only kind of justification we need for our actions. We do not have to keep our fingers crossed, as we nurture our children, hoping that we are doing something they would consent to. There is no reason for us to regret that we are not obtaining their permission to act on their behalf.

So, if we are to make sense of the idea that a wall surrounds each of us, protecting each individual from unwarranted interference, we should regard this wall as something that comes into existence when the powers of a human being—the cognitive, affective, and social powers that we have been discussing—are mature enough to make consent a meaningful act. Adults should not be treated like children: that is certainly an appealing slogan.

But the idea can be understood in two rather different ways. To see what they are, consider a concrete case. Suppose your mother loves to smoke, has no intention of stopping, and as a result is likely to shorten her life by five years if she continues. Would you be justified in depriving her of her cigarettes, merely on the grounds that this will improve her health and lengthen her life? One argument against your doing so rests on the simple and obvious point that health and longevity are only a small sample of what is good for a person. Keep in mind our assumption that she *loves* to smoke; she enjoys these tastes and smells, as others enjoy food and drink. An avid cigarette smoker has become accustomed to the way in which her sensory apparatus operates and gets great pleasure from her habit; her smoking has become part of her persona and her way of interacting with others. Once these habits have formed, it is not clear that we would do her more good than harm by taking away her cigarettes. How are the gains and losses to be compared? Much depends on how much she enjoys smoking. And who is in a better position to make that assessment than she? It would be presumptuous for others to substitute their judgment for hers on this matter. (This line of reasoning is entirely compatible with favoring antismoking statutes that discourage people from becoming smokers.)

This way of resisting paternalistic interference is entirely compatible with a good-centered conception of practical reasoning. We should not take away the smoker's cigarettes because smoking might, on balance, be good for her; and she is well equipped to decide whether it is. If that is the way we choose to think about the matter, we do not need the metaphor of a wall that protects each of us from the benevolence of others. We let individuals make the final decisions about their own well-being because they are better situated than others to know what is in their interests.

A second and entirely different approach would say that this is her decision to make because she and she alone has *jurisdiction* over matters that involve only her own well-being. We are allowed to intervene in someone's life in order to prevent her from harming others, but we are never allowed to do so merely to prevent her from harming herself. That is not because she is likely to be a better judge about her own good than others. Rather, it is because she is an adult, and adults have the prerogative to live their lives in whatever way they see fit, however harmful that may be to themselves, provided that others are not thereby made worse-off. This is a doctrine of pure antipaternalism—pure, in that it is untainted by any reliance on empirical assumptions about whether paternalistic interference is counterproductive. It should be distinguished from the strategic antipaternalism that underlies the first approach described above. A pure antipaternalist does not say: efforts to help people without their consent are often likely to be useless, because without their cooperation no good will be done. Nor does a pure antipaternalist say: people need to learn how to make decisions for themselves, and how to learn from their mistakes. These arguments are all based on the idea that intervening in the lives of others often does them harm over the long run. Similarly, it makes no difference, from the point of view of pure antipaternalism, that exercising control over major features of one's life is a component of well-being (section 53). The pure antipaternalist eschews all such considerations and talks instead in terms of jurisdiction, bypassing considerations of good and bad. All such appeals to well-being are unnecessary, because what a person does to himself and himself alone is not a matter for others to decide. (John Stuart Mill's *On Liberty*, incidentally, does not approach this subject in the manner of pure antipaternalism. Recall the title of Chapter 3: "Of Individuality, as One of the Elements of Well-being.")

This is not the simple idea that we should not treat adults as though they were children. Of course we should not, because adults know more and are better decision makers than children. But the pure antipaternalist does not suppose that adults have for the most part acquired some wisdom and have therefore earned the right to make decisions about their own well-being; that would imply that we are granted jurisdiction over our own good because we are more likely than we once were to use our authority well. Rather, pure antipaternalism holds that there is only this important distinction between children and adults: the latter are *capable* of understanding where their good lies. Even if an adult does not use that capacity, we must not do anything on his behalf and against his will.

A pure antipaternalist will have to agree that attempts to educate and persuade someone do not in themselves trespass on his territory. If S is intent on doing what T thinks will be harmful to S, T does not have to remain silent about this. Family members and friends of S would be remiss if they made no efforts to dissuade him from a self-destructive undertaking. No one supposes that S must give his permission to others before they can talk to him about his well-being. What they cannot do, according to pure antipaternalism, is to coerce S for his own good, so long as S is capable of understanding what is good.

But if other people should try to *shape* someone's will by talking to him, why must they never *bypass* his will for his own good? We bypass people's will all the time by preventing them from harming others and requiring them to contribute to the good of others, whether they want to or not (section 62). There is no merit in the general idea that we should all be allowed to do whatever we choose. So why suppose that there is some merit in the idea that an adult should not be coerced, when the grounds for doing so appeal solely to his well-being? Why is that, in principle, never a good enough reason for coercion? Pure antipaternalism cannot advert to the bad consequences that would occur were this the only basis for bypassing someone's will. It must say instead that this simply is wrong, but it cannot say *why* it is wrong. That puts pure antipaternalism in a weak position, because it must acknowledge that there is a powerful reason someone should be prevented from doing himself harm—namely, the harm done. That is a reason in favor of coercing someone for his own good, and so pure antipaternalism must give an intelligible reason that weighs on the other side. Merely affirming the wrongness of coercing someone for his good will not do, because coercion is acceptable in so many other cases.[31]

31. Joel Feinberg holds that a person's "right of self-determination . . . takes precedence even over his own good" (*Harm to Self,* p. 61), but he does not contest Mill's thesis that "the good is self-fulfillment and . . . development of the basic human faculties of choice and reasoned decision are components of self-fulfillment" (ibid., p. 58). That commits him to saying that it is not *because* exercising one's capacity for reasoned decision is good for one that one should be allowed to exercise it (provided no others are harmed). Why then should we refrain from paternalistic interference? His reply is that the right of self-determination "accords uniquely with a self-conception deeply imbedded in the moral attitudes of most people and apparently presupposed in many of our moral idioms . . . ('my life to live as I please,' 'no one else's business,' etc.)" (ibid., pp. 61–62). But if one grants, as he does, that it is good for a person to exercise control over his own life, why should that conception of the good not be used to explain the value and limits of these "moral idioms"? Feinberg's discussion is also weakened by

Pure antipaternalism is just as arbitrary as egoism (section 11). Egoism says that there is only one person—oneself—whom one should directly help; but it can give no good reason why this should be so. Similarly, pure antipaternalism says that there is only one person whose well-being never constitutes a grounds for coercion—the person coerced; but it can give no reason why. Antipaternalism, in many cases, is sound advice: it is often a bad idea to coerce people for their own good, because the consequences of trying to do so are often unfavorable. That kind of antipaternalism will examine proposals to protect people against their own ignorance or incompetence with a skeptical eye, but it will not reject all such ideas for purely jurisdictional reasons. (Surely when the harms a person would inflict on himself are immense and irreversible, and his powers of judgment are impaired, coercive intervention is justified. We would stop someone from killing himself if he has fallen into acute but curable despondency and has many good years ahead of him.) A reasonable—that is, an impure—form of antipaternalism is consistent with the thesis that good and bad are central to all good practical reasoning.

62. Moral Space and Giving Aid

Although pure antipaternalism is not a plausible doctrine, the jurisdictional image on which it rests is one that some contemporary philosophers find attractive. There are borders that surround each adult human being, protecting him from the unwarranted intrusions of others. Within that little kingdom, each individual has the authority to reject what others propose to or would like from her. One's status as an inviolable person entitles one to live as one chooses (provided one does not

---

his denial that a person can voluntarily aim at his own harm: "Presumably, if he genuinely chose the alternative that is in fact bad for him, he did not choose it because *he* believed it was bad for him. That would be so irrational that it would put the voluntariness of his choice in doubt" (ibid., p. 62, his emphasis). Underestimating the human will's potential for self-destruction, he invites his readers—people who always make choices under the guise of some freely chosen conception of the good—to recognize that they would not welcome the interference of someone who wishes to substitute his "better values" (Feinberg's phrase, ibid., which he places in scare quotes) for theirs. The more adept people are at choosing what is good for themselves, and the more dubious we are about the wisdom of those who interfere in the name of "better values," the easier it is to oppose paternalism. These features of Feinberg's argument must be distinguished from his insistence that there is a kind of value that has nothing to do with good (namely, the "right of self-determination"), and that takes precedence over it.

cross the borders of others). A person has that status not because it is *good* for a human being to have a certain zone in which his will reigns supreme, but because that is what is *due* to him as a matter of entitlement. Rights are not instruments for sustaining the good of each person; they are grounded in the authority each person has over his little part of the world—his body, his self, his life.

These are the ideas that Nozick is expressing when he says, "A line (or hyper-plane) circumscribes an area in moral space around an individual." He also speaks of "the classical liberals' notion of self-ownership" to convey the idea that there are things that each of us is entitled to control.[32] This, it might be said, is our birthright as persons. Locke, one of the classical liberals Nozick has in mind, writes: "Every man has a property in his own person; this nobody has any right to but himself. The labour of his body and the work of his hands we may say are properly his."[33] Similarly, Nozick says, "If people force you to do certain work, or unrewarded work, for a certain period of time, they decide what you are to do and what purposes your work is to serve apart from your decisions. This process whereby they take this decision from you makes them a *part-owner* of you."[34] Because you own yourself, it would be wrong for others to force you to aid another. That should be your decision. Giving aid may be the right decision, and if you never lift a finger for others, you may justly be accused of being mean, uncharitable, and cruel. Even so, others may not invade your space by requiring or forcing you to be of some use to them, and you may not be punished if you decline to do so.

For Nozick, respecting moral space has absolute priority over doing good. Note the consequences. Suppose a child is born with three kidneys and there is a completely safe procedure that would allow one of them to be removed and given to a child who needs one. (In fact, we are normally born with two and need only one; so the child whose kidneys are reduced from three to two still has a spare. Nearly all kidney disease affects both kidneys, so there is no medical value even in having one spare, let alone two.) Now if one owns oneself, that gives one a right to the disposition of one's body. That right cannot be overridden simply to promote the good of another. Presumably, then, Nozick must say that

32. Nozick, *Anarchy, State, and Utopia*, pp. 57, 172
33. John Locke, *Second Treatise of Government*, 5.27.
34. Nozick, *Anarchy, State, and Utopia*, p. 172, his emphasis.

taking an infant's kidney, without his permission, would be an invasion of his moral space. Are we simply to let the spare kidney go to waste, and to let the other child die?[35]

One might be tempted to say, on Nozick's behalf, that the child's parents should be consulted, and if they give their permission, the operation may proceed. But why should Nozick's theory be extended in this direction? After all, why should *both* parents be consulted? Why not just the mother? But, on second thought, why does *she* have sole authority, or any authority? Does she own her child because he was nurtured in her body during her pregnancy? Why does that give her the right to give away one of his kidneys? On the other hand, if she does own her baby, for how long does her ownership last, and why does her child's self-ownership begin at one time rather than another? In any case, suppose we ask her permission, and she refuses—not for any reason, but simply out of a stubborn unwillingness to do what is good for others. The child who needs a kidney dies. Why is that an outcome we must allow? Nozick's answer must be: to refrain from crossing the "line (or hyper-plane)" that "circumscribes an area in moral space" around the baby. It does not matter how much harm results from stepping back from that boundary; it does not matter that it would do no harm to cross it. We must not trespass into someone's moral space, whatever the consequences.

In effect, Nozick is postulating a system of taboos. The notion of the little moral kingdom, the hyper-plane that defeats all considerations of well-being, cannot survive reflection. It would make no sense to allow some children in need of kidneys to die when taking kidneys from other children, at no cost to them, would save those lives. When requiring some to aid others harms no one, it is justified.[36]

35. We can assume that both have been born in a hospital (in fact the same hospital), which has ready to hand a safe medical procedure to perform the organ transplant. An organ donation from a normal adult would no doubt disrupt his plans and thus impose a burden that is not present in the case of the newborn child. Of course, those who are convinced that the human body must not be violated without the consent of its "owner" will not agree that the donor's infancy makes any difference.

36. That one is legally required to V does not by itself show that it is, to some extent, bad for one to V. Admittedly, legal requirements are typically coercive; that is, their violation normally is penalized or punished. But that does not mean that they must be experienced as burdensome impositions that interfere with willing choices, and that they are therefore, to some extent, injurious. The law may, for example, require that parents provide their children with a minimal level of care. Parents who love their children would not regard such a law as a painful deflection of their will. It does not detract from their well-being that they are regulated in this

The political community is justified in assigning to certain people—typically they are biological parents, but they might be foster parents or others—the responsibility of caring for the very young. Since there is a younger generation, some people must go beyond merely refraining from making others worse-off: they must make certain people—the very young—better-off. But the very young are not the only ones who need the help of others. So do the very old, the very sick, the infirm, the uneducated, and so on. It properly falls to the political community to decide how much aid, and what sort of aid, each of us is to give to others. It is legitimate to use coercion not only to prevent us from making others worse-off, but also to induce certain people to make others who are in need better-off in this way or that.

One way to do this would be to allow the government to assign people to certain tasks: this group will be parents, these others the doctors, these will care for the elderly, these will be teachers, and so on. Thus Socrates, in Plato's *Republic*. But that would be a deeply defective arrangement because, as we saw earlier (section 53), it is good for people to exercise a large degree of control over the kind of work they do, whom they will marry, whether they will have children, and so on. It is a mistake to think of a person's control over the major features of his life as something that is *owed* him because there is a hyper-plane protecting his moral space. Rather, it is *good* for each of us to have a large degree of discretion over how we will live. How much discretion? And over which matters? There is no reason to think those questions can be answered once and for all, and answered the same way in every community. But if certain measures that require people to aid others impose only a slight burden, do much good, and do not unfairly distribute benefits and burdens, they can reasonably be adopted and enforced. Suppose, for example, that requiring people to donate blood were an effective way of maintaining a clean and ample blood supply. That would be a reasonable imposition; the small sacrifice would not substantially interfere with people's ability to fashion lives of their own choosing. We can go further: if donating a kidney were completely safe and required only a few days of recuperation, we could require that as well. But, at some point, we

way. More generally, laws that require citizens to give aid to others are not harms merely by virtue of being legal requirements backed by the threat of punishment. And if one objected to such laws merely on the grounds that one happens to experience them as impositions, that would hardly count as a reasonable complaint.

must stop requiring people to help others, because the cumulative burdens would substantially intrude upon the zone of freedom it is good for each to have. And there are some forms of aid that would, by themselves, involve a far greater loss to the donor than the loss of a kidney. (We can see with just one eye; should we be required to donate one, if that will give those who are blind one good eye?) A proper balance between requiring aid and leaving people alone is what we should look for, and there is no one right way to achieve this.

Rawls sometimes uses language that suggests that he too believes in a hyper-plane that protects the moral space of each individual. Recall what is perhaps his best known sentence: "Each person possesses an inviolability founded on justice that even the welfare of society as a whole cannot override."[37] Like Nozick, and in line with the liberal tradition, he is attracted by the image of human beings as separate choosers—as individuals who freely determine what kind of life they will lead. That image stands behind both his theory of what we must do as a matter of moral rightness and his theory (the conative theory) of what is good for us to do. Rawls appeals to these notions when he writes, against utilitarianism, that "the plurality of distinct persons with separate systems of ends is an essential feature of human societies."[38] To emphasize that you have your system of ends and I have mine is to imply that I cannot be drafted into a social scheme simply because my participation serves "the welfare of society as a whole." If any individual in the original position has reason to veto a proposed principle, then it cannot be right for society to enforce it, no matter how much good it does. That is another way of saying that moral rightness is prior to goodness.

But, in fact, Rawls does not take our "inviolability," our distinctness as persons, our "separate system of ends" to mean that no one can be required to help another. Rather, he uses the social contract as a device that protects each individual from being drafted into an unacceptable position of subordination to others—as a mere tool to be used for the purpose of producing the greatest aggregate good. In the original position, he thinks, we would choose a principle that requires each individual to help others when doing so does not involve substantial self-sacrifice.[39] The sense of security that comes to each person when there is widespread acceptance of such a principle would compensate for the oc-

37. Rawls, *A Theory of Justice*, p. 3.
38. Ibid., p. 25.
39. Ibid., pp. 98, 297–298.

casional intrusions it might sometimes require. But no one in the original position would accept a much more demanding principle of aid—for example, the utilitarian principle that we help others whenever doing so would maximize the good.

Why would a society that honors the utilitarian principle sin against the inviolability of each person—why would it fail to acknowledge our distinctness and the separateness of our plans—whereas the principle of mutual aid does not? The principle of mutual aid drafts us into social interactions that are not of our own choosing and impose a slight burden on us: why is that not a small offense against our inviolability, a small failure to recognize our distinctness and separateness? From Nozick's point of view, Rawls fails to take jurisdictional moral truths seriously—truths not about what is a benefit or a burden, but about who is entitled to make choices. He allows small intrusions into one's life, but not large ones, because the small ones do not substantially interfere with a person's ability to pursue his "separate system of ends." But why not say that there is a matter of principle here, and not merely a difference in quantity? Being drafted to a small extent by the good of someone else is nonetheless being drafted.

That critique of Rawls has no bite, however, because the metaphor of moral space is not apt. If taking a kidney from an infant does him no harm and benefits some other child, there can be no objection to doing so. To take one small step further: we can require someone to make a small sacrifice, if that is part of a fair system that yields great benefits. To take a larger step: we should support social arrangements in which all those who need help to live well receive help. But to make these ideas concrete, we of course need a conception of what is good and what is bad. It is because it is good to live a life of one's own choosing—a life in which one decides which of the many elements of flourishing one will especially love—that we should limit the demands we make on each other.

63. Slavery

Chattel slavery, once a widely accepted institution, is now generally assumed to be beyond the pale. What was objectionable about it? Why do we think we are well rid of it (to the extent that we are)?[40] One way of re-

---

40. See Kevin Bales, *Disposable People: New Slavery in the Global Economy* and *New Slavery:*

sponding to these questions is to criticize slavery for the grave harms it caused and the unjust way in which those harms were allocated. The severity and nature of the burdens borne by slaves varied greatly from place to place and time to time. Even so, the benefits and burdens of every system of slavery were ill distributed, the burdens falling exclusively on those who were the instruments of their owners.

This is a template for criticizing slavery that depends heavily on the notion of what is good and what is bad for human beings. Were it the case that it is good to be a slave, or a matter of indifference, we might not be greatly disturbed that it was not a role shared equally by all members of slave societies. If we took a slave's life to be good, we might suppose that slave societies ought to have been reformed so as to allow everyone to share in the benefits of being owned. But, in fact, when we think that enslaving someone was an unjust way of treating him, that is because we also think of it as bad for him.

Is it possible to avoid relying on any conception of what is good or bad for people, and to criticize slavery on other grounds, which have nothing to do with well-being? We might say: all human beings have rights, and among them is the right not to be enslaved. Or: it is morally wrong to be the owner of another human being. Or: each person is entitled to a zone of freedom over which he alone has jurisdiction. Or: no free and equal person would choose to be a slave.

The problem with such statements is not that they are false but that they are unilluminating. The objections they make to slavery proceed from a starting point that in effect already assumes that there is something objectionable about the subordination that is essential to the concept of slavery. Consider, for example, the critique of slavery that can be made by using Rawls's contractualist understanding of moral rightness and wrongness. Morally right institutions and principles, he claims, are those that would be chosen by individuals of a certain sort in an initial contractual situation.[41] What sort of individuals, and in what sort of situation? They are each other's equals, in that none is subordinate, formally or psychologically, to any other.[42] Unanimity is required, and so

---

A Reference Handbook. Contemporary discussions do not confine themselves to chattel slavery, but they include among the slave population all those who are coercively denied the opportunity to sell their labor.

41. Rawls, A Theory of Justice, p. 95.
42. Ibid., pp. 102, 131–132, 475.

each contracting party can veto any proposal. None defers to any others, or has more power than others. Furthermore, they are free persons in that they "give first priority to preserving their liberty" to alter or reaffirm their fundamental aims as they see fit.[43] When they evaluate principles to govern the basic political and economic structure of their society, they do so by looking for ways to secure such "primary social goods" as "rights, liberties, and opportunities."[44] Having described the contracting parties in this way, Rawls argues that they would choose social institutions that give each person "an equal right to the most extensive total system of equal basic liberties compatible with a similar system of liberty for all."[45] Obviously, slavery is ruled out by such a principle, since slaves are denied "basic liberties."

It would be misleading to express these ideas by saying that for Rawls the problem with slavery is that it is bad for slaves. Rather, the objection to slavery that can be constructed out of the materials of his political theory is that it is a violation of one of the principles of rightness. Those principles are chosen by free and equal individuals who deliberate in terms of a group of goods (the "primary social goods") that are appropriate for the problem of choice they must solve. The interests of the contracting parties are not affirmed by Rawls to be noninstrumentally good for all human beings, but they play a far more restricted role: they are the terms in which regulative principles are to be evaluated. They are tools to be used for solving a hypothetical problem of social choice; they need not be good, even instrumentally, for this or that real person. So the sin of slavery, from a contractualist perspective, does not consist in its badness for slaves, but on its ineligibility as a choice—its rejectability by the hypothetical choosers in the original position.

This is in effect to say that slavery is objectionable because it would not be chosen by equally situated freedom-loving people faced with a choice between freedom and subordination. But it is reasonable to look for a critique of slavery that does not already presuppose the equal moral standing of persons and the value that freedom has for them. Furthermore, it is hard to believe that we can understand why slavery is beyond the pale without appealing to a notion of how badly slaves typically

43. Ibid., p. 131.
44. Ibid., p. 79.
45. Ibid., p. 266.

fare—a notion, in other words, of what is noninstrumentally good for human beings.

Consider what a conative conception of well-being would require us to say about slavery. What is bad for someone, according to this approach, is his failure to get what he wants or seeks. So if slaves expected little from their lives and achieved what little they sought, there was nothing in their lives that was bad. And if, as a matter of historical fact, they wanted more than they had, it remains the case that slavery would not have been bad for them had they wanted less.[46]

It would be one-sided to consider the harm of an institution without also asking whether it had offsetting benefits. The conative theory holds that goodness consists in the successful execution of a rational plan; so if slaveholders planned to acquire great power, wealth, and luxury through the ownership of massive estates maintained by slave labor, and they succeeded in this plan, that was good for them. Accordingly, were we to adopt a conative conception of well-being, and were our critique of slavery cast, at least partly, in terms of the harm it did to slaves and the good it brought to slave owners, the force of our critique would be difficult to evaluate. Rawls believes that it is an advantage of his moral philosophy, in comparison with utilitarianism, that it rejects slavery without taking into account the happiness or unhappiness caused by the institution.[47]

But when we think of well-being as the development and exercise of our powers, it becomes obvious that slavery was immensely harmful, at least in the most common cases. A slave might have received humane treatment, food, and shelter—although the threat of whippings and beatings always stood in the background. Since slaves were commonly recruited for menial labor, their cognitive powers were allowed to operate at a minimal level, and it was not up to slaves to decide which among their powers should be developed. Family life could easily be disrupted through the sale of partners and children. Social life was atomized because of the masters' fear of collective slave rebellion. Being a piece of property, a slave had to negotiate and struggle to maintain some control over the most basic features of her life—the sort of work she did, the skills she acquired, the people with whom she associated, her sexual

46. Amartya Sen (*On Ethics and Economics*, pp. 45–46) makes a similar point in his discussion of developmental economics.
47. Rawls, *A Theory of Justice*, pp. 137–139.

partners, and the like. Every element of a flourishing life was jeopardized, and extraordinary courage and perseverance were required to assemble some shreds of well-being. (In some slave societies, the imbalance between masters and slaves was rationalized by the assumption of innate deficiencies among the slaves.)[48]

What of the good accomplished by slavery? Owning a slave was typically valued as a means to further ends—the production of basic necessities for some; great wealth, leisure, and gentlemanly status for others. None of these ends is by itself a component of well-being. Great wealth and leisure, properly used, can be means to other things that are components of well-being. So in some instances slaves may have been used in a way that did someone some good. In some of those cases, the good achieved by the use of slaves might have been achieved by other means. A wage laborer does not need to be housed and fed and is not tempted to run away.[49] But even if we acknowledge that in many cases a master's livelihood required his ownership of slaves, *we* who live in modern economies are certainly not in that situation. No good purpose would be served by slavery today. It would be a grave and unnecessary harm, and so we are well rid of it.

The badness of slavery for slaves is the most obvious normative fact about it. If a moral evaluation of slavery overlooks this point, if it examines slavery in terms that evade its effect on the well-being of slaves, it will be unable to explain why it is objectionable. Here, as elsewhere, the route to practical conclusions must pass through a conception of what is good and what is bad.

That does not mean that the only salient normative point to be made about slavery is the grave harm it so often did to slaves. The theories of innate deficiencies on which it sometimes rested (for example, in Aristotle's rationalization, and in theories that prevailed in the American South)[50] were false. Since those who were enslaved were fully capable of developing along all the dimensions of a flourishing life, but slavery

---

48. I have relied principally on Ira Berlin's nuanced portrait of slavery in North America, *Many Thousands Gone*. The conditions endured by Israelite slaves and Russian serfs, for example, were different in some significant ways. For an overview of slavery in ancient Greece, see N. R. E. Fisher, *Slavery in Classical Greece*. A magisterial survey is provided by David Brion Davis, *The Problem of Slavery in Western Culture*.

49. There is ongoing controversy regarding the economic efficiency of slavery in the American South. For a helpful guide, see Mark M. Smith, *Debating Slavery* (1998).

50. Aristotle *Politics* 1.4–7 and 13; Drew Gilpin Faust, *The Ideology of Slavery*.

made it difficult and often impossible for them to do so, there was a serious injustice in the way slave societies allocated good and evil. Just political communities must serve the common good of all their members—must be designed to benefit all of them equally—and slave societies unjustly counted slaves as nonmembers or had a misguided conception of the sort of good that slaves were capable of achieving.[51]

64. Torture

What can be said against torturing a human being? The place to start, obviously, is with the point that being tortured is bad. We would be misstating that point if we said that it is bad *that* someone undergoes torture. Rather, we should say that torture is bad *for* the person being tortured (sections 16–18)—very, very bad. The seriousness of the offense someone commits when he tortures another human being can be explained entirely in terms of the severity of the harm that is done. We all operate with an implicit theory of sensory and affective un-flourishing when we talk about torture: it is part of our commonsense framework that when we are in great pain or undergo other sensory afflictions (extreme fatigue, heat, cold), we are, in an important respect, doing extremely badly, because part of our well-being has to do with our nature as sensory beings (section 38). The condition of the sensory system of the victim of torture is the opposite of what it should be. So too his affective systems: torture involves not just pain and other sensory misfortunes but fear, humiliation, shame, and so on (section 39). The expe-

51. One might ask: "What if a significant portion of humankind had inherent mental deficiencies, and they were capable only of hard physical labor and incapable of self-governance? (That is, what if Aristotle were right that there are natural slaves, and many of them?)" Even in such a fantasy world, there would be no reason to recognize legal rights of ownership over human beings. Everything we know from history about where that kind of power leads tells us that these inherently limited human beings would be gravely injured by their diminished legal status. Their social, emotional, and physical good would be neglected. A just political community would have to give equal attention to the well-being of such individuals, even though some dimensions of flourishing would be beyond their reach. In saying this, I am drawing on both a conception of what is good for someone (there are other dimensions of flourishing besides intellectual competence), and an egalitarian political principle (limitations do not make one less deserving of care). If one could show that, the evidence of history notwithstanding, a system of ownership would in fact be the best way to serve the good of human beings incapable of self-governance, then, in that fantasy world, slavery would be justified. For it would be difficult to justify allowing these human beings to suffer from their limitations on the grounds that a system of ownership, despite all the good it would do them, would be wrong.

rience lives on in memory and continues to debilitate the victim of torture, as do the physical effects. Though an animal suffers very badly by being tortured, the emotional components of torture make this something far worse for a human being to endure. Where there are laws against torture (international and national), another objection can be brought against it—its illegality—but this offense pales in comparison with the damage the torturer intentionally causes.

Does it ever do any good for anyone when someone is tortured? Perhaps in some cases useful information is extracted. We can in any case invent hypothetical situations in which a great many lives are saved by torture. But if there can ever be a justification for deciding to torture someone, that justification would have to be cast in terms of the probability that torture would lead to results so good that they overwhelmingly compensate for the harm done. The person inflicting the torture would have to have good reason to believe that torturing *this* person would do great good. He would have to receive the authorization of a government, and proper controls would have to be in place, to safeguard against wanton torture. If all these conditions are present, there is a case to be made that torture would be justified. It contributes to such a justification that the intended victim of torture intends to withhold information in order to ensure the death of immense numbers. He hopes and intends to collaborate with mass murder; he is known by his torturer not to be an innocent victim.

Can the case in favor of torture, in this imaginary case, nonetheless be rebutted? An attempt to rebut it might consist simply in the thesis that one must never knowingly do what makes another human being worse-off—but that extreme position would make legal punishment unjustified. Perhaps then the rebuttal would be this: one should never do *that* much harm to a human being, no matter how much good comes of it. But that position is implausible. We should not fear that if we say that the decision to torture is sometimes justified partly because the great good it does compensates for the harm it inflicts, we are committed to utilitarianism. To hold that overwhelming good in some cases justifies doing some harm is not to agree that we should make all decisions by maximizing good.

Consider a case in which it is evident that the demanding conditions that must be met if torture is ever to be justified are not in fact met. It would be natural for us to say that in such a case torture is *morally wrong*. But notice that by using these words, we would not mean that the moral wrongness of the torture itself counts as part of the case against it. The argument against torture would consist entirely in the harm it does and its failure to be sufficiently likely to do enough good, and perhaps as well in the failure to follow proper procedures designed to prevent wanton torture. In light of those facts, we conclude that the person who authorized or committed torture should not have. To say "he should not have" is too mild a way of putting the point, and so we might strengthen the terms in which we describe the case: we say that it was morally wrong, and perhaps use still stronger terms. But the moral wrongness of what was done is no part of the case against torture.

It is of course possible to offend against someone by doing something to his body without going nearly so far as to torture him. We can hit someone without causing pain, push him, stare menacingly at him, stand unusually close to him in an uncrowded space, and so on. If we willingly do these things, and no features of the context in which we act justify what we do, then we have acted wrongly. How so? Has something bad happened to the person who was hit, pushed, stared at, approached too closely? That question is meant as a challenge either to the developmental conception of well-being presented in Chapter 3, or to the hypothesis of this chapter that all practical justification must proceed by way of what is good or bad for us. Either it is bad for you when someone stands too close, or there is something objectionable about standing too close that has nothing to do with what is bad. The reply to this objection is that all the actions mentioned are reasonably interpreted as threats of something worse—something that *is* a component of unflourishing (pain, physical injury, and so on). When threatening to harm someone (whether by gesture or word) is objectionable, the objection consists in the fact that it is *harm* (something that diminishes one's well-being) that is threatened. Here, as in all other cases, reasons that build a case for or against an action must advert to something that is good or bad for some individual.

65. Moral Rightness Revisited

We can now tie together several connected points that have been made in this chapter and in Chapter 1 about moral rightness and the role it should play in our thinking. We just noted that one cannot merely affirm, without support, the moral wrongness of torture in a good argument against it. If it is claimed that particular acts of torture, or a whole class of such acts, or all such acts whatsoever, are morally wrong, that assertion must be a conclusion of an argument, not an unsupported premise; and one premise that must always do a large portion of the work in supporting such a conclusion is the badness of torture for the victim. The moral wrongness of torture, when it is wrong, is not an additional reason against it, one that is added to the great harm torture does, thereby increasing the strength of a multifaceted argument against it. Since that is so, one can simply leave the moral wrongness of torture aside when one seeks reasons that might either support or oppose this kind of act, or particular instances of it.[52]

The same point can be made about slavery (section 63). Why should no one be a slave? Why should slave systems be dismantled and transformed into economies in which wage labor replaces involuntary servitude? A good answer to that question cannot begin with the unsupported assertion that slavery is morally wrong. It must instead begin with an argument that shows how bad slavery is for those who are enslaved. Having made that move, it must also consider whether slavery is needed in order that good be done. That is partly a philosophical question (what is good?) and partly empirical. The answer is that in modern economic systems no one need be a slave in order that others may flourish. The fact that slavery would do great harm and no good settles the matter: that decisively makes the case against this institution. Here, too, the moral wrongness of slavery can be left aside when one looks for reasons slavery should be prohibited.

Breaking a promise that should not be broken is typically not as serious an offense as torturing someone (when there is no good reason to do so) or owning slaves; and that of course is because the failure to deliver a promised good pales in significance when compared to the grave harm done by torture and many cases of slavery. Nonetheless, notice this structural similarity: the moral wrongness of breaking a promise can be left aside when one looks for reasons for keeping a promise. When

---

52. Using Scanlon's term (but dissenting from his view), we can say that moral rightness "passes the buck" (*What We Owe to Each Other*, p. 97). I side instead with Jonathan Dancy's thesis that "there are no independent overall qualities of rightness and wrongness; these supposed qualities are to be understood more in terms of verdicts on the way in which the reasons present in the case 'come down'" (*Ethics without Principles*, p. 141; see too p. 34).

a promise should be kept, the fact that one has made it does not, on its own, constitute a reason for keeping it (section 57). There must be some point in doing what one promised to do, or there must be some harm that would be done if the promise is broken. If honoring a promise can be supported on these grounds, then it can be concluded that one should keep it. But even if it is true of certain promises that it would be morally wrong to break them, or even if this is true of *all* promises that should be kept, the moral wrongness of violating them does not count as one of the reasons for keeping them.

These cases fit the pattern that we observed in Chapter 1 (section 8). Plagiarism should not be tolerated in the academy, not because it is morally wrong (though it may not be false to call it that), but because of the harm it does. Adultery in many cases does great damage and little or no good; *that* is why the moral rule against it is a good rule (not because it is morally wrong). Blinding a human being or an animal just for fun can never be justified, but we explain why this is so not by affirming the moral wrongness of doing so, but by pointing out that this is an act that does grave harm and no good.

The injustice of an act is unlike its moral wrongness in that it does constitute a reason for criticizing and refraining from it. If a parent loves only one of his two children, he treats his unloved child unjustly. His way of distributing what is good is seriously defective, and there is a far better pattern of distribution: not to stop loving the one, but to love the other equally. Analogously, we might say that the allocation of benefits and burdens in a slave system is unjust, and that the economy should be transformed for that reason. That criticism would of course rest on the prior claim that slavery is a severe impediment to flourishing.

Rawls notes that the classical utilitarians (Bentham, Mill, and so on) do not treat the proper distribution of what is good as itself something that is good. Instead, they take the satisfaction of rational desire as good and propose that this be maximized: "as much as possible" is their formula for the "pattern" of distribution that they favor. Rawls agrees with them that the way in which benefits and burdens should be distributed should not be conceived of as yet one more good—a higher-order good that consists in other goods arranged in a certain order. As he says, "The problem of distribution falls under the concept of right as one intuitively understands it."[53] Justice, for Rawls, belongs to a category of reasons that

---

53. Rawls, *A Theory of Justice*, p. 22.

are distinct in kind from reasons that advert to what is good for someone. That distinct category of reasons traffics in what is right, rather
than what is good. When we deliberate, justice or any other consideration that falls within the genus of moral rightness always take precedence over reasons that have to do with goodness. When Rawls says that
"the two main concepts of ethics are those of the right and the good,"[54]
he means that we must keep track of whether a reason belongs to the
category of rightness or the category of goodness, because those drawn
from the former class must be given priority to those drawn from the latter category.[55] His idea that justice is just one of many considerations of
the same type—all of them falling "under the concept of right as one intuitively understands it"—is supported by his thesis that the two principles of justice that play so important a role in his political theory are just
a few examples of the many principles that would be chosen by the parties in the original position. "The intuitive idea is this: the concept of
something's being right is the same as, or better, may be replaced by, the
concept of its being in accordance with the principles that in the original
position would be acknowledged to apply to things of its kind."[56] Promises of a certain sort—more precisely, what Rawls calls "bone fide promises"[57]—are to be kept because the principle that they are to be honored
would be accepted by the individuals in the original position. The moral
wrongness of an act, according to this way of thinking, does play a vital
role in good practical reasoning, because the fact that it violates a principle that would be chosen in the original position constitutes a reason of
the highest order against it.

    The crucial test for Rawls's theory is whether we need the device of
the original position, or of a social contract, to bring the fullest possible
order and clarity to our practice of practical reasoning as we reflect on it.
We have seen that there are reasons to doubt this. What we find is that
the strength of a practical reason varies according to the amount of good
or harm (properly understood) to which it refers. In certain circumstances, the reasons to keep a promise are extremely weak because what
one has promised to do makes little difference in terms of the good that
has been promised or the damage to a relationship that would be done
by breaking it. That individuals would, under certain conditions, agree

54. Ibid., p. 21.
55. Ibid., pp. 27–28.
56. Ibid., p. 95.
57. Ibid., p. 304.

to a principle of promising is not a consideration that turns every bona
fide promise (for example, to wear a silly hat to the party) into a matter
of great moment, trumping all or nearly all other considerations. It is
possible to reflect successfully on whether to keep a promise, and how
much weight should be attached to doing so, without placing promise
keeping into the category of rightness or noting that such a practice
would be chosen by hypothetical contractors. Similarly for torture, slavery, adultery, euthanasia, plagiarism, paternalism, and so on.

Rawls is right that when one conceives of good and bad in terms of
pleasure or the satisfaction of desire, reasons that allude to what is good
or bad for this person or that should often carry little or no weight in the
design of social institutions. Desires can have trivial or worthless objects, and they can be mere expressions of hostility. The utilitarian can
accept the point that satisfying a single desire may have little value, but
he insists that the satisfaction of all the desires of all people (or as many
as possible) can hardly be a trivial accomplishment. A central element of
the strategy Rawls uses against the utilitarian is to posit the existence of
a large category of reasons any one of which nullifies the force of reasons
that advert to what is good or bad. But there is no such category. When
we devote ourselves to doing good, we must be careful about the pattern
of good we bring about, and not merely the total quantity; that is why
the injustice of a distribution counts as a reason against it.[58] But justice is
not a member of a general category of reasons—the category of moral
rightness—each member of which takes priority over goodness precisely because it belongs to the superior category. The dichotomy that
Rawls proposes—either we must maximize the satisfaction of rational
desires, or we must place reasons of rightness above those of goodness—
is not exhaustive, and each of the two alternatives rests on a philosophical error. The utilitarian assumes that good is to be maximized, and that
it consists in the satisfaction of rational desire; both ideas should be rejected. Rawls mistakenly agrees that the good consists in the satisfaction
of rational desire; he holds, again mistakenly, that there is a general cate-

---

58. We must, in addition, not undermine the specific good to which an institution is devoted by violating its rules to pursue other types of goods. No amount of money received by a
teacher from a student would justify the falsification of a grade, for example. Similar points apply to the operation of the judicial and legislative system and to every other social office. Many
of our most important goods can be achieved only when their pursuit is governed by rules that
prohibit the substitution of goods alien to those that give the rules their point.

gory of reasons that take precedence over those that advert to good. We should reject both the good-maximizing and right-prioritizing alternatives (as well as the conative theory of well-being that both adopt). Practical reasoning must always proceed by way of premises that have to do with what is good (to that extent, utilitarianism is on the right track), but good must be understood developmentally.

When we describe a person as acting for moral reasons, the term "moral" often works by way of contrast with "prudential," "self-interested," "selfish," and so on. If, for example, someone decides to become a vegetarian for moral reasons, that means that he refrains from eating meat because he is opposed to the harm that is done to animals when they are raised for slaughter. If instead he is a vegetarian only because he is concerned with the effect of eating meat on his own health, we say that he acts not for moral but for prudential reasons. We can describe the moral vegetarian as someone who is moved by the moral wrongness of killing animals for food, but his objection of course has a great deal to do with the great and needless *harm* caused by this practice. When we say that he is motivated by the moral rightness of refraining from eating meat, we do not mean to imply that he believes there is some other type of reason, having nothing to do with good and harm, for being a vegetarian; we mean to say only that it is the good of *others*—not his own—that moves him.

Keeping track of someone's motivation by asking whether he acts prudentially or morally or from mixed motives is unobjectionable. But this way of talking can mislead us if we are not careful. When one says, "I do not eat meat because it is morally wrong," one might be asked by a philosopher to explain what this property, moral wrongness, is. It might be taken to be the property that certain acts of killing, assault, adultery, promise breaking, plagiarism, and so on, have in common, and that explains what is objectionable about them. For these are all cases of mistreating *others,* and what is defective in them cannot simply be that they are imprudent. Conversely, morally right acts would be those that are demanded of us precisely because they have the quality of moral rightness. Because "moral" and "prudential" are contrasting terms, they would not be acts in which one benefits oneself alone. Learning a new subject or taking up a sport are not usually counted as morally right, whereas acting justly, or keeping a promise, or giving assistance to a passerby in need are.

But what one is likely to have in mind when one says that one does not eat meat because it is morally wrong is that it is not one's own good but that of animals that one is thinking of. The criticism to be made of this practice is not that it has the property of moral wrongness, however that property is to be understood; it is simply that it willingly does great and unnecessary harm. The disproportionate balance of good and harm is what critics of this practice object to, and when the conclusion "It is morally wrong" is drawn, that conveys the thought that it is for the good of animals, not merely one's own, that one should be a vegetarian. The same point applies to the many other kinds of acts that are normally classified as moral wrongs. When we say, for example, that torture and slavery are morally wrong and that we should therefore never condone these practices, we mean that it is not merely the economic inefficiency of slavery that counts against it, and not merely the protection of one's own troops that stands behind the criticism of torture. We should not accept these practices because of what they intentionally do to *other* people, not merely because our acceptance of them will be contrary to our own interests. That way of using "morally right" and "morally wrong" keeps track of an important distinction—that between self-interest and altruism. This is the distinction we often presuppose when we say, "You should not—in fact, must not—do it, because it is morally wrong." There is no reason to abandon this way of talking. But we should not assume, simply because we know how to classify certain kinds of actions as morally wrong or morally right, that these terms play a reason-giving role—that it is precisely *because* slavery is wrong or torture is wrong that we must not accept these practices.

Not everyone agrees that we should reserve such terms as "morally right" and "moral reasons" to actions that benefit others or to altruistic motives. It could be said that this way of talking has the unfortunate effect of making self-interested actions and concern for one's own good dishonorable, or in any case of secondary importance. Perhaps this is what Ross has in mind when he writes: "The doctrine that morality is entirely social, that all duty consists in promoting the good of others, seems to me a profound mistake. Intellectual integrity, the love of truth for its own sake, is among the most salient elements in a good moral character. It is a thing which, with the other virtues, we should try to cultivate in ourselves and to promote in others."[59] Ross is claiming that

59. Ross, *The Right and the Good*, p. 153.

each person has a moral duty to acquire for himself two of the items that he regards as intrinsically good—knowledge and virtue. It would be *morally wrong,* according to his way of thinking, to pass up an opportunity to cultivate an intellectual skill, or to fail to acquire a body of knowledge, unless one had an overriding reason not to, deriving from some other duty. Of course, Ross is not alone here. Kant too holds that each person has a moral duty to cultivate his talents.[60]

The insight behind Ross's statement is that acting for one's good is not a reason that is inherently inferior to that of acting for the good of someone else. But if one wishes to call "morally right" every action that someone should undertake, the term will cover too large a territory to be of any value. There is nothing objectionable in abiding by the common distinction between moral and prudential reasons, so long as one is careful not to regard the latter category as inherently inferior. The more important question is whether there is a distinctive category of reasons—the ones that we invoke when we are concerned with moral rightness—that we must add to, and recognize as superior to, the kind that adverts to goodness and badness. We have not discovered any, and the common practice of distinguishing moral from prudential reasons gives us no reason to suppose that there are any.

66. Lying

We turn next to the topic of lying. As always, the question that drives our investigation is the role that good and bad should play in our practical reasoning. Do the lies that are to be avoided fall into that category because of the harm they do, or because of the way in which they disrupt practices that allocate what is good? Or is there some other factor, having nothing to do with good or harm, that determines when lies should be told (if they ever should be told)?

When one lies to someone, one intends to induce in him a false belief (or, less often, one allows him to continue believing what is false). Does that by itself tell us that something is going amiss whenever a lie is told—the very fact that it aims at *falsity* of belief? That would be so if having a false belief is always bad for the person whose belief it is. Lying to a person would in that case be comparable to causing him a physical

---

60. Kant, *Groundwork for the Metaphysics of Morals,* 4:423.

injury, and it would always count against an action that it involves telling a lie.

But is it *always* bad for someone to have a false belief? Before answering that question, we should distinguish two kinds of case: the instrumental badness of having a false belief, and its intrinsic badness. According to Ross, it is intrinsically good to have knowledge—no matter what
the object of knowledge is (section 42). If we accept a modification of
his theory, holding that it is always good *for* someone to have knowledge, we will arrive at the conclusion that every false belief is inherently
bad for the person who has the belief because in falsely believing that P,
one fails to know that it is not the case that P. Someone who believes
falsely is deprived of knowledge that he might have had; he has un-
knowledge instead. And that, we might suppose, is always bad, regardless of whether that un-knowledge leads to some further harm or depri-
vation.

The problem for such a view, as we noted (section 42), lies in its assumption that bits of knowledge, no matter how isolated and trivial
their objects, are good for someone to have. It is difficult to believe, for
example, that it is *intrinsically* good to know that such-and-such is
someone's telephone number. So it is reasonable to wonder: if I tell you
that such-and-such is someone's telephone number, and I realize that
what I tell you is false, have I already done something that merits criticism, regardless of whether there is any chance that you will need such
information? Of course, if you need to phone someone, and I knowingly
give you the wrong number, the falsity of your information will make it
more difficult for you to meet your need. But in that case, the objection
to what I have done does not lie merely in the fact that the belief I caused
you to have is false, but in the fact that the falsity of that belief led to a
bad result by impeding you in the pursuit of a worthwhile goal.

Here is another example of a harmless falsehood: whenever Mr.
Szycklewieski phones an American restaurant to make a dinner reserva-
tion, he identifies himself as Mr. Sanders. If the receptionist believes that
the caller is being truthful, has he been harmed because he has acquired
a false belief? Do we count it as one of the disadvantages of the receptionist's job that from time to time he is not given the real names of those
who phone to make reservations? It is hard to believe so.

If, on the other hand, these arguments are mistaken, and it *is* intrinsically harmful to have a false belief, that tells us that lying is always
objectionable, at least to some degree, and we have additional confirma-

tion of the hypothesis that good practical reasoning always proceeds by means of premises that advert to doing what is good or avoiding what is bad. I will assume, however, that Ross is wrong, and that it is not in itself bad for someone to have pieces of un-knowledge.

There are of course many cases in which it is instrumentally bad for someone to be lied to. The false belief induced by the person who tells the lie puts the person who is lied to at a serious disadvantage. For example, a prospective house buyer asks the current owner whether the basement has ever flooded, and the seller, lying, says it has not. It is bad for the buyer to believe that statement if his belief leads him to buy a house that he would not have otherwise bought, or to pay a higher price than he otherwise would have paid. Even if he decides not to buy the house, the owner can be faulted: he knowingly created a false belief in the hope that he would make himself better-off at the expense of the buyer. He intended to harm someone, merely for the sake of financial gain. The lie was an instrument by means of which he tried to take advantage of his superior knowledge of the item being sold. So we condemn the lie because of the instrumental role it played in an attempt to make someone worse-off. A large number of the lies that are told fit into this category. We need accurate information to deliberate well, and liars set us back, often for their own gain, when they feed us false information.

But that is not the only category of lies to which we properly object. Suppose a teacher tells his students that he has won several awards, but he is lying to them. He is seeking a certain good—their admiration, affection, and respect (section 41)—but does not deserve it, at least not on those grounds. The false information he feeds his students does not necessarily put them into a worse position to make practical decisions. But he gets from them something that he rightly thinks of as good for himself, and they would not have given it had they known the truth. The objection to lying in this sort of case is that something that is good for people to have is being misdirected; it goes to the wrong person because the teacher has not in fact earned the admiration he craves. Furthermore, his lie poisons the well of trust from which flows cooperative academic work, both his own and that of others. He makes this component of cognitive flourishing (section 42) more difficult for teachers and students to pursue. Lies have to do with good and bad in different ways: as instruments for appropriating goods and taking them from others (the homeowner), and as instruments for gaining goods that are undeserved (the teacher). (It is of course possible to lie on behalf of others rather than oneself: to gain a financial advantage for one's children, or to win admiration for one's father. They are no less objectionable for being altruistic.)

Other sorts of lies deserve criticism because the misinformation supplied by the liar is a displacement of information that should be shared by those who look to each other for intimate friendship. Suppose a child lies to his parents about where he has been and what he has done. In doing so, he induces them to believe that they are sharing in his life, whereas in fact they are being excluded. That subverts the basis of affection, even if the lies told are inconsequential and undetected. Parents and child in this case do not have the kind of shared life that it is good for families and close friends to have. These lies are inherently harmful not because of the falsity of the beliefs they induce, but because they are a denial of love. Similarly, the lies a husband tells his wife to conceal his adultery cut her out of a portion of his life that should be shared, and so even if they are not detected, both are harmed by this diminution in their intimacy.

Our catalogue of lies should not be unrepresentative, and so we need to remind ourselves that some lies are instrumentally valuable and contain nothing objectionable at all. The killer who is looking for his next victim should be supplied with misinformation. The person who lies to him is not performing a mixed action—good, in that a life is saved; bad, in that a lie is told. He is blameless, and the fact that his treatment of the killer involved a lie does not count as a strike against what he did.[61] Lies

61. Suppose one could have diverted a murderer just as effectively with a true statement as with the lie one told. Is one in this case blameworthy for having lied? I believe the answer is no. To see this, consider someone who uses an appropriate degree of physical force to prevent a murder. He is blameless for having done so; but had he inflicted far more physical harm than was necessary, that feature of his act would be blameworthy—even though, on balance, he might deserve more praise than blame. Now, the lie told to avert a murder does *not* seem comparable to the use of undue force, even when a truthful statement would have had the same effect. It is not a situation in which some blame but even more praise than blame is appropriate. Nonetheless, a scrupulous person who lies to a murderer to save a life will reasonably wish that he had had some truthful way of bringing about the same effect, and he may look for a truthful alternative before he decides to tell a lie. For being truthful in all one's relationships is an attractive ideal (because of the good achieved by those who participate in such relationships), and someone who is attracted to such an ideal will regret that some situations call for a lie. In the same way, relationships that do not involve the use of force or coercion are the ones that we wish we could enter into with all human beings; one may therefore wish that one did not have to use force or coercion, even when one is entirely blameless for having done so.

are not indelibly negative in value, retaining some stain regardless of how much good they accomplish. Cunning is, at times, entirely admirable; even when not admirable, it can be blameless because necessary. Hostile tribes competing for scarce economic resources, each justifiably suspicious of the other, cannot be faulted for using deception against each other.

Of course, there are mixed cases: situations in which one should regret telling someone a lie because of the harm it causes, but in which it is nonetheless the best thing to do. A dying grandparent asks whether his grandson has survived a plane crash, and the child's father, lying, says that he has. One should hate telling a lie to someone with whom one is intimate, because of the harm done to one's relationship; but that consideration is outweighed by the anguish one would cause by telling the truth. Here one is forced to weigh two evils: failing to share with a loved one, and causing him great pain. Lying may be the right choice, but a price is paid nonetheless. Another case of the same sort: a seventeen-year-old volunteers to risk his life in battle, but he lies about his age because the law sets the minimum age for soldiers at eighteen. The law reasonably aims to protect those who are not yet sufficiently mature, but it is a blunt instrument and excludes some who are far more capable, emotionally and physically, than their elders. The lie is told in order to do good, but penalties for telling such lies can also be justified.

The conclusion we should draw is that lies are objectionable or not according as their relation to good and bad varies. The nature of lies—the fact that they are devices for inducing false beliefs—does not make them inherently wrong. But the criticism that should be made of those lies that are subject to criticism rests in the harm they do or in their misallocation of what is good.

67. Honoring the Dead

When we honor the dead in ceremonies, or merely look for ways of reviving our memories of and affection for them, we do them no good. Of course, not everyone accepts that claim. Some think that the souls of the dead survive the destruction of their bodies, and they may also suppose that those we have lost to death are pleased by the honors and tokens of affection we bestow upon them. And even those who do not admit the possibility of life after death might claim that good things can happen to those who are dead. If it is good to be famous, then fame that comes posthumously does not come too late. If it is good for one's desires to be satisfied, then one's fortunes rise even after death as the things that one wanted to occur do occur. But if we reject these ideas about well-being in favor of developmentalism, and assume that the dead are truly dead, then honoring and loving those who are dead does them no good.

But it is not implausible to suppose that funerals and other occasions of remembrance do some good—to those who participate in them and are affected by them, emotionally and intellectually. It is widely assumed that it is bad for grief to be suppressed or hidden, and that it is healthy for those who have been close to someone recently deceased to express in common their sense of loss. But that is only one reason not to suppress our thoughts about those who have died. We do not stop loving someone merely because he has died. The expression of affection is one component of well-being (section 39), and it remains so after its object is no longer present. We enjoy reviving our fond memories and in this way sustaining, albeit in a one-sided way, the relationships that were important to us at an earlier time. The objects that are intimately associated with a person we loved—her remains, or her favorite piece of furniture—take on sentimental or symbolic value, and carving out a space for them in our lives is a way of continuing to express our love, just as a wedding ring acquires expressive significance (section 68). It is for our own good that we treasure these things and keep alive our affection for departed friends and family.

A radically different approach from the one proposed here would insist that one has a *duty* to honor certain people—parents, for example—when they have died. Whether it does one any good to participate in ceremonies of remembrance is irrelevant, according to this way of thinking. But the suggestion that we have this duty cannot survive scrutiny, unless it is backed by a systematic duty-centered theory—one that tells us how to recognize what our duties are and explains why we should do what we are said to owe to others, in spite of the fact that doing so does no good. As we noted long ago (section 8), widely accepted prohibitions (against killing, stealing, adultery) are ways of protecting people against certain kinds of harms. They are not mere taboos. Similarly, we have more recently seen that when promises should be kept, that is in part because it does some good to keep them (section 57); that pure antipaternalism should be rejected (section 61); that the case against slavery and torture cannot ignore the great harm they do (sections 63, 64); that lying is objectionable or not according to its relation to good and bad (section 66). It is difficult to believe that we have exactly one duty—to honor the dead—that must be performed, whether doing so is good for anyone or not.

Often people undertake or continue with certain activities because that is what a departed parent or spouse or friend would have wanted them to do, or did want them to do. That too, like memorial services, is a way to express one's continued affection for someone who has died, and because of that, such deference is a component of one's well-being. But suppose one knows that what one's father wanted, or would have wanted, does no good for oneself or anyone else, but rather does harm. To defer to the dead in such cases might be an expression of love—but, by hypothesis, it is an unhealthy love. There are better ways of honoring and continuing to love those whom we miss than being guided by their bad ideas.

There is a literary genre and intellectual discipline that takes the dead very seriously: history (although it is not by its nature confined to them). Part of its value is that through it we extend the range of people to whom we have emotional ties. The members of the English working class of the nineteenth century cannot feel anything for you, but you can feel something for them. History may have lessons to teach us, but it is a mistake to treat it as a mere means to making public policy. Through it one becomes a member of a larger affective and intellectual community, and the territory over which one's mental powers range is enlarged. There is no reason we should have affective ties only with those dead people whom we once knew or whose lifetimes overlap with our own. Our social world need not be limited to the people who have crossed our path or who might some day do so.

68. Meaningless Goals and Symbolic Value

We can easily underestimate the importance of what is good or bad for us if we attach too great a significance to the question "What should we care about?" For the proper answer to that question (as we are about to see) should *not* be: only about what is good for someone or avoiding what is bad for someone. But the centrality of good is revealed when we ask not about the appropriate *objects* of care, but about the very *caring* for those objects. The deeper question is not about which objects of love, concern, or interest should be present to our consciousness, but about how to evaluate the consciousness of those objects. Which caring states should a person be in? We should answer: only those that do some good for someone (not necessarily the subject who cares).

That point should be recognized as a commonplace. A basketball player wants the ball to go through the hoop, and he is filled with joy when it does. Is it good for him, or for anyone, that he made his shot? What is the good of having one material object pass through another? Of one team's putting a ball through a hoop more often than another's? Of running more quickly than everyone else? Of checkmating one's opponent? From a certain point of view, basketball and every other competitive game can seem absurd. But things come into proper perspective when we remember that working toward a goal can be good, even though, by itself, the act that constitutes the achievement of the goal is not. The enjoyment of running with speed and grace is good because it is the activation of our physical powers (section 36). But this, like many other goods, is easier and more pleasurable to achieve if one sets oneself a goal that is not, in itself, good to achieve. The attainment of the goal is not something that must be regarded by the agent as a means to a further end; efforts made to reach it will achieve something good, even if the agent has no idea what that good is and is indifferent to his well-being. The chess player's goal is to win games, not to deploy his spatial and strategic powers. If he is no moral philosopher, he may have no idea what is good for him or anyone else. In fact, when he checkmates his opponent, *that* does no good for anyone. The goal he aims at is worthless.

The variety of things we care about, and do well to care about, is enormous. It is not just people and activities that we love and hate. We become attached to physical objects and invest them with sentimental or symbolic value. If a wedding ring is missing, husband and wife are not likely simply to shrug their shoulders; they will spend an enormous amount of time searching for it. It may have no monetary value, but we say that nonetheless it does have value—sentimental or symbolic value. The ring has taken on a meaning in their lives. When it was sitting in the jewelry shop, before it was purchased, it lacked value. So it derives its value from their attitudes.

If the ring is lost, is that bad for them? This is not a question that asks:

should they be upset? Rather, it asks: *why* should they be upset? Is it because that loss is bad for them?

It is obvious that neither wearing a round object on one's finger nor owning such an object is a component of a flourishing life. No one is made better-off merely by possessing or wearing a ring. Nor is wearing such an object an effective method for bringing about some good. If there were no common custom of exchanging rings at a wedding and wearing them, human relationships would not necessarily take a turn for the worse. A marriage in which neither partner wears a ring is not, for that very reason, a marriage that is worse for each partner than it might have been.

Nonetheless, intimate and affectionate ties to other human beings are a component of well-being (section 39). These ties diminish in value if they are not expressed and affirmed. Spoken words and gestures are not the only way in which we do this. Wearing a ring is another way in which husbands and wives can express their love and commitment, since that is the conventional meaning that their society places on this kind of adornment. A ring that has been lost can of course be replaced by another, but that particular ring has a history, having been the object they exchanged as an expression of their bond and have continued to wear every day. Is it bad, then, for them to lose that particular object? Of course, but not because it is a mere means to an end, like checkmate or scoring a basket. That particular symbolic mode of expressing long-lasting affection will no longer be available to them, and the expression of that tie is a component of their well-being. That is why it is worth considerable effort to search for that missing ring. It can play an expressive role as no other ring can.

The practice of wearing rings and a person's attachment to a particular ring are not matters that are immune from critical assessment. We can ask whether these conventions and the investment of intense emotions in them are good for human relationships, whether they strengthen our ties in healthy ways, whether it is possible for someone to care more about these matters than is warranted, and so on. Here, as elsewhere, what is good for us is the central tool that we need for self-understanding. If wearing rings is a healthy convention, and our investment of meaning in these objects is justified, that must be because some human good is served by our doing so. Something goes badly amiss if someone devotes so much time searching for a lost ring that he no longer spends time with his spouse, and she suffers from neglect. Attachment to the ring and the good of the ring (guarding it against scratches and deterioration) should be subordinated to the good of the individuals whose relationship the ring symbolizes. The only cares we should have are those the having of which does some good.

Some physical objects, because of their history, evoke moral repugnance. One's revulsion at the sight or thought of an evil tyrant, long dead, spills over and spreads out to the objects with which he came into contact. No one should comfortably wear a sweater he knows was once worn by Hitler; it cannot be treated as simply another garment, to be worn because of its warmth and appearance. But what harm would it do to wear it? Why not do so? It would be bad for someone to be entirely without a capacity for moral revulsion—to be capable only of cold judgments of character unaccompanied by affect. That would be a deficiency in his affective powers. Any form of intimacy with an evil person should revolt us if our emotional reactions are as they should be. Our love and hatred of others naturally flow toward the physical objects they surround themselves with, and it would be a diminution of our affective life, a cold indifference to symbols and associative meaning, if objects did not take on affective coloration in this way. It is not the actual wearing of Hitler's sweater that would be bad for us, but rather the insensitivity that would have to underlie a cheerful willingness to do so.

69. Good-Independent Realms of Value

I return now to the place where we started: the use of "good" in which it serves to grade types of things—food, plans, friends, and so on (section 1). Here, too, our evaluations should proceed from premises that advert to what is good for someone. Without a notion of flourishing, we cannot properly determine what is a good member of a kind.[62]

That claim is far from obvious. When we ask, for example, whether a poem we are reading is a good poem, it may seem absurd to suppose that we should answer that question by finding out whether the poem is good *for* anyone—good, that is, for anyone to read, or listen to, or contemplate, or have written. To think that poems are meant to be good for

62. That leaves room for the possibility that a good thing of a kind might not be good for one person or another, because of special needs or circumstances. Good milk, for example, might be bad for someone because of her gastric deficiencies; but it must be good for *some*.

anyone, it might be said, is to misunderstand poetry. Poetry has its own internal standards of evaluation.

The same point could be made about many other evaluations. Good music does not have to be good for anyone. Nor does good painting, or good science, or good philosophy, and so on. Art is for art's sake; philosophy for philosophy's sake; science for science's sake.

Should we also say: duty should be done for duty's sake? That slogan can be construed as a denial that we should do only what is good for someone. It might mean, for example: do not ask whether any good is done by keeping a promise, or punishing a lawbreaker, or letting someone go his own way, or prohibiting slavery, or honoring the dead. These, it might be said, are our duties, and we should need no further reason for these acts and omissions than that.

We have rejected the notion of duty for duty's sake, so interpreted. We subject every moral rule and social role to this test: in what way, if any, does it enhance human life, or any life, by doing what is good for someone, or properly allocating what is good, or impeding what is bad, or properly allocating what is bad? That seems a reasonable question. Why then should we exempt poetry, philosophy, science, and other human pursuits from this challenge? And yet it *does* seem misguided to ask, "What good does this poem do?" Because of that, we might be tempted to talk about the poem's aesthetic *value*. We might then recognize or posit many other realms of value besides this: philosophical value, scientific value, historical value, athletic value, sentimental value, symbolic value, and so on. What we do or care about, it might be said, is validated if it has some kind of value. It need not be good *for* anyone, because to be good by being good for someone is only one kind of value—prudential value, we might call it. Human beings, we might say, are creators of these many realms of value: it is because we value things that they are valuable. That idea is of a piece with the conative approach to well-being, and with Rawls's proposal that moral rightness is whatever would be agreed to in the original position.[63] Human beings, we might add, are uniquely valuable, precisely because we give value to all else, and without us, nothing would have value (section 3).

We can also give many other examples, besides those drawn from the arts, in which we evaluate things without asking whether they are good

63. Rawls, *A Theory of Justice*, p. 95.

for anyone. Is someone a good thief? A good spy? A good rapist? It could be said that when we answer these questions, we ignore human well-being and use other standards of evaluation. A good thief, we might say, is simply a successful thief—someone who is good at thieving. When we judge someone a good thief, we are not approving of his thieving, merely evaluating it by reference to his goals, or the standards of thievery. So too for good instruments of torture, good land mines, and so on. We should not be taken aback, then, by the proposal that the arts and many other areas of human life are to be judged by standards that have nothing to do with human well-being. That, it might be said, is often what happens when we judge that S is a good member of a kind K. Often—but hardly always: surely a good watch must be good for someone, a good hotel good for someone, and so on. A believer in duty for duty's sake might say: a good person should no more be held to the standard of doing what is good *for* someone than is a good work of art or a good land mine. He is not like a good hotel or a good watch—not expected, in other words, to do any good for anyone; rather, he is to be judged by asking whether he does what he has a duty to do and does it for the sake of duty.

What are we to make of these ideas, which deny that well-being should be at the center of all evaluation? We should begin by returning to some recent examples (section 68). Competitive games are not organized around the goal of enhancing human well-being. A basketball player's goal is to get the ball through the hoop, to help his teammates accomplish that goal, and to stop the opposition from doing the same. The object of the game is not to do some good. So when we ask whether someone is a good basketball player, we do not respond—not immediately, at any rate—by talking about how he has contributed to the well-being of his teammates or the fans. We evaluate his skills as a player. But of course we can also look at the institution of basketball, or at competitive sports, and ask whether it is good for someone to be an athlete or to take an interest in sports. What is the good of being a good player, or an engaged and knowledgeable fan? It would be distressing if the answer were: these things do harm, not good. For in that case, we should worry about young people who aspire to play the game; about the wisdom of creating facilities—schools, gymnasia, public parks—that help them do so; and about the amount of time and money spent by those who follow the sport.

In the same way, when we judge whether a poem is a good poem, we look to the qualities of the poem, not something outside it—and in particular, not whether reading it does any good. Similarly, if asked whether a piece of writing is good philosophy, we evaluate the cogency of what it says and assess its ideas by standards internal to this style of thinking. But it is also intelligible to ask about poetry or philosophy, and the internal standards by which they are evaluated: why should we bother with such things? And it is sensible to respond to that question by considering the ways in which these practices enhance our powers and in this way constitute a form of human flourishing (section 47). A good poet is a poet who writes well, as assessed by standards of literary excellence, and the reason it is good to take pleasure in good poetry is that this is a component of well-being. The standards of literary excellence that are accepted by a community may themselves be evaluated: they may be thought to stifle the imagination, to confine rather than enhance our linguistic and affective powers and our comprehension of the world. Even so, two stages in the evaluation of a poem or a poet should be distinguished: are these words put together poetically? and what is the good of putting words together poetically? If we want to talk about the "aesthetic value" of a poem, we should use that phrase as an alternative way of calling something a good poem, or of talking about the way in which good poems are good for us. There is no independent aesthetic realm, a realm of art for art's sake, in which poetry is protected against the questions that should be asked about its connection to human flourishing. If that protection is what is sought by the ideal of art for art's sake, that ideal shares a defect with the notion of duty for duty's sake: it tries to establish a realm of human endeavor in which human good and harm are no longer the terms in which we assess whether something is worthwhile.

70. Good Thieves and Good Human Beings

What of the other examples, mentioned in the preceding section, in which the standards for deciding whether S is a good K seem to have nothing to do with human well-being? A good thief, we might say, is one who is good at thievery: stealing is his goal, and the only way to assess whether he is a good thief is to determine how well he progresses toward and achieves that goal. According to this way of thinking, the standards to be used for determining whether S is a good K are established by the aims of S.

But that cannot be right. A good dog is not one that achieves its aims, for it has none. A good dog is one who serves some human good—who is good *for* someone. A good wolf is one who acts in a way that is good *for* that wolf or for other members of his pack. A good poet, we saw in the previous section, also serves some human good, though that is not what he directly aims at in writing poetry. A good car is not necessarily one that achieves the purposes for which it was made; if it is dangerous, or becomes obsolete too quickly—if, in other words, it is a bad car for people to own or drive—then it is a bad car, however well it meets the manufacturer's specifications.

What, then, should we say about good thieves, good rapists, good instruments of torture, and so on? If we believe that no one should ever steal, because of the great harm theft always does, then we should say that there are no good thieves. All of them, in that case, would be bad thieves, though some may be far worse than others (namely the ones whose thievery is especially destructive). But if we think that theft can sometimes be justified, then we should say that a good thief is someone who knows, among other things, when to steal. He should also be good at stealing, of course. In addition to knowing what to steal, when to steal, how to steal, he must also have the physical skills needed for carrying out this task.

A torture instrument, correspondingly, can be a good one, only if torture can sometimes be justified in terms of the harm it avoids. It would be one that inflicts only as much pain as is needed in order to extract the information sought. It would be one that can be stopped immediately, as soon as the prisoner decides to cooperate. But if torture should not exist, then there are no good instruments of torture, and the least bad among them are the ones that are least painful. When we call something a good instrument of torture—or a good K in general—we are not merely evaluating, but approving.[64]

Good poetry, good wolves, good thieves, and good people are all good in the same way: in all cases, some contribution is made to what is good *for* someone, and that is what supports the judgment that S is a good K.

64. Rawls (ibid., p. 354) comes to a rather different conclusion because he adopts a perspectival approach (in the sense of section 24) to the analysis of the goodness of kinds. See especially the second stage of his definition of good (ibid., pp. 351–352): whether something is a good K for S depends on "his system of aims" (ibid., p. 351). Rawls's analysis commits him to the conclusion that a doctor who prescribes only such regimes as will promote the health of his patients is not a good doctor (*tout court*), but a good doctor for those who care about health and a bad doctor for those who do not.

Well-being, in some way or other, is the point of being a good K, or of there being such things as good Ks. The good qualities of a thing—its virtues—are those that prove their worth when assessed by the standard of what is good for someone. If courage, honesty, justice, and the like are indeed good qualities and partly constitute being a good person, that is not because they are universally thought of as virtues (section 52). Like everything else, they are not immune to critical assessment. About them too, we should ask: what good and what harm do they do?

71. Final Thoughts

By what route or routes can we properly arrive at the conclusion that we should, all things considered, do something? Certain philosophical systems propose an answer of astonishing simplicity. Egoism tells each person to maximize his own good. Utilitarianism says instead that it is the good of the entire universe that should be maximized. Neither theory survives reflection (sections 11, 12) because each has a maximizing structure that flattens the complex and rich terrain of practical life. But the good-centeredness of these doctrines is the baby that should not be thrown out with the bathwater. Practical reasoning has many tools at its disposal: it properly adverts to what one person owes another person, to considerations of merit, reciprocity, justice, commitment, obligation, duty, responsibility, impartiality, virtue, and so on. But a long tradition in moral philosophy accepts, in some way or other, Plato's hypothesis that the good is the sovereign object of all thought.[65] We find one variation on that theme in Aquinas's doctrine, which serves as the epigraph to this study, that "all other precepts of the natural law are founded" on the principle that "good is to be done and pursued, and bad is to be avoided." This way of thinking is not quantitative or reductive. It holds that it matters a great deal whether what we do is good or bad for this person rather than that; that the kind of good we create and the pattern according to which we do so, not merely the amount of good we do, are significant. One of the attractions of this approach is that it allows one to recognize a unity as well as the diversity in all justified practical thinking. The conceptual tools we bring to bear on practical life are not

65. Plato *Republic* Stephanus pp. 504–509.

a hodgepodge, but are focused on a central theme when we test every-thing we do and care about by asking, "What is the good of that?"

One need not be an especially reflective person, let alone a philoso-pher, to have a sound understanding of what is good and what is bad for human beings and other living things. Plato was utterly mistaken about that. Goodness is not an abstruse or abstract subject, requiring prelimi-nary training in mathematics, science, and dialectic. That is because the best way of thinking about good—that is, thinking of it as a matter of flourishing—lies ready to hand in commonsense, practical thought. All normal parents know, at least in outline, what is good for their children, because a developmental picture of how life should go is almost an ines-capable part of our conceptual framework.

But as I noted from the start (section 1), common sense is an unreli-able guide to action, because if one has no other guide but this, one can easily be led to accept conflicting pictures of human well-being. It is all too easy to misconceive the relationship between pleasure and good, and not only because of our natural love of pleasure—there are also intellec-tual reasons for supposing that all that is good is pleasant, and that all pleasure is good (sections 32, 33). Similarly, it is not only because de-sires have motive power, often of great force, that we may fall into think-ing that our good lies in their satisfaction. The conative theory, like he-donism, has a basis in common ways of thought (section 30). So it is not surprising that people make mistakes about what goodness is—about what it is for G to be good for S—when they rely on nothing but unre-flective intuitions and conventional wisdom. And because assumptions about what is good are and ought to be pervasive in our deliberations, one can do much harm to oneself and others if one simply accepts what-ever ideas lie ready to hand about well-being. Even if one does no dam-age, one can waste one's time by pursuing goals that are not worth caring about.

That is why the good-centered ethical theories that prevailed in Greece and Rome assigned a special role to philosophy in the life of a community. These philosophical schools, deeply indebted to Socrates, acknowledged, in one way or another, the risks taken by those who live unexamined lives—lives that are not guided by reflection about what is worth aiming at. Good intentions and the ethical training everyone re-ceives as a child can by themselves take one only so far. To act well, one must bring to bear on what one does a sense of what is worthwhile, and if that sense is merely a product of what one happens to want or like, one can easily go astray. Common sense must be informed by ethical reflection; and such reflection, systematized and intensified, is what moral philosophy is.

Works Cited

Adams, Robert Merrihew. *Finite and Infinite Goods*. Oxford: Oxford University Press, 1999.

Anderson, Elizabeth. *Value in Ethics and Economics*. Cambridge, Mass.: Harvard University Press, 1993.

Anscombe, G. E. M. *Intention*. 2nd ed. Ithaca, N.Y.: Cornell University Press, 1963.

———. "Modern Moral Philosophy." In Roger Crisp and Michael Slote, eds., *Virtue Ethics*. Oxford: Oxford University Press, 1997. Pp. 26–44. Originally published in *Philosophy* 33 (1958): 1–19. Citations refer to the reprint.

———. "On Promising and Its Justice, and Whether It Need Be Respected *in Foro Interno*." In *The Collected Philosophical Papers of G. E. M. Anscombe*. Vol. 3, *Ethics, Religion, and Politics*. Minneapolis: University of Minnesota Press, 1981. Pp. 10–21.

Bales, Kevin. *Disposable People: New Slavery in the Global Economy*. Berkeley: University of California Press, 1999.

———. *New Slavery: A Reference Handbook*. Santa Barbara, Calif.: ABC-CLIO, 2000.

Bales, R. Eugene. "Act-Utilitarianism: Account of Right-Making Characteristics or Decision-Making Procedure?" *American Philosophical Quarterly* 8 (1971): 257–265.

Bentham, Jeremy. *An Introduction to the Principles of Morals and Legislation*. Ed. J. H. Burns and H. L. A. Hart. London: Athlone Press, 1970.

Berlin, Ira. *Many Thousands Gone: The First Two Centuries of Slavery in North America*. Cambridge, Mass.: Belknap Press of Harvard University Press, 1998.

Blackburn, Simon. *Being Good: An Introduction to Ethics*. Oxford: Oxford University Press, 2001.

Brandt, Richard B. *A Theory of the Good and the Right*. Oxford: Clarendon Press, 1979.

Brink, David O. *Moral Realism and the Foundations of Ethics*. Cambridge: Cambridge University Press, 1989.

275

Broad, C. D. *Five Types of Ethical Theory.* London: Routledge and Kegan Paul, 1930.

Cullity, Garrett. *The Moral Demands of Affluence.* Oxford: Clarendon Press, 2004.

Dancy, Jonathan. *Ethics without Principles.* Oxford: Clarendon Press, 2004.

Darwall, Stephen. *Welfare and Rational Care.* Princeton: Princeton University Press, 2002.

Davis, David Brion. *The Problem of Slavery in Western Culture.* Ithaca, N.Y.: Cornell University Press, 1986.

Diogenes Laertius. *Lives of Eminent Philosophers.* Vol. 2. Cambridge, Mass.: Harvard University Press, 1979.

Dworkin, Gerald. *The Theory and Practice of Autonomy.* Cambridge: Cambridge University Press, 1988.

Faust, Drew Gilpin. *The Ideology of Slavery: Proslavery Thought in the Antebellum South, 1830–1860.* Baton Rouge: Louisiana State University Press, 1981.

Feinberg, Joel. *The Moral Limits of the Criminal Law.* Vol. 1, *Harm to Others.* New York: Oxford University Press, 1984.

———. *The Moral Limits of the Criminal Law.* Vol. 3, *Harm to Self.* New York: Oxford University Press, 1986.

Feldman, Fred. *Pleasure and the Good Life.* Oxford: Clarendon Press, 1994.

Finnis, John. *Natural Law and Natural Rights.* Oxford: Clarendon Press, 1980.

Fisher, N. R. E. *Slavery in Classical Greece.* London: Bristol Classical Press, 1993.

Fleischacker, Samuel. *A Third Concept of Liberty: Judgment and Freedom in Kant and Adam Smith.* Princeton: Princeton University Press, 1999.

Foot, Philippa. *Natural Goodness.* Oxford: Clarendon Press, 2001.

———. "Utilitarianism and the Virtues." In *Moral Dilemmas.* Oxford: Clarendon Press, 2002. Pp. 59–77.

Fowler, H. W. *A Dictionary of Modern English Usage.* 3rd ed. New York: Oxford University Press, 2000.

Frankfurt, Harry G. *The Reasons of Love.* Princeton: Princeton University Press, 2004.

Frey, Bruno S., and Alois Stutzer. *Happiness and Economics: How the Economy and Institutions Affect Human Well-Being.* Princeton: Princeton University Press, 2002.

Geach, P. T. "Good and Evil." In Philippa Foot, ed., *Theories of Ethics.* London: Oxford University Press, 1967. Pp. 64–73. Originally published in *Analysis* 17 (1956): 33–42. Citations refer to the reprint.

Gert, Bernard. 1998. *Morality: Its Nature and Justification.* New York: Oxford University Press.

Geuss, Raymond. "Happiness and Politics." In *Outside Ethics.* Princeton: Princeton University Press, 2005. Pp. 97–110.

Gilbert, Margaret. 1989. *On Social Facts.* Princeton: Princeton University Press.

Griffin, James. "Incommensurability: What's the Problem?" In Ruth Chang, ed., *Incommensurability, Incomparability, and Practical Reason.* Cambridge, Mass.: Harvard University Press, 1997. Pp. 35–51.

———. *Well-Being: Its Meaning, Measurement, and Moral Importance.* Oxford: Clarendon Press, 1986.

Haidt, Jonathan. *The Happiness Hypothesis: Finding Modern Truth in Ancient Wisdom.* New York: Basic Books, 2006.

Hardin, Russell. "The Free Rider Problem." In Edward N. Zalta, ed., *The Stanford Encyclopedia of Philosophy.* Summer 2003 ed. http://plato.stanford.edu/entries/free-rider/.

Hooker, Brad. *Ideal Code, Real World.* Oxford: Clarendon Press, 2000.

Hurka, Thomas. *Perfectionism.* New York: Oxford University Press, 1993.

Hursthouse, Rosalind. *On Virtue Ethics.* Oxford: Oxford University Press, 1999.

Jeffrey, Richard C. *The Logic of Decision.* 2nd ed. Chicago: University of Chicago Press, 1983.

Kagan, Shelly. *Normative Ethics.* Boulder, Colo.: Westview. 1998.

Kahneman, Daniel, Ed Diener, and Norbert Schwarz, eds. *Well-Being: The Foundations of Hedonic Psychology.* New York: Russell Sage Foundation, 1999.

Kamm, F. M. *Morality, Mortality.* Vol. 1, *Death and Whom to Save from It.* New York: Oxford University Press, 1993.

Kant, Immanuel. *Critique of Pure Reason.* Trans. Norman Kemp Smith. New York: St. Martin's Press, 1929.

———. *Groundwork for the Metaphysics of Morals.* Trans. Arnulf Zweig. Oxford: Oxford University Press, 2002.

———. *Lectures on Ethics.* Trans. Peter Heath. Cambridge: Cambridge University Press, 1997.

Kitcher, Philip. "Biology and Ethics." In David Copp, ed., *The Oxford Handbook of Ethical Theory.* Oxford: Oxford University Press, 2006. Pp. 163–185.

———. "Ethics and Perfection." *Ethics* 110 (1999): 59–83.

Kornblith, Hilary. *Knowledge and Its Place in Nature.* Oxford: Clarendon Press, 2002.

Korsgaard, Christine M. *The Sources of Normativity.* Cambridge: Cambridge University Press, 1996.

Kraut, Richard. *Aristotle: Political Philosophy.* Oxford: Oxford University Press, 2002.

———. "Desire and the Human Good." *Proceedings and Addresses of the American Philosophical Association* 68 (1994): 39–54.

———. "Doing without Morality: Reflections on the Meaning of *Dein* in Aristotle's *Nicomachean Ethics.*" *Oxford Studies in Ancient Philosophy* 24 (2006): 169–200.

———. "How to Justify Ethical Propositions: Aristotle's Method." In Richard Kraut, ed., *The Blackwell Guide to Aristotle's* Nicomachean Ethics. Malden, Mass.: Blackwell Publishing, 2006. Pp. 76–95.

Layard, Richard. *Happiness: Lessons from a New Science.* New York: Penguin Press, 2005.

Mill, John Stuart. *On Liberty.* In J. M. Robson, ed., *The Collected Works of John Stuart Mill.* Vol. 18, *Essays on Politics and Society.* Toronto: University of Toronto Press, 1977. Pp. 213–310.

———. *Utilitarianism.* In J. M. Robson, ed., *The Collected Works of John Stuart Mill.* Vol. 10, *Essays on Ethics, Religion and Society.* Toronto: University of Toronto Press, 1969. Pp. 203–260.

Moore, G. E. *Principia Ethica.* 2nd ed. Cambridge: Cambridge University Press, 1993.

Mulgan, Tim. *The Demands of Consequentialism.* Oxford: Clarendon Press, 2001.

Murdoch, Iris. *The Sovereignty of Good.* London: Routledge and Kegan Paul, 1970.

Murphy, Liam B. *Moral Demands in Nonideal Theory.* Oxford: Oxford University Press, 2000.

Nagel, Thomas. "Death." In *Mortal Questions.* Cambridge: Cambridge University Press, 1979. Pp. 1–10.

———. *The View from Nowhere.* New York: Oxford University Press, 1986.

Nozick, Robert. *Anarchy, State, and Utopia.* New York: Basic Books, 1974.

Nussbaum, Martha C. *Frontiers of Justice: Disability, Nationality, Species Membership.* Cambridge, Mass.: Belknap Press of Harvard University Press, 2006.

Overvold, Mark Carl. "Self-Interest and the Concept of Self-Sacrifice." *Canadian Journal of Philosophy* 10 (1980): 105–118.

Parfit, Derek. *Reasons and Persons.* Oxford: Oxford University Press, 1984.

Pieper, Josef. *Leisure: The Basis of Culture.* Trans. Gerald Malsbary. South Bend, Ind.: St. Augustine's Press, 1998. German ed., Munich: Kösel-Verlag, 1948.

Platts, Mark. *Ways of Meaning: An Introduction to a Philosophy of Language.* London: Routledge and Kegan Paul, 1979.

Prichard, H. A. *Moral Writings.* Ed. Jim MacAdam. Oxford: Clarendon Press, 2002.

Railton, Peter. "Facts and Values." In *Facts, Values, and Norms.* Cambridge: Cambridge University Press, 2003. Pp. 43–68.

Rawls, John. *A Theory of Justice.* Rev. ed. Cambridge, Mass.: Belknap Press of Harvard University Press, 1999.

Raz, Joseph. *Ethics in the Public Domain: Essays in the Morality of Law and Politics.* Oxford: Oxford University Press, 1994.

———. *The Morality of Freedom.* Oxford: Clarendon Press, 1986.

Ross, W. D. *The Right and the Good.* Oxford: Clarendon Press, 1930.

Scanlon, T. M. *What We Owe to Each Other.* Cambridge, Mass.: Belknap Press of Harvard University Press, 1998.

Sen, Amartya. *Development as Freedom.* New York: Alfred A. Knopf, 1999.

———. *On Ethics and Economics.* Oxford: Basil Blackwell, 1987.

Shafer-Landau, Russ. *Moral Realism: A Defence.* Oxford: Clarendon Press, 2003.

Shaver, Robert. *Rational Egoism: A Selective and Critical History.* Cambridge: Cambridge University Press, 1999.

Sidgwick, Henry. *The Methods of Ethics.* 7th ed. 1907. Reprint, Indianapolis: Hackett, 1981.

Slote, Michael. *Morals from Motives.* Oxford: Oxford University Press, 2001.

Smith, Adam. *The Theory of Moral Sentiments.* Ed. D. D. Raphael and A. L. Macfie. Indianapolis: Liberty Classics, 1979.

Smith, Mark M. *Debating Slavery: Economy and Society in the Antebellum American South.* Cambridge: Cambridge University Press, 1998.

Smith, Michael. *The Moral Problem.* Oxford: Blackwell, 1994.

Sumner, L. W. *Welfare, Happiness, and Ethics.* Oxford: Clarendon Press, 1996.

Thomson, Judith Jarvis. *Goodness and Advice.* Princeton: Princeton University Press, 2001.

Watson, Gary. "Free Agency." In *Agency and Answerability: Selected Essays.* Oxford: Clarendon Press, 2004. Pp. 13–32.

Wilde, Oscar. *De Profundis.* New York: Modern Library Paperback Edition, 2000.

———. "The Soul of Man under Socialism." In *The Soul of Man under Socialism and Selected Critical Prose.* 1891. Reprint, London: Penguin Books, 2001. Pp. 125–160.

Williams, Bernard. *Ethics and the Limits of Philosophy.* Cambridge, Mass.: Harvard University Press, 1985.

———. "Internal and External Reasons." In *Moral Luck.* Cambridge: Cambridge University Press, 1981. Pp. 101–113.

———. "Modernity and the Substance of Ethical Life." In Geoffrey Hawthorn, ed., *In the Beginning Was the Deed.* Princeton: Princeton University Press, 2005. Pp. 40–51.

———. *Morality: An Introduction to Ethics.* New York: Harper and Row, 1972.

———. *Truth and Truthfulness.* Princeton: Princeton University Press, 2002.

Index

Good-centered ethical theory. *See* Primacy of good

Good for, 1–21, 66–99. *See also* Reason-giving force of "good for"

Good of a kind, 1–2, 16–18, 67–68, 69, 75, 136n4, 209–210, 266–271

Good that, 71–81

Griffin, James, 5n5, 46n56, 96n32, 97n33, 98n35

Haidt, Jonathan, 8n11, 126n48

Happiness, 158–161. *See also* Flourishing: affective

Hardin, Russell, 147n12

Health, 3, 5, 9, 90, 106, 133, 204

Hedonism, 13, 19–20, 34, 120–130, 144–145, 150, 166, 168, 170, 173, 202, 272

History, 263

Hitler, Adolf, 34, 266

Hobbes, Thomas, 40n50, 158–161

Honesty, 192–194. *See also* Plagiarism

Honor, 139n9, 261–263

Hooker, Brad, 17n24

Humanitarian aid, 45–48, 55, 60, 66n1

Human nature, 4, 50n58, 52, 88, 90–91, 91–92, 100–101, 135–201

Hume, David, 204, 231

Humor. *See* Laughter

Hurka, Thomas, 4n3

Hursthouse, Rosalind, 5n4

Ideal self, 109–113

Imagination, 112, 141, 177–178, 197, 269. *See also* Flourishing: cognitive

Imitation, 102, 110, 199–200

Inclusiveness. *See* Rawls, John: on principle of inclusiveness

Independence of mind. *See* Autonomy

Indifference to good and bad, 37

Indifferent (neither good nor bad), 150, 183

Insufficiency of good, 14–15, 60–61, 208, 210, 211–215, 271. *See also* Primacy of good

Interest. *See* Good for

Intrinsically good for, 6nn6,7

Intrinsic value, 212n7, 266–269. *See also* Absolute goodness

Jeffrey, Richard, 12n15, 20n26

Justice, 30–31n45, 75n17, 163n20, 180,

191–196, 200, 209, 225–234, 244, 247–248, 252, 254

Kagan, Shelly, 12n15, 13n18, 26n40

Kahneman, Daniel, 126n48

Kamm, Frances, 139n9

Kant, Immanuel, 27n42, 28n43, 35–36, 132n2, 224n22, 228n25, 257

Kidney transplants, 239–243

Kitcher, Philip, 4n3, 147n12

Korsgaard, Christine, 8n11, 151n13

Language learning, 91, 106–108, 113, 140, 180

Laughter, 35, 156, 170

Layard, Richard, 126n48

Leisure, 200, 247

Liberalism, 197, 201, 239, 242

Literary activities, 45–47, 87, 176–180, 266–269. *See also* Flourishing: cognitive

Locative reading of "good for," 81–85

Locke, John, 239

Loneliness, 161–162

Love, 156, 162–163, 169, 181–182, 252, 260, 262–263, 265–266. *See also* Friendship; Self-love

Lying, 257–261

Marriage, 30, 143, 201, 221, 265. *See also* Adultery; Children; Parents

Master value, 36, 210. *See also* Primacy of good

Masturbation, 170

Materialism, 188. *See also* Wealth

Maximization. *See* Quantification of good

Methodology of ethics, 137–138n8. *See also* Common sense

Mill, John Stuart, 12–14, 15, 16, 27n41, 121, 123–124, 125, 127n49, 136n4, 198n37, 204, 236, 237n31, 252

Mind-independence of good, 8–10, 116. *See also* Plants

Moore, G. E., 68n5, 69–71, 75, 88

Moral realism. *See* Mind-independence of good

Moral reasons, 27, 255–256

Moral revulsion, 266

Moral rightness: alleged priority of, 21–24, 34, 61n63, 254; distinguished from non-moral rightness, 24, 27, 255–256;